Springer Wien New York

T0137892

Sabine Coquillart · Guido Brunnett
Greg Welch
Editors

Virtual Realities

Dagstuhl Seminar 2008

SpringerWienNewYork

Editors
Dr. Sabine Coquillart
INRIA Rhône-Alpes
ZIRST
avenue de l'Europe 655
38334 St.Ismier
France
sabine.coquillart@inria.fr

Prof. Dr. Guido Brunnett
TU Chemnitz
Fak. Informatik
Professur für Graphische
Datenverabeitung und Visualisierung
Straße der Nationen 62
09107 Chemnitz
Germany
guido.brunnett@informatik.tu-chemnitz.de

Dr. Greg Welch
University of North Carolina
Dept. Computer Science
Sitterson Hall
27599-3175 Chapel Hill North
Carolina
Campus Box 3175
USA
welch@cs.unc.edu

SpringerWienNewYork is a part of Springer Science+Business Media
springer.at

Cover: WMXDesign GmbH, Heidelberg, Germany

Typesetting: SPI Publisher Services, India

Printed on acid-free and chlorine-free bleached paper
SPIN: 12530366

With 78 Figures

ISBN 978-3-211-99177-0   ISBN 978-3-211-99178-7 (eBook)
DOI 10.1007/978-3-211-99178-7
SpringerWienNewYork

Preface

During the week of June 1–6, 2008, the Schloss Dagstuhl – Leibniz Center for Informatics held a first-of-its-kind seminar in the area of *Virtual Reality*. Being the first seminar in this area, both the organizers and the participants were not completely sure what to expect from this event beforehand. In retrospect, we rate this Dagstuhl seminar as a great success: it was the ideal venue to define and discuss key topics and to initiate new collaborations.

What is Virtual Reality?

The definition of Virtual Reality (VR) depends on whom you ask and in what context. For the purpose of planning this seminar, we defined it as *a multidisciplinary area of research aimed at interactive human–computer-mediated simulations of artificial environments*. This definition captures applications ranging from simulation, to training, to scientific visualization, and to even entertainment. An important aspect of such VR-based systems is the stimulation of the human senses – typically sight, sound, and touch – such that a user feels a sense of *presence* (or immersion) in the virtual environment. Different applications require different levels of presence, with corresponding levels of realism, sensory immersion, and spatiotemporal interactive fidelity. These requirements lead to research ranging from human perception, to psychological aspects, to physical simulation, and to VR technologies including tracking, displays, user interfaces, rendering, and modeling.

Who Attended the Seminar?

We succeeded in bringing together a good mix of leading researchers and promising young scientists. In total, 50 researchers from 11 different countries participated in the seminar; nine of them were women. The attendees were mostly affiliated with universities, with a few coming from research institutes (e.g., MPI, Fraunhofer) or industry.

What Transpired During the Seminar?

The format of the seminar sessions changed during the week. Based on the responses from the participants, the organizers tried to adapt to evolving needs for more discussions or lectures. One idea that turned out to be very fruitful was to concentrate the discussion toward the end of each session, i.e., the talks were presented without the usual question part. Instead at the end of the session, all speakers took a seat in front of the audience and answered questions in panel style. This format allowed questions to bridge between the talks, and stirred very lively discussions. These discussions were considered to be so productive that the lengths of the talks had to be reduced in order to free up time.

On Wednesday morning, the entire group met for discussion of the "grand challenges" facing VR. Based on the results of this session, different topics were defined for further discussion in subsequent parallel sessions. On Thursday afternoon, the group split up to discuss the following themes: Latency, Augmented Reality, Experience Design, Virtual Humans, and Perception. As these themes were selected by popular vote from a larger list, it is an indication that these topics were considered some of the most important in VR.

Major VR Themes Discussed

Latency is recognized by VR researchers as a topic that is important but underreported in the field. The group identified the main sources of latency: tracking and other input devices, interface buffering, network delays, device driver and operating system overheads, application simulation time, rendering (software and hardware), and display devices. In a typical system, the end-to-end latency is the sum of these. It is this end-to-end timing that was identified as the key measurement for comparing different systems, and for understanding the impact of varying levels of latency on task performance. There is also a need to measure the latencies in the contributing components.

The discussion of existing methods for measuring and reporting end-to-end latency made clear that these methods will have to be straightforward to use if they are to be adopted widely by the VR researchers and practitioners. Two variants were proposed: one for HMDs and the other for screen/projector-based systems, and the group agreed to further develop these for dissemination. More generally, it was agreed that there is an urgent need for a 'field guide to latency'.

In **Augmented Reality**, the observer's view of a real scene is enhanced by virtual objects. Examples include to blend in repair instructions into the field of view of a car mechanic, or to project MRI data onto a patient during a surgery. Obviously, AR requires accurate tracking of the user. In moving environments, it might be necessary to combine different kind of tracking devices in order to avoid situations, where the tracked markers are lost. To make use of the full potential of AR, it is important to install AR infrastructure not only in laboratories but also in usual environments (e.g., offices). In this context, the concept of AR-ready buildings was discussed.

The group that worked on **Experience Design** focused on the creative use of existing VR equipment to create compelling experiences. This extremely fruitful discussion took advantage from the different views of engineers, psychologists, and practitioners in multimedia design.

The discussion made clear that not only the technical possibilities but also the script of the presentation has a strong effect on the experience made by the user. Visitors of virtual worlds are usually more impressed when technical explanations (how it is done) are not given in advance. Depending on the application, it can also be advantageous to leave certain details to the imagination of the observer. Also, the element of surprise is an effective means for getting the observer involved in the virtual environment.

An extremely important research topic in VR is that of **virtual humans**. Similar to the Turing test of AI, the goal is here to design the appearance of virtual humans and their interaction with the user so life-like that emotions are invoked similar to those in interhuman interactions. One application presented in Dagstuhl was a training environment for medical doctors. To improve their interaction with patients, a virtual environment has been created in which difficult situations between doctors and patients can be simulated.

In the **perception** group, it was discussed how recent results from perceptual psychology could be used for the design of intuitive 3D human computer interfaces. Another issue of this group was the problem of simulation sickness, and the question of how the length of time humans can be exposed to virtual environments can be extended.

This Book

This book comprises a collection of position papers, documentation of breakout discussions, or extended research papers related to VR. The position papers include topics such as constrained 3D user interfaces, social gaming and learning applications, and future VR software platforms. The breakout discussion papers included the next generation of Augmented Reality systems, and the importance of experiential fidelity. The extended research papers include topics ranging from fundamental methods to compelling applications. All of the submissions were peer-reviewed for appropriateness and quality.

TU Chemnitz, DE	*Guido Brunnett*
INRIA Rhône-Alpes, FR	*Sabine Coquillart*
University of North Carolina, Chapel Hill, US	*Greg Welch*

Contents

Contributors

Heni Ben Amor VR and Multimedia Group, Institute of Informatics, TU Bergakademie Freiberg, Freiberg, Germany, amor@informatik.tu-freiberg.de

Steffi Beckhaus im.ve, Department of Informatics, University of Hamburg, Vogt-Kölln-Str. 30, 22767 Hamburg, Germany, steffi.beckhaus@uni-hamburg.de

Torsten Bierz University of Kaiserslautern, D-67663 Kaiserslautern, Germany, bierz@cs.uni-kl.de

Mark Billinghurst The HIT Lab NZ, University of Canterbury, Christchurch, New Zealand, mark.billinghurst@hitlabnz.org

Wolfgang Broll Ilmenau University of Technology, D 98693 Ilmenau, Germany, wolfgang.broll@tu-ilmenau.de

Bruce Cairns The Department of Surgery, The University of North Carolina at Chapel Hill, Campus Box 7228, Chapel Hill, North Carolina 27599-7228, USA, bruce_cairns@med.unc.edu

Matthias Deller German Research Center for Artificial Intelligence (DFKI), D-67663 Kaiserslautern, Germany, matthias.deller@dfki.de

Ralf Dörner RheinMain University of Applied Sciences, D 65197 Wiesbaden, Germany, ralf.doerner@hs-rm.de

Achim Ebert University of Kaiserslautern, D-67663 Kaiserslautern, Germany, ebert@cs.uni-kl.de

Henry Fuchs The Department of Computer Science, The University of North Carolina at Chapel Hill, Campus Box 3175, Chapel Hill, North Carolina 27599-3175, USA, fuchs@cs.unc.edu

Hans Hagen University of Kaiserslautern, D-67663 Kaiserslautern, Germany, hagen@cs.uni-kl.de

Nils Hasler Weta Digital, Wellington, New Zealand, nhasler@wetafx.co.nz
and
MPI Informatik, Saarbrücken, Germany

Guido Heumer VR and Multimedia Group, Institute of Informatics, TU
Bergakademie Freiberg, Freiberg, Germany,
guido.heumer@informatik.tu-freiberg.de

Adrian Ilie The Department of Computer Science, The University of North
Carolina at Chapel Hill, Campus Box 3175, Chapel Hill, North Carolina
27599-3175, USA, adyilie@cs.unc.edu

Bernhard Jung VR and Multimedia Group, Institute of Informatics, TU
Bergakademie Freiberg, Freiberg, Germany, jung@informatik.tu-freiberg.de,
http://vr.tu-freiberg.de

Srinivas Krishnan The Department of Computer Science, The University of
North Carolina at Chapel Hill, Campus Box 3175, Chapel Hill, North Carolina
27599-3175, USA, krishnan@cs.unc.edu

Tobias Langlotz Institute for Computer Graphics and Vision, Graz University
of Technology, Graz, Austria, langlotz@icg.tugraz.at

Robert W. Lindeman HIVE Lab, Department of Computer Science, Worcester
Polytechnic Institute, 100 Institute Rd., Worcester, MA 01609, USA,
gogo@wpi.edu

Benjamin Lok University of Florida, 32611-6120, Gainesville, FL USA,
lok@cise.ufl.edu

Sebastian Manten Center of Information and Media Technology, Heinrich Heine
University Duesseldorf, 40225, Duesseldorf, Germany,
manten@uni-duesseldorf.de

Ketan Mayer-Patel The Department of Computer Science, The University
of North Carolina at Chapel Hill, Campus Box 3175, Chapel Hill, North Carolina
27599-3175, USA, kmp@cs.unc.edu

Stephan Olbrich Regional Computer Center and Department of Computer
Science, Scientific Visualization and Parallel Processing, University of Hamburg,
20146 Hamburg, Germany, stephan.olbrich@rrz.uni-hamburg.de

Peter-Scott Olech University of Kaiserslautern, D-67663 Kaiserslautern,
Germany, olech@cs.uni-kl.de

Bodo Rosenhahn Institut für Informationsverarbeitung, Hannover University,
Hannover, Germany, rosenhahn@tnt.uni-hannover.de

Dieter Schmalstieg Institute for Computer Graphics and Vision, Graz University
of Technology, Graz, Austria, schmalstieg@tugraz.at

Hanna M. Söderholm The Swedish School of Library and Information Science,
Göteborg University and the University College of Borås, 50190 Borås, Sweden,
Hanna.Maurin@hb.se

Diane H. Sonnenwald School of Information and Library Studies, University
College Dublin, Belfeild, Dublin 4, Ireland, Diane.Sonnenwald@ucd.ie

Hans-Peter Seidel MPI Informatik, Saarbrücken, Germany,
hpseidel@mpi-inf.mpg.de

Andrei State The Department of Computer Science, The University of North
Carolina at Chapel Hill, Campus Box 3175, Chapel Hill, North Carolina
27599-3175, USA, andrei@cs.unc.edu

Anthony Steed Department of Computer Science, University College London,
London, UK, A.Steed@cs.ucl.ac.uk

Daniel Steffen German Research Center for Artificial Intelligence (DFKI),
D-67663 Kaiserslautern, Germany, daniel.steffen@dfki.de

Wolfgang Stuerzlinger York University, Toronto, Canada, http://www.cse.yorku.
ca/~wolfgang, wolfgang@cse.yorku.ca

Sebastian Thelen University of Kaiserslautern, D-67663 Kaiserslautern,
Germany, s_thelen@cs.uni-kl.de

Herman Towles The Department of Computer Science, The University of
North Carolina at Chapel Hill, Campus Box 3175, Chapel Hill, North Carolina
27599-3175, USA, herman@cs.unc.edu

Michael Vetter Department of Computer Science, Scientific Visualization and
Parallel Processing, University of Hamburg, D-20146 Hamburg, Germany,
michael.vetter@uni-hamburg.de

Arnd Vitzthum VR and Multimedia Group, Institute of Informatics,
TU Bergakademie Freiberg, Freiberg, Germany,
vitzthum@informatik.tu-freiberg.de

Greg Welch The Department of Computer Science, The University of North
Carolina at Chapel Hill, Campus Box 3175, Chapel Hill, North Carolina
27599-3175, USA, welch@cs.unc.edu

Rene Weller Department of Computer Science, Clausthal University, D-38678
Clausthal-Zellerfeld, Germany, rwe@tu-clausthal.de

Chadwick A. Wingrave University of Central Florida, Orlando, FL, USA,
cwingrav@eecs.ucf.edu

Ruigang Yang The Department of Computer Science, The University of Kentucky,
232 Hardymon Building, Lexington, KY 40506-0195, USA,
ryang@cs.uky.edu

Gabriel Zachmann Department of Computer Science, Clausthal University,
D-38678 Clausthal-Zellerfeld, Germany, zach@tu-clausthal.de

Chapter 1
Proposals for Future Virtual Environment Software Platforms

Anthony Steed

Abstract The past two decades have seen the development of a plethora of software solutions to support virtual environments. Many very capable software platforms, toolkits and libraries have been built, but the rate of development of new software continues to increase. There is very significant functional replication amongst these software, and there are few possibilities to migrate anything other than simple content from one piece of software to another. In this chapter we discuss why there are so many software solutions for virtual environments.

We make some suggestions to software developers that might facilitate code re-use at the platform building stage, with the aim of moving towards platforms that support content re-use.

1.1 The Problem

The term virtual environment (VE) has been applied to many types of media and forms of presentation over the years. The area of software to support VEs is thus broad, but it almost always includes software for real-time graphics, real-time audio, interaction based on user input and time-based animation. Often it includes networking between processes, haptic device control, physical simulation or multi-display control. Less commonly it includes interfaces to unusual input devices such as brain-computer interfaces, ubiquitous sensors, remote sensing, microscope controls, etc. Whilst integration of specialist facilities will always require specialist software, even at the core (graphics, audio, interaction and animation), there is a plethora of potential software solutions, from open-source scene-graph libraries through to full-solution commercial packages.

The first problem that developers in the area encounter is that almost none of these toolkits inter-operate in more than a superficial way. Whilst static assets can

A. Steed
Department of Computer Science, University College London, London, UK
e-mail: A.Steed@cs.ucl.ac.uk

S. Coquillart et al. (eds.), *Virtual Realities*, DOI 10.1007/978-3-211-99178-7_1,

be committed to files, and ported across to other software, this is almost never trivial in practice and sometimes crucial implicit knowledge is lost. Moreover, animation and interaction descriptions are almost certainly not portable between different systems. Standards such as Collada and X3D do help in this area, but neither supports the description of full applications using a range of input and output devices. There is thus a constant battle to keep demos working and there is little generic content that works in many systems. In our own lab, we have lost the ability to run most of the demos we have written, sometimes within a few months of creation, because they stop working for an unknown reason and the author has moved on. More importantly, best practice, case studies and benchmarks have to be reproduced from secondary sources such as the papers written about them.

The second problem is that creation of applications remains a complex process, with users needing to learn specific programming interfaces, sometimes even new languages in order to create content. Whilst there are simple platforms available, these do not generally scale up to support the full range of applications that a typical lab or facility needs.

Whilst there is almost certainly no single platform that can satisfy a broad range of requirements, this chapter highlights some potential ways forward for software in the area. The chapter reflects the position of a system designer, attempting to balance functional requirements against the needs of users (programmers) who want to build applications. The paper thus starts by highlighting the range of conflicting requirements of VE systems. It covers both functional differences, and also programmer interface differences. It suggests that there are some common themes of development and this leads to some suggestions for coordinated effort in software engineering in the field.

1.2   Requirements and Constraints

There are many hundreds of 3D engines, games engines and VE toolkits out there. Most laboratories will use several systems to power their applications and demos. In a previous paper I listed over 40 that students and staff in our lab have used over the past 15 years [10]. In the 2 years since, that list has grown by 3 or 4 systems. In no particular order, we present some general distinguishing characteristics of these platforms:

- The range of support on different operating systems. There are several middleware vendors that target broad support across different software. This contrasts with the very specific middleware that is supplied by game console vendors. The former targets common functionality and acceptable performance; whereas the latter targets optimal performance and match to the facilities provided by the console hardware.
- Assumed level of graphics support. Some engines make assumptions about their being a certain level of graphics capacity that might be found only in high-end workstations. For example, engines that are targeted at scientific visualization

might require graphics cards with a minimum amount of graphics memory. This can be contrasted with the relatively low capacity of platforms for mobile graphics. Whilst an engine might scale up from low resources; they might not scale down.

- The ability to launch from within web browsers. Most VE engines are standalone applications, but several target integration as web resources. It is relatively easy to create a web plugin, but even then there are constraints imposed by the web browser context. More importantly there need to be good methods to deploy content.
- The flexibility of the display and interface descriptions. Some platforms, especially VE platforms targeted at immersive virtual reality, require very flexible systems to describe displays and interfaces. Other, such as typical game engines, make assumptions such as there being only one screen and a fixed, small, number of input controllers.
- The range of media types supported. Some engines support artist-create media from standard packages such as Autodesk 3DS Max. Others focus on procedural graphics, such as might be generated to visualize data.
- The need to support heavily scripted animation as well as real-time data-processing. Platforms that target user experiences such as games need to support heavily scripted content such as cut-scenes that last several minutes. Contrast this with visualization systems or systems that employ significant vision-processing or other remote sensed data that are only reactive to user input.
- The need to support users with varying programming experience. Some systems are very focused on content production and thus support designers and artists in creating applications. Others require experienced C++ programmers.

This thus sets us up with some hard technical choices. Unfortunately these choices give us constraints that then lead us to exclude potential systems, some of which might have served us very well in the past:

- Choose a specific rendering engine because it supports a specific visual effect that we need. Alternatively, we might choose an engine because it supports a specific shading language.
- If we require to run with a web-browser context then we'll need to choose one of a few completely mutually incompatible web scripting systems (Flash versus ActiveX versus Java)
- If we need to support a range of users, then we'll probably need to choose a platform supporting a simple scripting language. Common examples include Lua or simple Python scripts.
- Interaction and animation code is tricky to debug, so we may wish to choose a platform with interactive, online visualization or debugging facilities.
- We may want to support import of models from other sources, which may constrain us to choose a particular library that supports that model or provides good module support for writing importers. Several game engines require all data to be exported from a modeling package. This shifts the problem but doesn't make it easier.

- If we want to support specific interaction techniques such as augmented reality, multi-touch or multi-user, we may be constrained to choose a particular toolkit that supports this novel functionality.
- If we need to support multiple display devices, we will need a system that is at least aware of clustering, or for which someone else has done the work to make cluster-aware. This constraint means that many promising game engines are not usable in the aim is to supporting CAVE-like displays or even stereo displays.
- If we want multi-user or distributed processing support, we may want to adopt a particular networking engine which will imply some platform constraints.
- We might want guarantees on real-time performance or end-to-end latency. This is highly desirable for immersive systems but less necessary for desktop or web-based applications. It implies some form of internal monitoring capacity.

There may be other requirements, but fitting a particular application inevitably leads to excluding a range of potential platforms. Once a choice is arrived at, one may find that a host of functionality that was relied on in other applications needs to be ported across to the new platform. A case in point: as this chapter was being written one of my students was implementing an inverse-kinematics model to construct a jointed avatar that can represent the body of a user inside a HMD. To my reckoning this is the 10th or 11th implementation of this type of functionality in our lab (I did five implementations myself). Whilst any particular platform may have been pushed to fill a variety of roles, we would be doing a disservice to the community if we claimed that any platform was emerging as a generic solution: the design space is much too large and the constraints too various.

There are other pressures on choice of a more social nature:

- Collaboration with the authors of the software.
- Good fit to student or engineer knowledge.
- System was highly popular at the time, and students or engineers came wanting to use a specific system.

And of course, it goes without saying that good marketing, good documentation and lots of examples are also key in persuading users to adopt a system. By far the greatest incentive is that there is an existing demonstration that is close to your particular requirements; a complete system that can be demonstrated to all eventual users to solicit more design constraints.

Also of importance is the open status of the software. Whilst there seems to a polarization in to Open Source versus commercial software, the actual implications are much more subtle. For example, some libraries and systems come without any licensing information at all and thus are a little risky to touch; others come under the GPL which has important implications for onward use; others come under a mixed-license. One example problem that is that any particular system might involve code from several sources, and thus it may simply not known if the toolkit can be used. For example, what happens if code under GPL, LGPL and Apache licenses is mixed? In the past, we have had need to completely re-implement a demonstration because although we were a university we wanted to do some commercial exploitation, and we simply couldn't get a cost of a commercial license from the author of a particular library. Other times, we've wanted to use commercial software for short-term consultancy work, but have only been offered the same per-seat deal as games developers expecting to shift thousands of units.

Of course, many of the issues highlighted are common across the software engineering domain. Languages and application programming libraries change relatively rapidly. As noted, VE software has picked up on major themes such as object-oriented programming, and to a lesser extend patterns. The development of VE software might follow development processes established elsewhere (pair-programming, test-first programming). However, compared to other domains, in our opinion, the VE and real-time graphics community has not done as good a job of establishing common practice or even common models for comparing architectures.

1.3 A Strawman with the Display-Loop Model

At this point it is worth reflecting on the model that is still taught in basic virtual environments modules and which still holds for a few systems. This is the display-loop model as shown in Fig. 1.1. There are a few separated code modules with different responsibilities (this might be modules in the code sense, or simply

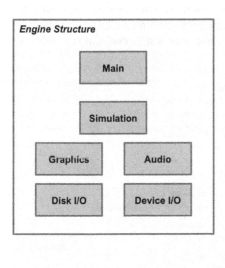
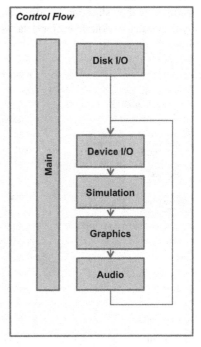

Fig. 1.1 A simple system model. *Left*: code is split in to several modules with different responsibilities. *Right*: The main loop

different functions that access different parts of an API). The main module is actually a loop that calls these other modules in order.

This model is still embodied in a few systems. It is conceptually easy to understand; data is input, processed and output. A common design pattern in VE software is to give the programmer callbacks so that they can insert code in to different phases of the display loop. There are a few notable systems that are targeted at artists and designers hinting that this model is attractive for less-experienced programmers.

The display-loop model does not map well to more complicated applications. It does not support concurrent programming directly. Whilst certain facilities might be spawned off to separate CPU cores, the model itself doesn't deal well with the maintenance of large state, slow calculations or asynchronous communication over the network or to a hardware resource.

Thus, possibly inevitably, the architecture diffuses in to a concurrent process model, an example of which is shown in Fig. 1.2. This is not based on any particular architecture, but highlights two main features. Some common calculations, such as physics are commonly centralized, because the solution needs to be globally consistent, and is more expensive if solved piecemeal. Other modules such as planning for characters (or data analysis) might take several seconds. Some modules are run with the expectation to complete at certain times (input device I/O), others only need to complete, or at least be in a consistent state by the start of the next frame (motion interpolation).

Such an architecture is somewhat inevitable as functional requirements rise. Unfortunately they start confounding simple programming models: it is almost certainly necessary to double buffer data, as some data will be committed to processes

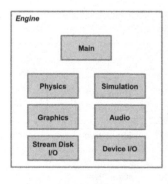
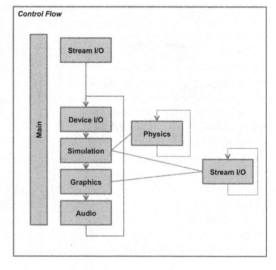

Fig. 1.2 A more complex system model. *Left*: A significantly expanded set of code modules. *Right*: A set of concurrent processes monitored by the main loop

(e.g. rendering) whilst other processes need to alter it (e.g. physics). Thus it very soon becomes difficult to provide a very simple interface to a shared repository of data.

These issues are only compounded by the need to move to distributed processing, either to support a cluster or to provide multi-user system.

1.4 Response of the Community

In the previous section we purposefully critiqued without reference to any particular system. This is because we don't wish to criticize any package: we have been the happy users of many systems and much of our own academic work has built on the significant and often under-appreciated work of system builders. However, there has been a very significant theme over the past few years of building better and more powerful tools. We identify a few themes that have emerged in recent work.

1.4.1 Device Abstractions

If there is one problem that has a reasonable solution, it is the issue of interfaces to devices. There are several libraries and systems including VRPN, CAVElib VRJuggler and DIVERSE which provide broad support for a range of devices. It is rare that one needs to write a device driver these days. All of the afore-mentioned systems provide daemon-like services where application processes get data transparently across the network if necessary. The only constraint is that labs, like ours, prefer not to start and restart devices drivers to run specific systems. Thus we have written several bridging systems, or extended systems to use the device abstraction that we've used.

1.4.2 Time-Oriented Programming

One area that has received considerable attention is animation and interaction programming. Although event-based programming is productive, for very frequent calculations, such as interaction techniques that run at the frame rate of the display, it leads to a lot of events, and leads to complexity in managing lots of interaction techniques. Thus dataflow languages have been investigated (e.g. [2, 12]), and other types of time-based programming. Unfortunately, although it would seem appropriate, there is rarely a strong concept of timing and synchronization in VE systems, as might be found in other time of real-time simulation or multimedia playback. X3D does address some data-flow and timing concerns, but planning and timing are still, in our opinion, poorly supported in most systems.

1.4.3   Modular Code and Frameworks

VE systems have been around for a while, and programming styles and practice
has moved on. Whilst new languages have emerged, the main impact on VE systems has been the adoption of object-oriented programming models, design patterns
and framework-based systems (e.g. see [6, 11]). This does allow some efficiencies
for the programmer and the ability to overload functions on abstract types and other
inheritance techniques does provide a useful way to hide complexity. However these
don't address two common properties of VE systems: the range of services or modules that are required, and the need to manage many instances of objects ensemble.
Another key problem is how modular code interacts with other common programming models. For example, how does event-based programming, interface with
data-flow based programming; each assumes a particular locus of control (events
are processed in event order, dataflow is processed in cascade order) (e.g. see [7,8]).

1.4.4   Scripting Languages

A common facility in many systems is a high-level scripting system which sits
on top of a set of native code modules. The scripting is usually done as part of a
simulation module (refer to Fig. 1.2), whereas other modules, being more compute
heavy, would run separately. Scripting is commonly done to separate or encapsulate
repetitive code, to generate behavior based on data input, or to schedule sequences.
Systems vary in how much of the system is exposed to the scripting interface,
from having the scripting language being able to load and save modules and reflect
the system architecture, through to a simple limited interface to asset loading and
property control.

1.4.5   Object-Sharing and Distributed Programming

Despite the increased power of individual PCs, distributed systems are being more
important to support multiple displays in clusters, complex interfaces, real-time
visualization or multiple users. There are no general standards for inter-networking
between systems, though there are many toolkits that can be used. Whilst some systems are designed from the ground-up to support distributed applications [1], the
choice of a networking library can have pervasive implications for an architecture,
and networking requires asynchronous I/O. This then usually implies a thread-
ing model and operating system abstraction. Another approach that is becoming
more widely used is local or wide-area sharing of data through a distributed object
paradigm (e.g. [9]), a variant on the distributed shared memory approach [5]. This
is a good fit to the architecture of many systems that have some sort of object repository consists of lots of instances of a relatively small number of types of objects.

Each object type can be derived from a super-class that supports object cloning and distribution of copies over a network. This makes the actual management of shared data very easy for the programmer; instance variables on local copies of objects can be transparently mirrored on other systems.

All of these development strategies have simplified programming or allowed more complex systems to be built. However, they are difficult to integrate.

1.5   Some Suggestions for System Builders

Given the discussion so far, it is tempting to claim that there is no possibility of a generic platform or core of all virtual environment systems. However there are several commonalities which lead us to suggest that there could be several potential areas that could be mutually developed to facilitate inter-operation at a modest level between different tools.

The first suggestion is motivated by the observation that although scene-graphs are still being written, there is actually a potential common thread is the trend towards compiled data structures and shaders. Scene-graphs are now distinguished more by their support for rendering passes and particular global illumination formats than they are by the actual data types they support. Whilst we aren't suggesting that there should be a single scene-graph, there is definitely an opportunity for shared code that loads assets in to in-memory data structures that can easily be converted in to the specific representations that a scene-graph uses. For example, most scene-graphs directly support mesh data-structures that closely follow the under-lying array structures that OpenGL and DirectX support. There are example asset loaders for several file formats, what would be required, is a library that could amalgamate these libraries and provide simple methods for accessing the in-memory representations. Bindings in to existing scene-graphs would then be straight-forward.

The second suggestion is to build your scripting API as if you don't actually know the scripting language that will be used. Whilst this sounds impossible on first hearing, scripting APIs are often wrapped around engine interfaces. There are many options to choose, such as what classes or methods to expose, what functionality should the scripting be responsible for, etc. In one platform that the author has used, scripts could be written, and call other scripts, in two different scripting languages. They did this via a well known event API. Plugins in C/C++ could also be treated like the scripting language. Thinking through the implications of this can lead to some very clear separation of data versus code in the system.

One theme that has run through many of our systems is the struggle to decouple the behavior of the virtual environment from the description of how any particular user interacts with the system. The most successful system here was, in our opinion, DIVE, where the world description was completely decoupled from considerations of input devices, by the concept of the vehicle [3,4]. The vehicle concept meant that any interface must provide a way to move around the world and provide abstract interaction signals in to the world, such as Select, Grab, etc. This was coupled with a mandatory description of each user as an avatar, with each interface, desktop or immersive, moving this avatar about the world. This meant that all interactions could be described by reference to a user and their limbs, not to devices. This meant the same worlds could be loaded on desktop or immersive interfaces without any change at all [13]: the vehicle code was bound into an application through plugin and run-time configuration, not the world. The majority of the worlds scripted in DIVE originally intended to run on the desktop interface would work just as well on a CAVE-like display or HMD. The same can not be said for many VE systems, where knowledge of the actual devices is bound in to the application code.

Whilst many systems are very good at managing assets, one stumbling block can be meta-data or generic relations between objects. Many VEs are constructed from multiple instances of similar types, so having good object management through naming, metadata and search facilitates encapsulation of code. For example, a virtual vehicle might be assembled from several objects, and some of these will be instances of common parts such as wheels, doors, etc. Knowledge about function is implicit in relative location, but programming is facilitated by naming and meta-data (name=front left wheel, wear=5). But then, when multiple vehicles are instantiated, we need to be able to refer to specific front-left wheels. Again this can be considered implicit using a nearness metric in scene-graphs terms, but hierarchical naming and searching functionality facilitate the management of complex assemblies.

1.5.1 Longer Term Goals

Amongst our longer term goals would be to encourage greater re-use of code, assets and services between systems and to improve the usability of virtual environments software. Although this will need further reflection amongst the community, we offer five suggestions:

The first is to reflect on the success of web APIs for large and diverse services such as Google Location, Facebook or even something such as the Spore Creature API. These have allowed external users to build custom applications very easily, a type of application that is often known as a mash-up. The web APIs are focused not on the specifics of presentation of media, but on access and retrieving data. For example, web services APIs in this area typically return either assets (2D images, movies and audio), or XML documents. The expectation is that there is a HTML/Javascript document that then embeds this data which can then be rendered within a web browser. What is the VE equivalent of such flexibility? How can existing web API models be extended to richer sets of assets?

A second suggestion is a facility that would aid many systems users is reflection of the system through external APIs. This would allow an engine (a running system) to be controlled remotely. By providing a core set of services that can be accessed by other processes, the engine could be slimmed down.

A third suggestion is to reflect on the difference between a VE system and an operating system. As systems become more and more rich, they take on many of the same roles as operating systems (e.g. thread management, asset caching, etc.). Whilst some VR systems are described as having kernels, this isn't true in a number of ways, not least of which is process isolation under failure. Thus although there is a notion of services and modules, they are all loaded and shutdown as the system starts and stops.

To ensure the usability of systems, we need to learn lessons from the 2D media field, and systems such as Flash and Processing. At one level these systems hide system complexity, but then authors have built wonderfully complex applications on top. Part of this may be down to code legibility; part of may be down to very tight author-test cycles. Of course, these applications tend not to be very data intensive, but they have APIs to access other functionality so the author who is familiar with graphics can focus on that, and rely on services provided elsewhere.

A final suggestion to move towards our longer-term goals is to focus less on building systems, and more on interfaces between modules of code. Because that in order to run VE simulations in our labs and facilities, we need full systems that provide broad support for interfacing, graphics, etc., VE systems have tended to cover a broad range of facilities, but have typically been weak in some areas. The exceptions are device drivers, and possibly, though the interfaces are quite low-level, physics engines. Software writers might think about how to isolate pieces of functionality and make interfaces to them can be made broadly compatible with existing systems.

1.6 Conclusions

In conclusion, I want to emphasise that I believe that we have a range of excellent tools and platforms for building virtual environments at our disposal, but as a community we would benefit from being able to share more code. I would not personally call for more standards (yet), nor a unified platform, but for system and API builders to think about how their code could be reused across different systems. Essentially, this boils down to a call for more compile-time and run-time interfaces to code, less actual code.

References

1. Allard, J., Gouranton, V., Lecointre, L., Limet, S., Melin, E., Raffin, B., & Robert, S. (2004) FlowVR: a Middleware for Large Scale Virtual Reality Applications. In: Proceedings of the International Conference EUROPAR 2004, Springer, LNCS, vol. 3149, 497–505.
2. Figueroa, P., Green, M., & Hoover, H. J. (2002) InTml: A description language for VR applications. In: Proceedings of the Seventh International Conference on 3D Web Technology, ACM, New York, NY, 53–58.

3. Frécon, E. (2004) DIVE on the Internet, PhD Thesis, IT University of Göteborg.
4. Frécon, E., Smith, G., Steed, A., Stenius, M., & Ståhl, O. (2001) An Overview of the COVEN Platform. Presence: Teleoperators and Virtual Environments, 10(1), 109–127.
5. Nitzberg, B., & Lo, V. (1991) Distributed Shared Memory: A Survey of Issues and Algorithms. Computer, 24(8), 52–60.
6. Oliveira, M., Crowcroft, J., & Slater, M. (2001) Components for Distributed Virtual Environments. Presence: Teleoperators and Virtual Environments, 10(1), 51–61.
7. Ponder, M. (2004) Component-Based Methodology and Development Framework Virtual and Augmented Reality Systems. PhD Thesis No 3046, EPFL.
8. Ponder, M., Papagiannakis, G., Molet, T., Magnenat-Thalmann, N., & Thalmann, D. (2003) VHD++ Development Framework: Towards Extendible, Component Based VR/AR Simulation Engine Featuring Advanced Virtual Character Technologies. In: Proceedings of Computer Graphics International (CGI), 2003, IEEE Computer Society Press.
9. Roth, M., Voss, G., & Reiners, D. (2004) Multi-Threading and Clustering for Scene Graph Systems. Computers & Graphics, 28(1), 63–66.
10. Steed, A. (2008) Some Useful Abstractions for Re-Usable Virtual Environment Platforms. In: IEEE Virtual Reality Workshop for Software Engineering and Architectures for Realtime Interactive Systems.
11. Steed, A., & Frécon, E. (2004) Construction of Collaborative Virtual Environments. In Maria-Isabel Sanchez Segura (ed), Developing Future Interactive Systems, Idea Group, 235–268.
12. Steed, A., & Slater, M. (1996) A dataflow representation for defining interaction within immersive virtual environments. In: Proceedings of IEEE Virtual Reality Annual International Symposium 96, 163–167.
13. Steed, A., Mortensen, J., & Frécon E. (2001) Spelunking: Experiences using the DIVE System on CAVE-like Platforms. In: Immersive Projection Technologies and Virtual Environments 2001, Springer/Wien, 153–164.

Chapter 2
Augmented Reality 2.0

Dieter Schmalstieg, Tobias Langlotz, and Mark Billinghurst

Abstract Augmented Reality (AR) was first demonstrated in the 1960s, but only recently have technologies emerged that can be used to easily deploy AR applications to many users. Camera-equipped cell phones with significant processing power and graphics abilities provide an inexpensive and versatile platform for AR applications, while the social networking technology of Web 2.0 provides a large-scale infrastructure for collaboratively producing and distributing geo-referenced AR content. This combination of widely used mobile hardware and Web 2.0 software allows the development of a new type of AR platform that can be used on a global scale. In this paper we describe the Augmented Reality 2.0 concept and present existing work on mobile AR and web technologies that could be used to create AR 2.0 applications.

2.1 Introduction

Augmented Reality (AR) is an area of research that aims to enhance the real world by overlaying computer-generated data on top of it. Azuma [Azu97] identifies three key characteristics of AR systems: (1) mixing virtual images with the real world, (2) three-dimensional registration of digital data and (3) interactivity in real time. The first AR experience with these characteristics was developed over 40 years ago [Sut68], but mainstream adoption has been limited by the available technologies.

Early Augmented Reality applications ran on stationary desktop computers and required the user to wear bulky head mounted displays (HMDs). Despite the ergonomic shortcomings with this configuration, there have been successful

D. Schmalstieg (✉) and T. Langlotz
Institute for Computer Graphics and Vision, Graz University of Technology, Graz, Austria
e-mail: schmalstieg@tugraz.at, langlotz@icg.tugraz.at

M. Billinghurst
HIT Lab New Zealand, University of Canterbury, Christchurch, New Zealand
e-mail: mark.billinghurst@hitlabnz.org

S. Coquillart et al. (eds.), *Virtual Realities*, DOI 10.1007/978-3-211-99178-7_2,
© Springer-Verlag/Wien 2011

applications developed in certain domain areas, such as industrial assembly [Miz00], surgical training [Sie04] or gaming [Son09]. However the cost of these systems, and the technical expertise needed to use them has prevented widespread use. Despite this, monitor-based AR advertising applications by companies such as Total Immersion[1] and Metaio[2] are beginning to be available for non-expert users.

Recently, AR experiences have begun to be delivered on mobile phones. Researchers such as Möhring [Mh04] and Wagner [Wag08b] have shown how phones can be used for computer vision based AR tracking, while companies such as Layar[3] are deploying compass and GPS based mobile outdoor AR experiences. However, widespread use of AR-based mobile technology that allows "Anywhere Augmentation" away from the desktop has not yet been realized.

In this paper, we describe how recent developments in mobile and web technologies allow Augmented Reality applications to be deployed on a global scale and used by hundreds of thousands of people at the same time. We call this approach *Augmented Reality 2.0,* a combination of the terms *Augmented Reality* and *Web 2.0.* Although our focus is on mobile AR, we also realize that there will be continued developments in HMD and monitor based AR applications that will increase their ease of use and deployment.

Like mobile phone AR, Web 2.0 is itself a recent development. O'Reilly[4] mentions that the main difference between Web 1.0 and Web 2.0 technologies is that Web 2.0 enables end user creation of web content, and thereby encourages social networking. In contrast, the original web technology was mainly used for one-way information retrieval. Only few people made content, while most users accessed information without creating or modifying it. Web pages were mostly static and did not allow the users to interact with them or provide additional information.

The advent of Web 2.0 substantially changed the way people use the Internet. Instead of only retrieving content, users are engaged in creating and modifying web material. Web interfaces have become simplified to a point that even people with no technical skills could create content. This has opened the way for services based on user participation, like Flickr,[5] YouTube[6] and Facebook,[7] among others.

In a similar way, the goal of AR 2.0 is to provide widely deployable location-based mobile AR experiences that enhance creativity, collaboration, communication, information sharing and rely on user generated content. With an AR 2.0 platform a user should be able to move through the real world and see virtual overlays of related information appearing at locations of interest, and easily add their own content. Figure 2.1 shows how this might look.

This information overlay will be dynamically generated from a variety of sources and seamlessly fused together on the users handheld display. In addition, the

---

[1] www.t-immersion.com.

[2] www.metaio.com.

[3] http://layar.com/.

[4] http://www.oreillynet.com/pub/a/oreilly/tim/news/2005/09/30/what-is-web-20.html.

[5] http://www.flickr.com/.

[6] http://www.youtube.com/.

[7] http://www.facebook.com/.

Fig. 2.1 Contrary to traditional map displays (*left*), AR 2.0 will augment navigation information on top of the images captured by mobile phones (*right*). Users will also be able to create and update 3D registered content, creating a location-based social network. (Image courtesy of Graz University of Technology)

Table 2.1 Comparison of Web 2.0 and AR 2.0 characteristics

Web 2.0 Characteristics	AR 2.0 Characteristics
Large number of users and web sites (already true for Web 1.0)	Large-scale in number of users as well as working volume
No clearly visible separation between accessing local data and remote data	No clearly visible separation between visualizing local data or remote data
Applications running in a browser behave like local applications, encouraging the user to interact with them	Applications locally running on the device can transparently download modules or new features from remote servers
A huge amount of non technical people retrieve data and contribute or modify it as well	Users can create or update the AR content at specific locations
Information from different sources can be combined and create a new value-added application, in so-called *Mashups*	*Mashups* which access data from sources like traditional web services and combine them with AR content to display them in three-dimensional space

user will be able to generate their own location-specific virtual content, that can then be uploaded to content servers and shared with others. Finally, the platform will provide support for social networking through synchronous and asynchronous context-sensitive data sharing. AR 2.0 as a user experience and networked medium has many parallel characteristics to Web 2.0 (See Table 2.1).

If AR applications are going to be deployed on a massive scale in an AR 2.0 approach, there are several key areas of technology that are needed:

1. A low-cost platform that combines AR display, tracking and processing
2. Mobility to realize AR in a global space
3. Backend infrastructure for distribution of AR content and applications
4. Easy to use authoring tools for creating AR content
5. Large-scale AR tracking solutions which work in real time

In the remainder of this chapter we first discuss the related work that provides the enabling technologies for AR 2.0. We then explain the use of AR for social networking, end-user authoring for AR 2.0, and finally present several case studies of early AR 2.0 applications.

2.2 Related Work

AR 2.0 builds on earlier work in several areas, in particular research in mobile AR, social networking, and location-based services. In the late 1990s, the first experiments were conducted on presenting geo-referenced content in AR applications. The Touring Machine [Fei97] was the first mobile outdoor AR application and was used as a campus tour guide by showing virtual annotations on real university buildings. Although simple, this prototype showed the power of in-situ presentation of geo-referenced information.

Since then the increasing computing capability of personal mobile devices has made it possible to move AR systems from the backpack AR systems of the mid-nineties to Tablet PCs [New06], PDAs [Wag03] and then mobile phones [Mh04]. Nokia's MARA[8] project is an example of the Touring Machine idea ported to the mobile phone. Figure 2.2 shows sample systems in this evolution. Most recently, commercial applications such as Wikitude [Mob09] can show location-tagged AR content on a mobile phone in much the same way as the Touring Machine.

While the mobile AR hardware platform was changing, there was also progress being made on the software platforms. The emergence of the Web as a mass phenomenon prompted Spohrer to suggest the "WorldBoard" [Spo99], a combination of distributed online information systems and geo-referenced indexing. Information could be published in a traditional web form, but was indexed by geographic position rather than by a symbolic URL. The short-term goal of the WorldBoard was to allow users to post messages on every cubic meter of space humans might go to on the planet, while the long-term goal was to allow users to experience any information in any place, co-registered with reality.

Unfortunately, the WorldBoard vision was not fully realized, partly because key technologies such as community content creation tools were not mature enough. Later work, such as the Nexus project in Stuttgart [Hoh99], has similar concepts but

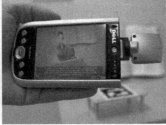

Fig. 2.2 Evolution of Mobile AR Systems: Desktop Windows driven Tablet PC with weight about 1.2 kg, ∼ 1,500 Dollar (*left*), PDA with external camera and limited communication capabilities (*middle*), Smartphone with built-in camera and various communication channels (GSM/3G and Wi-Fi) and low weight (100 g), ∼300 Dollar (*right*). (Image courtesy of Graz University of Technology)

---

[8] http://research.nokia.com/research/projects/mara/.

targeted coarse geo-referenced information systems rather than Augmented Reality presentation.

Today, we see a new mass phenomenon, which has been dubbed Web 2.0. This is characterized by open communication, decentralization of authority, and the freedom to share and re-use Web content [Bar06]. It is also driven by collaboration between users and provides a platform offering open APIs and applications that can be combined in sophisticated applications integrating information from multiple sources [Ore08].

One of the key innovations that can be supported through Web 2.0 is social networking and crowd-sourced content. Without revolutionary changes, the availability of the web has reached a point that the voluntary joint effort of literally millions of users can produce databases of a size and quality that has previously been considered impossible. For example, Wikipedia[9] has already surpassed many traditional encyclopaedias in coverage and richness, and Flickr is one of the largest collections of digital images worldwide. As a side effect, it was found that simple keyword tagging is powerful enough to replace sophisticated semantic web techniques as an organizational principle. The open architecture of the Web 2.0 services allows everybody to enrich these experiences with *Mashups* (Information from different sources that can be combined to create a new value-added application), while advertising pays for the underlying infrastructure. It is important to note that all these results are based on simple existing technologies such as HTTP and *Asynchronous JavaScript and XML* (AJAX).

As part of the Web 2.0 movement, digital globe and map services have become very popular – Google Earth,[10] Google Maps[11] and Microsoft Virtual Earth[12] among others. While the primary source of data of these applications is produced by large enterprises at a high cost and level of effort, it is noteworthy that the results are still made freely available via the Web 2.0 ecosystem.

Using these map services, next generation web technologies may be used to link physical places, objects and people to digital content. This is often called Ambient Intelligence (AmI) [Aar01], a research field that explores the convergence of mobile, ubiquitous and intelligent systems (e.g. context-aware systems) and interaction with real objects. Another project is Deusto Sentient Graffiti [Deu09], which consists of an application that allows users to create annotations associated to real places using context and location data with Web 2.0 infrastructure. It aims to show the potential of Mashups, using the capabilities of mobile devices, Web 2.0 as a platform, ubiquitous computing web paradigms and social annotation of objects and places.

Deusto Sentient Graffiti is based on AJAX technology and using real objects to offer URL tags to XML virtual post-its. These post-its have multimedia content or a pointer to a web service and contextual attributes. Users of the system can

---

[9] http://www.wikipedia.org/.

[10] http://earth.google.de/.

[11] http://maps.google.de/.

[12] http://www.microsoft.com/virtualearth/.

move through an annotated environment, and browse and consume the available annotations according to the user's current context, profile and preferences. Servers store, index and match user annotations against the user's current context published.

The final key area of related work is social networking. Many mobile devices have adapted versions of web-based social networking applications such as Facebook for the Apple iPhone.[13] However, with mobile devices, social networking applications can also be developed based on the device location and other context cues.

There are many popular mobile social applications, which use these context cues. In Dodgeball [Dod09] users receive text messages of friends, and friends of a friend if they are within ten blocks of each other. The location-awareness is implemented by user's entering their location and time or using the IDs of cell towers. Plazes [Pla09] is a location/context-aware system that relies on the Internet infrastructure to serve information about services and nearby friends. Localization is based on GPS, and MAC addresses of networks and WiFi access points. Rumble [Rum09] helps mobile users locate nearby friends, or even strangers with the same interests and offers them access to location-related data. Jabberwocky [Jab09] performs repeated Bluetooth scans to create the sense of the "familiar stranger" in an urban community. Familiar strangers are people that are always nearby in an urban region but are acquaintances. Serendipity [Eag05] uses Bluetooth technology to facilitate interactions between physically proximate people through a centralized server. Through the identification of Bluetooth IDs and support of on-line profile matching, Serendipity identifies new people to become acquainted with.

As can be seen there has been related work developed in a number of areas, including social networking, location-based services, and mobile AR. However, there have been few examples of applications that combine all these areas. In the next section we discuss how this previous work can be integrated into a platform for developing AR 2.0 applications.

2.3 Augmented Reality for Social Networking

A low-cost hardware platform for AR is important for realizing our vision of AR 2.0. Today's smartphones satisfy all basic requirements of a hardware platform for AR 2.0. They combine networking, a display, and graphics hardware capable of 3D rendering. Furthermore, smartphones offer enough computing power to track the device using the build-in camera, with the optional assistance of various other sensing technologies like GPS, WiFi triangulation and accelerometers. Smart phones are inexpensive as they are produced for a mass market and there are currently hundreds of millions sold per year. This momentum ensures a large-scale in terms of number of users and broad geographic coverage.

---

[13] http://iphone.facebook.com/.

A further feature of smart phones over older mobiles phones is their capability to communicate over various channels. They use third-generation mobile phone communication technology (3G), which is optimized for data rather than voice traffic, while WiFi and Bluetooth complete the set of supported fast communication channels. This makes it possible to access the Internet using higher bandwidth to request additional content or program modules, and allows applications to remove the separation of local and remote data.

Spohrer's vision of "information in places" can be realized by using smart phones as the hardware platform and Web 2.0 as the backend infrastructure. Web 2.0 owes its success largely to open standards, which allow interested parties to easily partake in an economy of scale. Likewise, the success of AR 2.0 will require a federated approach and especially open formats for content description and content exchange.

An interesting common standard is the *Keyhole Markup Language* (KML), an open and extensible XML dialect utilized by Google Earth. It incorporates Placemarks which describe geo-referenced information, and also refers to other web standards for multimedia content. For example, 3D models (essential for AR) are described as COLLADA files, an XML-based 3D exchange format increasingly supported by digital content creation tools. However, while KML is an open format it still has a lot of properties that are proprietary to Google Earth. Thus it is only partially suitable for describing AR content, which could be referenced in many ways (geo-referenced, using barcodes, other AR tracking systems, etc.). Consequently, we suggest adopting ideas from KML into a new open format called *Augmented Reality Markup Language* (ARML), which describes the AR content and its spatial reference system.

As shown in Fig. 2.3, a location-based AR application uses data and services remotely stored and served by web Mashups, visualized on the mobile device. Data and services offered to the user must be related to geospatial information corresponding to user location – using GPS, WiFi or a vision-based tracked scene, for example – and a geo-database web services. Content authoring can be performed using a desktop computer or directly on the mobile device while on location. Taking advantage of open APIs and Mashups, complex applications can be easily broken down into smaller components and leverage existing online services. Given appropriate sources of geo-referenced data, developers can focus on the user experience of AR 2.0 applications.

Specific AR data types can easily be integrated into the XML dialects, and hosted using standard web-based databases, accessible via HTTP. New types of Mashups, which are specifically designed to be consumed by AR clients, can be derived from a mixture of existing (conventional) content and content specifically created for AR. This will include visual objects, other multimedia data, application code and the feature database necessary for local tracking.

The selection of content by the user can be performed using either a push mechanism or a pull mechanism such as a webserver capable of accepting simple HTTP queries encoding the current location or area. This allows everybody with access to a server to provide geo-referenced AR content, either genuine or based on data accessed via mash-up. In addition, larger service providers (the "YouTube of AR")

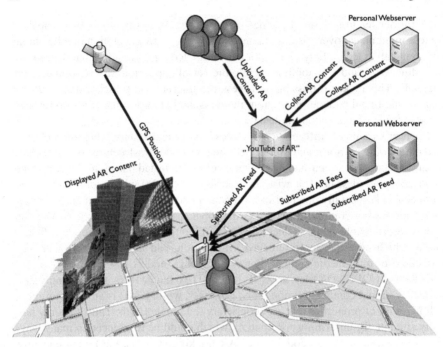

Fig. 2.3 Data flow of end-user provided content in an Augmented Reality 2.0 scenario. (Image courtesy of Graz University of Technology)

can syndicate content provided by many users and organized through tagging. Such syndicated content-hosters would allow a wide audience to publish their material, and also provide easy access for the mainstream audience.

For consuming the AR content, we expect that an end-user device has subscribed to content feeds from a number of AR service providers, based on personal taste and recommendations from others. At a given location, the device sends a request containing its current position and other context information to all these service providers and receives an index of available content. The request can ask for all information in a user-defined radius around the current point of interest, or it could describe an area in an alternative form, for example all data along a route to a given destination. The exact details on which information to download and/or to present to the user and how the user interface lets the user control what he or she sees, is entirely up to the client. All of these approaches are possible without modifying the server side infrastructure.

For example, if an online service for image recognition from a large database of geo-referenced images is available, this service would act as a filter: The client device takes a picture and sends it to the recognition service, possibly assisted with GPS coordinates to reduce the search space. If the image is recognized successfully, the recognition service returns an exact position match, which can then be used by the client to query for content.

Fig. 2.4 QR-code based AR advertising application. (Image courtesy of Graz University of Technology)

Another approach is the use of 2D barcode markers, such as DataMatrix[14] or QR-Code[15] (see Fig. 2.4), which contain enough information to point to a specific web address of an AR content service. This can substitute the need for GPS or image recognition, and directly point to specific content rather than having to know a specific server feed or channel beforehand. It is also a suitable method for non geo-referenced content, for example downloading an AR game board game printed and advertised in a newspaper. If barcode markers are used, they can also initialize tracking, and thereby establish a common frame of reference (for a shared space of multiple users), while ongoing tracking can be based on natural features in the surroundings.

2.4   Application Development and Authoring

Although mobile devices provide a good hardware platform for AR experiences, there is still a need to create the content that is going to be viewed and also author the AR 2.0 application. Most web-based social services provide tools for easy content creation. However, there are no such tools yet for AR 2.0 experiences.

In developing AR 2.0 applications there are several aspects that must be considered; the application data, programming the mobile AR client interface and creating a representation of the real world. In this section we consider each of these aspects in turn.

---

[14] http://datamatrix.kaywa.com.

[15] http://www.denso-wave.com/qrcode/index-e.html.

Authoring in an Augmented Reality 2.0 ecosystem can be transformed from a monolithic problem into one that can be simultaneously addressed with a multitude of tools. Authoring activities range from genuine creation of new applications from ground up to simple Mashups with only minimal original contribution. The key factor is that standard file formats can be used at least for passive content. Work on actual content creation will likely be done primarily on the desktop, while layout may either be performed on the desktop (e.g., using a map of the area), or in-situ. For many instances of application logic, wizards can be created (for example, for AR Magic Books or a timeline-based self-running presentation), which makes the task accessible for end users with little programming experience. Complete integrated development environments for code-centric applications are also conceivable.

2.4.1 Application Data

As described in the previous section, AR 2.0 applications involve the aggregation of multiple data sources depending on users' needs. Combining multiple data sources through open APIs into a complex "Mashup" application makes it easier to create mobile social software:

1. Complex social network algorithms and huge databases can be processed on servers, offering light-weighted data and services to clients.
2. Mash-ups can use the benefit of existing social networking applications and other related applications to concentrate in designing features truly related to mobility, pervasiveness, location and context awareness.
3. APIs (like GoogleMaps[16]) and geo-databases can be used to create geospatial mash-ups, simplifying the development of location-aware social software.
4. User preferences and other data that might be used to infer context can be gathered from web sources and combined with mobile client acquired data.

A possible extension is the use of AJAX for live client-server collaboration. If the content is represented at the client side as a document object model, for example as an X3D compatible scene graph, then a client-server connection, e.g., based on XML and Javascript, can be used to shift the execution of parts of the application logic to the server. This avoids lengthy downloads, allows exploitation of the greater computational power of the server and facilitates multi-user applications. In many cases it should be possible to mask the latency of network transmission using the asynchronous, multi-threaded execution model of AJAX. Applications that are not just passive browser of AR information and that cannot be encoded with a simple approach such as Javascript, will have to be provided in binary form, forsaking platform independence. However, even platform-specific downloads are a large step forward towards the interoperability of AR applications compared to current approaches.

---

[16] http://code.google.com/apis/maps/.

2.4.2 In-Situ Reconstruction and Authoring

One of the most important aspects of AR 2.0 is how the representation of the real world is captured. This is necessary so that AR 2.0 content can be attached to real world locations and objects. Of course, simple configurations can be created from markers, and environments that are planar (such as a wall) or near-planar (such as a façade) can simply be photographed and then turned into tracking targets with an automated tool. We also assume that wide-area geo-referenced information sources, such as a database of streets and even textured 3D models of buildings, are available through large geo-data providers. Moreover, large collections of geo-referenced photos are already available through image services. However, this does not solve the immediate problem of creating 3D models of specific environments or registering user-generated content in such an environment.

Early work in in-situ authoring focused on placing virtual objects in the real scene and supported users through triangulation from different views [Bai01] or working plane constraints [Pie04]. Another approach, which allows the user to create AR applications in place, was presented in [Lee04]. Here the designer can interact with the virtual world by using a marker-based tangible interface. Another example is sketchand+ [Sei03] an AR collaboration tool geared towards urban planner and architects. The approach was to annotate design proposals with 3D sketches, text snippets and audio clips in order to communicate processes, design decisions and other spatial artefacts to peers.

More recently, systems have been demonstrated that simplify the task of arranging virtual objects in 3D through constrained modelling. Wither et al. [Wit08] presented a system that uses a single point laser range finder to measure the object surface. Afterwards an annotation can be stuck to that object and automatically aligned to the surface of the object. A pure camera-based approach to specifying the location and orientation was demonstrated by the University of Cambridge [Rei06, Rei07] by integrating an online model estimation framework to extract the 3D geometry of the real world and place annotations automatically with respect to it.

2.4.3 Client Application Development

There has been little previous research on client authoring tools for end-user AR 2.0 applications, although there are several existing authoring tools for building AR applications and for mobile phone applications that provide a useful starting point. These can be broadly organized into two types: (1) AR authoring tools for programmers, (2) AR authoring tools for non-programmers. These categories can be further organized into low-level tools which require coding/scripting skills, and higher-level application builder tools which use higher-level libraries or visual authoring techniques (see Table 2.2).

Low-level AR computer vision tracking libraries such as ARToolKit [Kat99] can be used to calculate camera position relative to physical markers. However,

Table 2.2 Types of desktop AR authoring tools

	Programmers	Non-programmers
Low-level	ARToolkit [Kat99]	DART [Mac04]
	arTag [Fia05]	ComposAR [Don08]
High-level	Studierstube [Sza98]	AMIRE [Gri02]
	osgART [Gra05]	BuildAR [Bui09]

Table 2.3 Authoring tools for mobile phones

	Programmers	Non-programmers
Low-level	Studierstube Tracker [Sch08]	Python[17]
	ARToolkit for Symbian [Hen05]	
High-level	Studierstube ES [Sch08]	FlashLite[18]
	M3GE[19]	

in order to develop a complete application more code needs to be added for 3D model loading, interaction techniques and other utility functions. High-level programming libraries such as Studierstube [Sza98] and osgART [Gra05] provide a complete system for developing AR applications. Studierstube includes all of the functions needed for building an AR application such as scene graph rendering, networking, window management and support for input devices, etc.

There is another set of authoring tools that have been developed for non-programmers. At the most basic level, tools such as BuildAR [Bui09] allow users to associate virtual models with visually tracked AR markers, but there is no support for object interaction or more complicated behaviours. A more complete system is DART [Mac04], the Designers AR Toolkit. DART is a plug-in for the popular Macromedia Director software which allows non-programmers to create AR experiences using the low-level AR services provided by the Director Xtras and to integrate them with existing Director behaviours and concepts.

Although there are several tools for building desktop AR applications, there is less support for mobile AR. These tools can be summarised in Table 2.3. At the low-level, the ARToolKit tracking library has been ported over to the Symbian operating system [Hen05] while the Studierstube tracker library [Wag08a] runs on multiple mobile platforms such as Symbian, iPhone and Windows Mobile.

One of the few higher level programming libraries for mobile AR applications is the Studierstube ES [Sch08] (StbES) library. This is a C/C++ based application framework for developing AR applications for mobile devices. Studierstube ES provides support for 2D and 3D graphics, video capture, tracking, multimedia output, persistent storage and application authoring. For non-AR applications there are mobile 3D game engines such as the Java M3GE library that can be used for image loading, input, output, and general functions like AI, collision detection and other 3D rendering facilities.

---

[17] http://www.forum.nokia.com/Resources_and_Information/Tools/Runtimes/Python_for_S60/.

[18] http://www.adobe.com/products/flashlite/.

[19] https://m3ge.dev.java.net/.

For non-programmers, there is no mobile AR authoring tool but Python is available for rapid development of non-AR mobile applications. The Symbian version of Python[20] has support for 2D and 3D graphics, camera input, file handling, networking and many other functions for rapidly prototyping mobile applications. Users can develop python scripts on their desktop and then run them on their phone using a native interpreter. Other high-level visual design tools are available to author mobile graphics applications. The most popular is FlashLite,[21] a version of the Adobe Flash Player that has been specifically designed for use on mobile phones. With this a developer can use a combination of visual authoring and ActionScript scripting to build interactive phone applications.

Developing an AR 2.0 authoring tool for non-programmers is an active area of research, but as can be seen there are a number of options for developing AR 2.0 applications using existing low-level and high-level tools.

As it can be seen, there are currently no ideal tools for authoring AR 2.0 applications. This is an active area of research. However, there are methods that can be used for content aggregation, rapid prototyping and in-situ authoring. Over time these will progress from being low-level developer libraries to tools that can be easily used by non-programmers.

2.5 Case Studies

Although large-scale deployment of AR 2.0 applications has not occurred, there have been several mobile AR experiences that display features that are needed in such applications. In this section we report on several mobile AR case studies that teach important lessons for developing complete AR 2.0 applications.

2.5.1 Mobile AR Advertising

For AR 2.0 applications one of the challenges is how to deliver AR experiences to mobile devices on a massive scale. Traditionally AR applications have been preinstalled on devices or just distributed to a small number of users. However, recently researchers have begun to explore mobile AR advertising experiences that need to be widely distributed and so address the AR 2.0 deployment challenge.

In 2007 the HIT Lab NZ delivered the world's first mobile AR advertising campaign. Working in collaboration with Saatchi and Saatchi[22] and the Hyperfactory,[23] they developed a marketing campaign for the Wellington Zoo in Wellington, New Zealand. For 3 days in a local city paper an advertisement was printed with a number

---

[20] http://www.forum.nokia.com/python.

[21] http://www.adobe.com/products/flashlite/.

[22] http://www.saatchi.com/worldwide/index.asp.

[23] http://www.thehyperfactory.co.nz/.

Fig. 2.5 Wellington Zoo Mobile AR campaign: Printed AR Advertisement (*left*), Virtual Zoo Animal Appearing (*right*). (Image courtesy of the HIT Lab NZ)

that a code could be texted to (see Fig. 2.5, left). When the reader sent a text message to the number they were sent back a small 200 K application that they could run on their mobile phone. When the application was running they could point their mobile phone at the printed advertisement and see a virtual zoo animal, such as a cheetah, popping out of the newspaper page (see Fig. 2.5). This appeared overlaid on a live video view from the phone camera. To achieve this, a mobile AR application was written using the Symbian port of ARToolKit [Hen05], which combined a 3D model loader with marker-based tracking.

Although the AR application being delivered was very simple (just a single static model), there were challenges in being able to freely distribute a mobile AR advertisement outside of the lab environment. In this case the application was built for Nokia N-series mobile phones running the Symbian operating system, such as the N95 and N72 phones, etc. This meant that code on the application server needed to detect the type of phone that the text message came from. If the phone was not an N-series phone then the AR application was not sent since it could not be run. Instead a picture was sent back showing what the AR application would have looked like if the phone could have run it. There were also different versions of the application that needed to be developed depending on the N-series phone model that was being used. If the text message was sent from a Nokia phone then there was a specific executable sent to the mobile phone depending on the model of phone it was.

In addition there were challenges in creating the AR content. The initial virtual models delivered were designed for desktop applications. Significant work needed to be done to reduce them down to the size that they could be rendered in real time on the mobile phone.

Despite the work involved, the advertising campaign was a success. Attendance at the zoo increased, there was a large amount of press generated and Saatchi and Saatchi won several advertising awards for the innovative use of leading edge technology. Since that time several more campaigns have explored different aspects of AR marketing. In all cases the most challenging aspects have been the content creation and application distribution, not the application programming.

Although not a complete AR 2.0 application, this simple application shows both the impact that mobile AR applications can have and also the challenges that must be addressed in terms of content creation and application distribution.

2.5.2   Content Delivery

One of the key challenges of AR 2.0 applications is how to provide location-based delivery of software and services. For example, when a person is visiting a new city location they may want to be able to automatically download AR tags of building names and virtual comments that other visitors have left at that location.

Mobile service providers typically use 3G or GPRS to deliver content to the handset. However, this is often expensive (especially with service providers that charge for data transfer) and the 3G service isn't location-specific.

Researchers at the Australasian CRC for Interaction Design (ACID)[24] have been exploring an alternative delivery method that could be useful for AR 2.0 applications. The first version of this is an embedded device supporting transfer of digital content to and from nearby mobile phones. Called the InfoPoint, this is a small Linux computer connected to wired networking and Bluetooth hardware than can detect when mobile phones are within range and then use Bluetooth to automatically push content on the phone. In this way location-specific applications or data (such as text, image, audio and video files) can be delivered to phones at no cost to the end user, exploiting the use of the mobiles as "third screens" [Gog06]. The design intention behind InfoPoint is to manage and deliver situated content for mobile phone users without the need for custom software.

The InfoPoint access hardware was tested in a heritage trail tourist application in the Fishing Boat Harbour in Fremantle, Perth in 2008. This was an adaptation of a guidebook prototype that supported the upload and download of situated content by mobile phone users running custom software. The prototype used LightBlue to support Bluetooth features (OBEX) that avoided the need for users to install client software [Che05, Sch06]. The unit was solar-powered, sealed for protection against the coastal climate and mounted on a traffic pole (see Fig. 2.6). It also included a web interface for Fremantle Council to remotely manage content and review logs.

When users with Bluetooth enabled mobile phones walked within 30 m they were asked if they would like to receive historic information about the site. If they accepted, they received an mp3 file with an audio dramatization of a letter written by a Captain D.B. Shaw in 1892 describing Fremantle as "the worst damn hole I ever saw."

The system was tested over several months during which the InfoPoint detected an average of 600 distinct phones each day. The installation highlighted issues related to long-term real-world deployments. Only around 5% of users accepted the offer to receive the digital content, showing reluctance on the part of users to download unsolicited content. There were also major variations found in Bluetooth interfaces between mobile phone models and wide variations in familiarity with Bluetooth-based interaction, with a strong generational bias.

As can be seen, the InfoPoint prototype delivers rich media content to visitors' mobile phones, providing a platform for research into mobile experiences

---

[24] http://www.interactiondesign.com.au/.

Fig. 2.6 InfoPoint Hardware. (Image courtesy of ACID)

and interactions, user-generated content and system architectures. In the future the platform can be used to understand mobile phone users' experiences of situated content, and to explore interfaces for managing this content, with a longer term aim of exploring options for user-generated situated content.

2.5.3 Signpost

Signpost is an indoor navigation system, which takes advantage of associating locations with markers, thereby providing an inexpensive, building-wide guide executing solely on the end user's camera-enabled mobile phone. While previous work on barcode-based location tracking, such as applications requiring 2D-barcodes (e.g. QR Codes), rely on non real-time "snapshot" processing, our approach continuously scans an environment in search for navigation hints. The navigation therefore scales from sparse, strategically placed fiducial markers to continuous navigation in 3D with AR overlays.

Pose tracking-based on fiducial markers is a well-established mechanism in AR. Unlike natural feature tracking it is highly robust and works well under varying lighting conditions. Furthermore, efficient algorithms for detecting and estimating the pose of these markers exist, making the approach highly suitable for devices with minimal processing capabilities such as mobile phones. Although marker tracking systems can do 6 degree-of-freedom (DOF) pose estimation, in Signpost we typically use only 3DOF to reduce the effort in creating a building model (map), thus making the system more practical. Full 6DOF tracking can still be used for advanced interaction mechanisms. Deploying our system to a new location consists of three

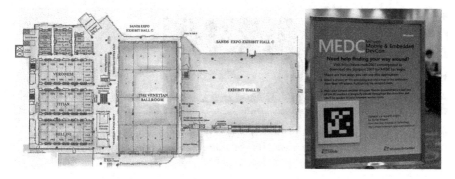

Fig. 2.7 Marker placement for Signpost 2007 at the MEDC 2007 conference in an area of roughly 100 × 200 m. Red dots mark locations of posters with instructions and markers (*left*). Poster with instructions and marker for tracking (*right*). (Image courtesy of Graz University of Technology)

steps: (1) creating a map and database of marker locations, (2) deploying markers on-site and (3) finally making the software available to potential users.

The mobile phone software activates the phone's built-in camera and continuously scans for markers at video frame rate. Since the phone is not a dedicated appliance, it was important to achieve a performance allowing the phone to remain highly responsive without disrupting regular cellular services.

Based on the technology presented in the previous section, we created a location-based conference guide, Signpost, which was deployed at several large trade conferences with thousands of attendees. The application is designed to work typically with sparse tracking to limit deployed markers to a manageable number. The left image in Fig. 2.7 shows the location of 37 markers that were installed at the conference site in the Venetian Hotel Las Vegas, an area of roughly 100 × 200 m.

While the 6DOF tracking can deliver centimetre-level accuracy when markers are tracked, presenting only 2D location on a map reduces accuracy requirements considerably. This was found important as conference organizers have to consider the logistics of deploying and inspecting marker placement. The most efficient way that was developed after consulting conference organizers was to stick markers onto poster stands which can be quickly deployed on-site at pre-planned locations (see Fig. 2.7). The poster stand also attracts attention and provides details on how to download the application from the local Wi-Fi network.

The core function of Signpost is its combination of a conference calendar and a navigation system. The conference calendar can be browsed using various filters such as per-day, per-session or full-text indexing. Live RSS updates from the Wi-Fi network make sure the latest changes are reflected in the schedule. All calendar entries are linked to locations, so that the navigation module can compute the fastest route from the current location (sampled from the last seen marker) to the desired lecture hall. The results are displayed on a map that can be freely navigated by panning, rotating and zooming relative to a marker or using phone hotkeys.

For large events in venues with multiple levels or buildings, a single map is no longer sufficient. Signpost therefore supports multiple maps linked to a 3D overview,

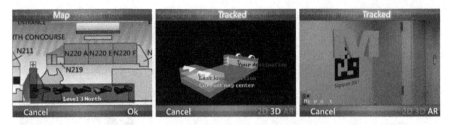

Fig. 2.8 Switching between maps (*left*), 3D view of the building with the current user's location (middle), Built-in AR mini-game (*right*). (Image courtesy of Graz University of Technology)

or alternatively an interactive 3D representation of the building showing the global geographic relationship of the current location and the target location (see Fig. 2.8).

A built-in Augmented Reality mini-game challenges users with a treasure hunt. In this game, each marker in the environment holds a specific 3D game object such as a company logo (see right image in Fig. 2.8). The game objects only appear in the AR video view. A user managing to collect all game objects may register for a prize drawing or win a conference hat.

2.6 Next Steps

In this chapter we have described the concept of the AR 2.0 platform and have also discussed some early case studies that show technology that could be used to develop that platform. However before AR 2.0 applications become commonplace there are an important number of next steps that must take place. In particular important work needs to be conducted in the following areas, among others; Localization and Registration, Application Development, and User Evaluation.

2.6.1 Localization and Registration

In order to provide compelling AR 2.0 applications there is a need for research on better methods for outdoor localization and registration. Early AR systems developed for outdoor use relied on GPS for position measurements and magnetic compasses and inertial sensors for orientation [Fei97, Hoe99, Bai01, Tho98, Pie01]. Recent examples, such as Nokia's MARA project [Gre06] and Wikitude [Mob09] work on mobile phones and exploit the embedded sensors, including GPS, accelerometers and a compass. However, GPS is only typically accurate to about 10 m, creating large registration errors for virtual objects and its reliability significantly deteriorates in urban environments due to shadowing from buildings. Indoors, the GPS signal is usually unavailable. Similarly, inertial sensors are prone to drift and magnetic sensors are disturbed by local magnetic fields encountered in urban environments.

Computer vision techniques can be used to overcome these limitations. These directly rely on the image to be augmented, so the placements of virtual images can be accurate up to the pixel. The camera pose is estimated by matching image features and minimizing the re-projection error of these features in the image. This is an active area of research. The University of Cambridge has demonstrated a fast edge-based 3D tracking algorithm [Dru99] and successfully applied it to Augmented Reality in [Kle03] and [Kle04]. EPFL developed a feature-point-based system that matches points with reference images and also tracks feature points over time to prevent drift and jitter [Vac03].

The recent developments of feature point descriptors such as SIFT [Low04] or SURF [Bay06a] allow for fast matching of the captured image against a set of reference images. EPFL also developed an approach called Ferns that is computationally more efficient but requires more memory [Ozu07]. These techniques can be used for accurate, autonomous and robust initialization. These techniques have been tried in localization methods by matching captured images against databases of geo-referenced images [Siv03, Nis06, Mob09b]. Some authors demonstrated that techniques from this category perform relatively well with large datasets of city landmarks [Phi07, Phi08]. However, these approaches require large amounts of memory, and are not feasible on mobile devices.

Both sources of information, image matching and geo-location sensors, represent a promising area of research but the final goal should be to develop systems combining both sources. Reitmayr developed one of the first handheld augmented reality devices that rely on a combination of edge-based tracking, inertial sensors and GPS to perform robust and accurate 3D tracking in outdoor conditions [Rei06, Rei07]. More recently, [Tak08] uses the SURF local descriptor and fast computation of near-neighbour using kd-trees to match images. Running feature extraction and matching on the client-side against a local database of features determined by the current GPS estimate allowed real-time performance. Schall et al. showed a system that compensated the error of a digital compass and inertia sensors using a vision based panorama tracker [Sch09] presented in [Wag10].

One of the main problems is that mobile phones have limited processing power, while computer vision algorithms typically perform heavy computations. Hence we require improved computer vision tracking algorithms for AR. In 2003 the ARToolKit library was ported to Windows CE [Wag03] and creating the first self-contained AR application on an off-the-shelf embedded device. This evolved into the ARToolKitPlus [Wag07] and heavily optimized Studierstube Tracker [Wag08a] libraries. Most recently the first natural feature tracking solution running at frame rate on mobile phones was developed. Wagner et al. [Wag08b] modified the SIFT [Low04] and Ferns [Ozu07] approaches and created the first real-time 6 Degrees-of-Freedom natural feature tracking system running on mobile phones.

2.6.2 AR 2.0 Application Development Areas

Once AR 2.0 hardware and software platform technology has been developed there is future work that can be conducted in exploring possible application areas. Some of the possible application areas include the following:

Personal city exploration: Users can create and browse recommendations, comments and hints about tourist places, restaurants, bars and shops and leave personal, user-generated content created by tourists and citizens for others in the community. This would form an ideal test-bed for the usefulness of the interfaces for selecting and creating content, and system scalability.

Urban sub-culture: Providing tools for young people to express themselves creatively, such as virtual graffiti, where the mobile phone can be used as a spray can, city tagging with exciting media, or video and image diaries that are related to a certain location. In this way a virtual dimension is added to street art. It can also be used to mark cool locations and organise events.

Culture information: Professional content can be experienced for cultural highlights and sight-seeing spots in the city. Cultural objects can be enriched by virtual media that explains its origin and significance for the city. The accurate overlay of digital 3D reconstructions or adequately historical images can simulate a view into the past. Users can contribute with their annotations, post comments or recommendations.

Urban planning: Planned, virtual architecture can be viewed within the real environment of the city. This provides a completely novel way in which architects and urban planners can visualise and examine their visions. The same data can be kept open for the public to give interested citizens the chance to comment on planned constructions.

Urban maintenance: People responsible for maintenance of the city infrastructure can retrieve important status information on site, coordinate with other staff members and create and anchor their own situation assessment and status reports. Here AR makes it possible to accurately mark critical spots or objects and provide valuable annotations for an efficient and flawless handling of maintenance or emergency cases.

2.6.3 User Evaluation

An important part of AR 2.0 development will be to evaluate prototype interfaces and provide guidance to on-going application development. Evaluation methods for handheld augmented reality applications are only beginning to emerge. Early examples are the evaluation of AR Tennis [Hen06] and the Virtual AR Guide [Wag06b] applications. However, those tests were performed with only small user groups in very formal test setups. In the future there will be a need to move beyond the state of the art by developing novel methods for evaluating AR user interfaces designed for large-scale use and social networking applications with many simultaneous users.

Most of the published AR research has been on enabling technologies (tracking or displays, etc), or on experimental prototype applications, but there has been little user evaluation of AR interfaces [Dun07]. For example, in 2005 Swann et al. [Swa05] produced a literature survey reviewing all of the AR research papers from leading journals and conferences and they found that less than 8% had any formal user evaluation as part of them. Thus there is a need for examples of user evaluations of AR applications and development of new methods for AR user evaluation. The HIT Lab NZ has since then developed a report reviewing all of the known AR user studies to the end of 2008, again identifying key gaps in the research literature [Dun08]. One of the areas with smallest amount of research is on evaluation of collaborative systems with only 10 out of total of 161 AR papers with user evaluations focusing on collaborative applications, or just 6% of all known AR user studies.

There is research that needs to be conducted in the evaluation of the social network and collaborative communities facilitated by the AR 2.0 platform. Numerous papers have been published on the evaluation of social networks, the effectiveness of social networking visualization tools [Hen07, Tur05], social network user interfaces [Riv96], impact on collaboration [McD03, Don99] and user behaviour in social networks [Acq06, Vie04], among other topics. However, there has been little previous work on user studies of location-based social networking, such as [Bur04], and no work on the evaluation of augmented reality for location-based collaboration. Many of the evaluations of social networks have been focused on qualitative methods such as user surveys and interviews, and not quantitative measures. There is a need to conduct research in evaluation of augmented reality for location-based collaboration and also develop new evaluation methodologies that can be used by the broader research community for these types of user studies.

2.7 Conclusions

In this chapter we have described the concept of AR 2.0 and showed that Augmented Reality technology has developed to the point that it can be widely deployed on handheld devices and consumer-level hardware. Furthermore, we showed how the Web 2.0 infrastructure and tools allow user-generated content to be created and shared with social networking communities. Taken together these recent developments allow us to create location-based AR experiences that can be enjoyed on a global scale.

Early case studies show the potential for using mobile phones for experiencing AR content, for widespread deployment of AR applications and for experiencing AR real world navigation tasks. However, these studies have also identified important issues that need to be addressed in terms of the user experience, installing applications and tracking user location.

In the future, before AR 2.0 applications become commonplace, there are important research issues that must be solved in terms of device localization and registration, building demonstration applications, and conducting user evaluation.

Acknowledgements This work was sponsored partially by the Austrian Science Fund FWF under grant no. Y193 and grant no. W1209, the Christian Doppler Laboratory for Handheld Augmented Reality as well as the EU funded project MARCUS (FP7-PEOPLE-IRSES-2008-230831). The authors would like to thank Istvan Barakonyi for contributing many important ideas.

References

[Aar01] Aarts E., Harwig R., and Schuurmans M., Ambient intelligence, The invisible future: the seamless integration of technology into everyday life, McGraw-Hill, New York, 2001

[Acq06] Acquisti, A. and Gross, R., Imagined Communities: Awareness, Information Sharing, and Privacy on the Facebook. PET 2006, LNCS 4258:36–58, 2006

[Azu97] Azuma, R.T., A Survey of Augmented Reality. Presence: Teleoperators and Virtual Environments 6, 4 (Aug 1997), 355–385, 1997

[Bai01] Baillot, Y., Brown D., and Julier S., Authoring of physical models using mobile computers. In Proc. of ISWC 2001, pages 39–46, 2001

[Bar06] Barsky E. and Purdon M., Introducing Web 2.0: social networking and social bookmarking for health librarians. Journal of the Medical Library Association 2006

[Bay06a] Bay, H., Tuytelaars, T., and Van Gool, L., SURF: Speeded up robust features. In Proc. of the European Conference on Computer Vision, 2006

[Bui09] BuildAR website: http://www.buildar.co.nz/

[Bur04] Burak, A. and Sharon, T., Usage patterns of FriendZone: mobile location-based community services. In Proc. MUM '04, vol. 83. ACM, New York, 93–100. 2004

[Che05] Cheverest, K., et al., Exploring Bluetooth based mobile phone interaction with the Hermes photo display, MobileHCI05, 47–54, ACM, New York, 2005

[Deu09] Deusto Sentient Graffiti Project website: http://www.smartlab.deusto.es/dsg/

[Dod09] http://www.dodgeball.com

[Don99] Donath, J.S., Visualizing Conversation. Journal of Computer-Mediated Communication, 4(4). 1999

[Don08] Dongpyo, H., Looser, J., Seichter, H., Billinghurst, M., and Woontack, W. 2008. A Sensor-Based Interaction for Ubiquitous Virtual Reality Systems. In Ubiquitous Virtual Reality, 2008. ISUVR 2008. International Symposium on, 75–78

[Dru99] Drummond, T.W. and Cipolla, R., Visual tracking and control using Line algebra. In Proc. of CVPR 1999, Ft. Collins, CO, USA, June 23–25, 1999

[Dun07] Dünser, A., Grasset, R., Seichter, H., and Billinghurst M., Applying HCI principles to AR systems design, presented at MRUI'07: Workshop at IEEE VR 2007, 2007

[Dun08] Dünser, A., Grasset, R. and Billinghurst M., A Survey of Evaluation Techniques Used in Augmented Reality Studies. HIT Lab NZ Technical Report TR-2008–02, 2007

[Eag05] Eagle N., Pentland A., "Social Serendipity: Mobilizing Social Software," IEEE Pervasive Computing, vol. 4, no. 2, pp. 28–34, 2005

[Fei97] Feiner S., MacIntyre B., Höllerer T., and Webster A.: A touring machine: Prototyping 3d mobile augmented reality systems for exploring the urban environment. Proceedings of the First International Symposium on Wearable Computers (ISWC), pp. 74–81, 1997

[Fia05] Fiala, M., ARTag, A Fiducial Marker System Using Digital Techniques. In Proc. of the 2005 IEEE Computer Society Conference on Computer Vision and Pattern Recognition (CVPR'05) – vol. 2, pp. 590–596, 2005

[Gog06] Goggin G., Cell phone culture: Mobile technology in everyday life, Routledge, New York, 2006

[Gra05] Grasset R., Looser J., and Billinghurst M., 2005. OSGARToolKit: tangible + transitional 3D collaborative mixed reality framework. In Proc. of the 2005 international Conference on Augmented Tele-Existence (Christchurch, New Zealand, December 05 – 08, 2005). ICAT '05, vol. 157. ACM, New York, 257–258

[Gre06] Greene K., Hyperlinking reality via phones. MIT Technology Review, 2006

[Gri02] Grimm P., Haller M., Paelke V., Reinhold S., Reimann C., and Zauner J., AMIRE – Authoring Mixed Reality, The First IEEE International Augmented Reality Toolkit Workshop, Germany, 2002

[Hen05] Henrysson A., Billinghurst M., and Ollila M., Face to Face Collaborative AR on Mobile Phones. Proceedings International Symposium on Augmented and Mixed Reality (ISMAR'05), pp. 80–89, Austria, 2005

[Hen06] Henrysson A., Billinghurst M., and Ollila M., AR Tennis. ACM Siggraph, ACM, Boston, USA, 2006

[Hen07] Henry N. and Fekete J., MatLink: Enhanced Matrix Visualization for Analyzing Social Networks. In Interact 2007, LNCS 4663, Part II, pp. 288–302, 2007

[Hoe99] Höllerer T., Feiner S., Terauchi T., Rashid G., and Hallaway D., Exploring MARS: developing indoor and outdoor user interfaces to a mobile augmented reality system. Computer & Graphics, 23(6):779–785, 1999

[Hoh99] Hohl F., Kubach U., Leonhardi A., Rothermel K., and Schwehm M., Next century challenges: Nexus–an open global infrastructure for spatial-aware applications. In Proc. of International Conference on Mobile Computing and Networking, pp. 249–255, 1999

[Jab09] http://www.urban-atmospheres.net/Jabberwocky/

[Kat99] Kato H. and Billinghurst M., Marker Tracking and HMD Calibration for a video-based Augmented Reality Conferencing System. In Proc. of the 2nd International Workshop on Augmented Reality (IWAR 99), pp. 85–94, USA, 1999

[Kle03] Klein G. and Drummond T.W., Robust visual tracking for non-instrumented augmented reality. In Proc. of ISMAR 2003, pages 113–122, Tokyo, Japan, 2003

[Kle04] Klein G. and Drummond T.W., Sensor fusion and occlusion refinement for tablet-based AR. In Proc. of ISMAR 2004, pages 38–47, Arlington, VA, USA, Nov 25 2004

[Lee04] Lee G., et al., Immersive Authoring of Tangible Augmented Reality Applications. Proceedings of the IEEE and ACM International Symposium on Mixed and Augmented Reality 2004. 2004

[Low04] Lowe D.G., Distinctive image features from scale-invariant keypoints. International Journal of Computer Vision, 60(2):91–110, 2004

[Mac04] MacIntyre B., Gandy M., Dow S., and Bolter J.D., DART: A Toolkit for Rapid Design Exploration of Augmented Reality Experiences, User Interface Software and Technology (UIST'04), Sante Fe, New Mexico, 2004

[McD03] McDonald D.W., Recommending collaboration with social networks: a comparative evaluation. In Proc. CHI '03. ACM, 593–600, 2003

[Miz00] Mizell D., Augmented Reality Applications in Aerospace, IEEE and ACM International Symposium on Augmented Reality (ISAR'00), 2000

[Mob09] Mobilizy, Wikitude – AR Travel Guide, Website: http://www.mobilizy.com/wikitude.php, visited Mar 25, 2009

[Mob09b] IST Mobvis, FP6-511051, Website: http://www.mobvis.org/, visited March 26, 2009

[Mh04] Möhring, M., Lessig, C. and Bimber, C. Video See-Through AR on Consumer Cell Phones. Proceedings of International Symposium on Augmented and Mixed Reality (ISMAR'04), pp. 252–253, 2004

[Nis06] Nister, D. and Stewenius, H., Scalable recognition with a vocabulary tree. In Proc. of CVPR, 2006

[New06] Newman J., Schall G., Barakonyi I., Schürzinger A., and Schmalstieg D., Wide-Area Tracking Tools for Augmented Reality. In Proc. of the 4th International Conference on Pervasive Computing, 2006

[Ore08] O'Reilly T. What is Web 2.0? Design patterns and business models for the next generation of software http://oreillynet.com/pub/a/oreilly/tim/news/2005/09/30/what-is-web-20.html (accessed Jul 2008)

[Ozu07] Ozuysal M., Fua P., and Lepetit V., Fast Keypoint Recognition in Ten Lines of Code. In Proc. of IEEE Conf. on Computer Vision and Pattern Recognition, 2007

[Pie01] Piekarski W. and Thomas B.H., Tinmith-evo5 – An Architecture for Supporting Mobile Augmented Reality Environments. In 2nd Int'l Symposium on Augmented Reality, pp 177–178, New York, Oct 2001

[Pie04] Piekarski W. and Thomas B.H., Augmented Reality Working Planes: A Foundation for Action and Construction at a Distance. In 3rd Int'l Symposium on Mixed and Augmented Reality, Arlington, Va, Oct 2004

[Phi07] Philbin J., Chum O., Isard M., Sivic J., and Zisserman A., Object retrieval with large vocabularies and fast spatial matching. In Proc. of CVPR, 2007

[Phi08] Philbin J., Chum O., Isard M., Sivic J., and Zisserman A., Lost in quantization: Improving particular object retrieval in large scale image databases. In Proc. of CVPR, 2008

[Pla09] http://www.plazes.com

[Rei06] Reitmayr G. and Drummond T., Going Out: Robust Model-based Tracking for Outdoor Augmented Reality Proc. IEEE ISMAR'06, Santa Barbara, California, USA, 2006

[Rei07] Reitmayr G. and Drummond T., Initialisation for Visual Tracking in Urban Environ- mentsProc. IEEE ISMAR'07, Nara, Japan, 2007

[Riv96] Rivera K., Cooke N. and Bauhs J., The effects of emotional icons on remote commu- nication, Conference companion on Human factors in computing systems: common ground, pp. 99–100, Apr 13–18, 1996

[Rum09] http://www.rummble.com/

[Sch06] Scheibe M., Meissner F.W., Tunbridge I., Investigating clientless mobile phone inter- action with a Bluetooth public display, CS06–14–00, University of Cape Town, 2006

[Sch09] Schall G., Wagner D., Reitmayr G., Wieser M., Teichmann E., Schmalstieg D., and Hofmann-Wellenhof B., Proceedings of the 2009 8th IEEE International Symposium on Mixed and Augmented Reality (ISMAR), pp. 153–162, 2009

[Sch08] Schmalstieg D. and Wagner D., Mobile Phones as a Platform for Augmented Reality. In Proc. of the IEEE VR 2008 Workshop on Software Engineering and Architectures for Realtime Interactive Systems, IEEE, Reno, NV, USA, Shaker Publishing, 43–44, 2008

[Sie04] Sielhorst T., Obst T., Burgkart R., Riener R., and Navab N., An augmented real- ity delivery simulator for medical training. In International Workshop on Augmented Environments for Medical Imaging – MICCAI Satellite Workshop, 2004

[Siv03] Sivic J. and Zisserman A., Video google: A text retrieval approach to object matching in videos. In Proc. of ICCV, 2003

[Sei03] Seichter H., Araya C., Ekasidh C., Kamol K. and Walaiporn N., sketchand+, In CAADRIA 2003, 209–219, 2003

[Son09] Eye of Judgement: http://www.us.playstation.com/PS3/Games/THE_EYE_OF_ JUDGMENT

[Spo99] Spohrer J., Information in Places, IBM System Journal 38(4):602–628, 1999

[Sut68] Sutherland I., A head-mounted three-dimensional display. In Proc. of the Fall Joint Computer Conference. AFIPS Conference Proceedings, vol. 33. AFIPS, Arlington, VA., 757–764, 1968

[Swa05] Swan J.E. and Gabbard J.L., Survey of User-Based Experimentation in Augmented Reality, presented at 1st International Conference on Virtual Reality, Las Vegas, Nevada, 2005

[Sza98] Szalavari S., Schmalstieg D., Fuhrmann D., and Gervautz M., "Studierstube" – An Environment for Collaboration in Augmented Reality, Virtual Reality – Systems, Development and Applications, vol. 3, No. 1, pp. 37–49, Springer, New York 1998

[Tak08] Takacs G., Chandrasekhar V., Gelfand N., Xiong Y., Chen W.-C., Bismpigiannis T., Grzeszczuk R., Pulli K., and Girod B., Outdoors Augmented Reality on Mobile Phone using Loxel-Based Visual Feature Organization. In Proc. of the 1st ACM International Conference on Multimedia Information Retrieval, pp. 427–434, 2008

[Tho98] Thomas B.H., Demczuk V., Piekarski W., Hepworth D., and Gunther B., A wearable computer system with augmented reality to support terrestrial navigation. In Proc. of ISWC'98, pages 168–171, Pittsburgh, PA, USA, Oct 19–20, 1998

[Tur05] Turner T., Smith M., Fisher D., and Welser H., Picturing Usenet: Mapping Computer-Mediated Collective Action. Journal of Computer Mediated Communication. 10(4), 2005

[Vac03] Vacchetti L., Lepetit V., and Fua P., Stable real-time 3d tracking using online and offline information. IEEE Trans. PAMI 26(10):1385–1391, 2000

[Vie04] Viegas F.B. and Smith M.A., Newsgroup Crowds and Author Lines: Visualizing the Activity of Individuals in Conversational Cyberspaces, 2004

[Wag03] Wagner D. and Schmalstieg D., First Steps Towards Handheld Augmented Reality. In Proc. of the 7th IEEE international Symposium on Wearable Computers (Oct 21–23, 2003). ISWC. IEEE Computer Society, Washington, DC, 2003

[Wag06b] Wagner D., Billinghurst M., and Schmalstieg D., How Real Should Virtual Characters Be? Conference on Advances in Computer Entertainment Technology 2006 (ACE 2006), 2006

[Wag07] Wagner D. and Schmalstieg D., ARToolKitPlus for Pose Tracking on Mobile Devices. In Proc. of 12th Computer Vision Winter Workshop (CVWW'07), pp. 139–146, 2007

[Wag08a] Wagner D., Langlotz T. and Schmalstieg D., Robust und Unobtrusive Marker Tracking on Mobile Phones. In Proc. of ISMAR'08, pp. 121–124, 2008

[Wag08b] Wagner D., Reitmayr G., Mulloni A., Drummond T.W., and Schmalstieg D., Pose tracking from natural features on mobile phones. In Proc. of ISMAR'08, 125–134, 2008

[Wag10] Wagner D., Mulloni A., Langlotz T., and Schmalstieg D., Real-time Panoramic Mapping and Tracking on Mobile Phones. In Proc. of Virtual Reality'10, pp. 211–218, 2010

[Wit08] Wither J., Coffin C., Ventura J., and Höllerer T., Fast Annotation and Modeling with a Single-Point Laser Range Finder In Proc. ACM/IEEE Symposium on Mixed and Augmented Reality, Sept. 15–18, 2008

Chapter 3
Experiential Fidelity: Leveraging the Mind to Improve the VR Experience

Steffi Beckhaus and Robert W. Lindeman

Abstract Much of Virtual Reality (VR) is about creating environments that are believable. But though the visual and audio experiences we provide today are already of a rather high sensory fidelity, there is still something lacking; something hinders us from fully buying into the worlds we experience through VR technology.

We introduce the notion of Experiential Fidelity, which is an attempt to create a deeper sense of presence by carefully designing the user experience. We suggest to guide the users' frame of mind in a way that their expectations, attitude, and attention are aligned with the actual VR experience, and that the user's own imagination is stimulated to complete the experience. This work was inspired by a collection of personal magic moments and factors that were named by leading researchers in VR. We present those magic moments and some thoughts on how we can tap into experiential fidelity. We propose to do this not through technological means, but rather through the careful use of suggestion and allusion. By priming the user's mind prior to exposure to our virtual worlds, we can assist her in entering a mental state that is more willing to believe, even using the limited actual fidelity available today.

3.1 The Quest

Much of Virtual Reality (VR) is about creating virtual environments that are believable. But though the visual and audio experiences we provide today approach the limits of human sensory systems, there is still something lacking; something beyond

S. Beckhaus (✉)
im.ve, Department of Informatics, University of Hamburg, Vogt-Kölln-Str. 30, 22767 Hamburg, Germany
e-mail: steffi.beckhaus@uni-hamburg.de

R.W. Lindeman
HIVE Lab, Department of Computer Science, Worcester Polytechnic Institute, 100 Institute Rd., Worcester, MA 01609, USA
e-mail: gogo@wpi.edu

S. Coquillart et al. (eds.), *Virtual Realities*, DOI 10.1007/978-3-211-99178-7_3,
© Springer-Verlag/Wien 2011

sensory fidelity hinders us from crossing the uncanny valley [18], keeping us from fully buying into the worlds we experience through VR technology.

Working on improving realism has been a driving force behind much of VR research. The breadth of work the VR community has used to attack the problem includes improving visual characteristics (e.g., resolution, field of view, field of regard, model fidelity, rendering speed), audio attributes (e.g., bit rate, number of simultaneous audio sources, faithfulness, spatialization [30]), haptic cues (e.g., direction and magnitude of forces, coverage of the human body, delay), olfactory displays (e.g., scent generation, scene delivery, and scent variety [7, 32, 33]), and even gustatory output (e.g., consistency, sample delivery [12]).

These all contribute to increasing the sensory fidelity and thus provide for an increased level of immersion, aiding in evoking the illusion of a place [24]. Better immersive technology, however, does not necessarily provide a better VR experience. Asking "how much immersion is enough," Bowman and McMahan point out the possibilities, but also the limits, of just investing more in improving the match between visual fidelity and reality. Their research showed that this does not always, for example, also improve the results of learning [3].

While sensory fidelity is important from a *technical* point of view for immersion, the user's sense of "being there" is *qualitative* in nature. Presence, the user's subjective psychological response to a VR system, is an individual and context-dependent user response [23]. The level of presence invoked in users is also one of the most common measurements of the quality of effectiveness of a virtual environment (VE) [27]. This suggests that one of the factors for effective VEs is content. Whitton phrases this in the way that it is a combination of *immersing technologies* and *well-designed applications* that will then let users experience real, recreated, abstract, or imaginary places [31]. Here, she also points out the necessity of paying attention to the delivered *content*. A lot of research has been done on content-driven factors, such as realism of virtual characters [13, 15] and environments [16], naturalness of user interaction [2], evaluation of performance [20], presence [25], and perception [11], to name a few.

This, however, might not be enough. Entertainment is not the only area needing effective, emotion-evoking scenarios [28, 31]. The relevancy of such scenarios extends much further: education applications, communication and persuasion needs, and also phobia and pain treatment require a VR application that provides a deep and meaningful experience. In educational applications, studies have shown that an immersive learning experience creates a profound sense of motivation and concentration conducive to mastering complex, abstract material [5]. VR Phobia training strongly relies on evoking responses and experiences similar to that of the real threat [8]. VR pain treatment showed great success in distracting the minds of patients during their highly painful daily burn wound care procedures [9]. All of these obviously involve the user deeply in some kind of experience, motivating learning, or distracting them from the real world. What is this experience, and what level of experiential fidelity do these applications need and provide?

At the perceptual level, the various human sensory systems (e.g., vision, audition) are fed stimuli that reach the brain, where they are interpreted through a "lens" of previous experience, and tempered by the current state of the user [14]. The experience is simultaneously stored for later retrieval and further interpretation. In addition, the new experience could alter the user state, moving her from one of relaxation to anticipation, for example.

While this is a fairly simplistic model, it allows us to think about ways of designing for the user experience beyond altering the sensory stimuli. While some work has been done on trying to interpret the state of the user, another approach would be to coerce the user into a state of mind that is receptive for her to more-easily believe what the VR experience is designed for.

This is one aspect of what we mean by the term Experiential Fidelity:

improving the user experience by increasing the alignment of what the VR experience provides with that which the user is likely to believe.

In game design the driving force is the user experience. Game designers often seek to keep players engaged by creating various levels of goals: short-term (collect the magic keys), lasting seconds; medium-term (open the enchanted safe), lasting minutes; and finally, long-term (save the world), lasting the length of the game [28]. Swartout and van Lent describe that in entertainment, simply because it is a game, people are more willing to suspend their disbelief and subsequently will have a deeper immersion (in the commonly used sense) in the game. Game designers thus craft every aspect of the player's experience to support the desired effect and avoid breaking their sense of immersion. For example, simple scripted virtual characters that always behave believably are more desirable, than complex autonomous characters that occasionally make stupid mistakes, thus breaking the sense of immersion [28].

Many of the features in games can be applied to serious-minded applications, ultimately providing a deep, memorable user experience. It is, however, not clear what the fabrics of a user experience in general are and what this means for VR. It is clear by now that there is more to creating an experience than providing high-fidelity, multi-sensory stimuli to our VR participants. To induce a sense of deep realism and believability, high fidelity is not even required. "Low-tech" media such as books, music, and film regularly transport us to fantastic situations, and engross us to the point of willing suspension of disbelief that we are not actually in the worlds they conjure. Many filmmakers understand the power of the human mind for rounding out the experience. For example, Ridley Scott taps into this in his movie *Alien* [22], whereby instead of explicitly showing the audience the creature, we only get to see quick flashes of it, its shadow, evidence that it had been there (residue slime), and what it does (dead victims).

This points at another aspect of Experiential Fidelity:

the extent to which a person is able to fill in gaps in perception is related to the amount and richness of previous material from which to draw.

The question remains, what a user experience then is and, moreover, how we can aid in creating a valid, valuable, deep user experience for VR. This question made us look at the far end of user experiences: real-world, personal magic moments.

3.2 Where Does the Magic Come From?

In the Dagstuhl seminar on Virtual Realities attended by more than 50 leading VR researchers in 2008, we explored the notions outlined above in a group session by way of describing personal "Magic Moments," and identified several diverse factors that potentially stimulate and trigger great experiences. Magic moments are arguably very rare and will not be the ultimate goal for many of our VR applications. But if we begin to understand the diversity and fabrics of these deep experiences, then we might get hints about how to design for the "ordinary experiences" useful for education, therapy, or any other domain. We might also gain a better understanding into why users experience our installations in a specific way.

3.2.1 Magic Moments

Some of the situations that participants listed as magic moments are presented below. These descriptions are by people who have been working on VR research for a significant number of years with great investment into thinking about this issue. The answers, on purpose, were mostly personal and descriptive of a personal event. The question posed to everybody was, what was the most memorable, magic moment of your life? The answers were:

- Sitting with friends listening to music, I am often struck with surprise by the sense of openness between us, because of the ease of interactivity and intimacy.
- Achievement of flow [4] constitutes magic moments for me.
- For me, it usually has some element of surprise or novelty. Magic often happens for me when I can get time alone, for quiet relaxation, a lack of demands, and solitude.
- I most remember full-body experiences, and living in the moment, such as sitting in a hot tub while really stressed, or standing in the rain and getting that full experience.
- I was a spectator at a unique theatre show that had a huge outdoor stage (1 km wide) with airplanes, boats, fire, video walls and such, set up by a river. This was true full-sensory stimulation.
- Some of these are an escape from reality, and are in stark contrast to the real world; maybe the key is being in the moment and knowing you are doing so.
- For me, memorable moments are those with high anticipation, followed by achievement of a goal (performance).
- Visiting the Oklahoma City bombing site was unforgettable, because of the weight of the event that happened there.
- I had the good fortune of fulfilling a childhood dream of playing hockey in a famous stadium.
- For me, it is when I am so engaged in an activity that I lose track of time and space; my focus is drawn in to what I am doing.

- Sometimes, though rarely, I experience a focus of consciousness and self-sense of the scale of things, extreme hypersensitivity, a heightened awareness and lack of distraction.
- The book "Blink" by Malcolm Gladwell [6] describes situations where things slow down and sometimes you don't pay attention to other senses. This gets at one aspect of it for me.
- For me, it's about emotions, experiencing a range of them, and feeling the extremes.
- Environmentally appropriate music enhances experience; environmental sounds can be of even more benefit.
- Doing "The Wave" at a stadium is an example of a large group engaged in a shared experience.

These statements show the diversity of situations that are capable of evoking deep emotions and engagement in people. Some experiences are highly personal and the invoking situation was built up over a long time, others have to do with social interaction, others with specific states of mind. In short, the non-exclusive factors mentioned in the statements are living in the moment, flow, personal achievement, surprise, novelty, relief following anxiety, ambient responsiveness, awareness and mindfulness, engagement, release of pressure, focus of consciousness, multi-sensory experiences, and dream fulfillment.

3.2.2 Bringing Magic into Virtual Environments

Most of these experiences are difficult to create for a general audience and in the short amount of time people usually experience a Virtual Environment (VE). However, some content-oriented factors that might be prerequisites to prepare for a more generally applicable magic experience were named as: provide for a *new* kind of experience, let users do something they always wanted to do but cannot do in the real world, enable learning, and enable the creation of something.

3.2.3 Providing Personal Value in Applications

The most important factor, however, is that we create applications that offer a *personal value* to the user. Something that can be *achieved*, *experienced*, or *learned* by the user in the environment. An application might then be most memorable if it taps into a personal or collective need that is not otherwise fulfilled, provides personal value, or even fulfills a heart's desire. These factors will largely influence the motivation to use the VE in the first place.

3.3   Factors Supporting the User Experience

This first round of statements collecting magic moments also prepared us to collect a list of more-general approaches that influenced those experiences, or that could aid in creating memorable experiences in VR. Following some discussion, we found that it is, for example, important to pay attention to: the invitation, context, and surrounding (the lab), the third-person view (people using the VE before you), the transition to the virtual world, safety (actual and felt), and distractions (from technology, people, cabling, furniture, noise etc.).

All these influence the mindset of the users and contribute to shaping the experience of the participants. While most of them also involve some physical actions, like writing invitations or removing cables, they all are about creating and supporting a backstory for the experience in the user's mind. Safety, for example, is about making a user feel safe and happy to use the environment. This is, however, not only to avoid harm to people but also to ensure them that they can relax into what will follow. Distractions can be dealt with either by removing them, by covering them or by including them into a story and, by this, re-framing how they are experienced. The phrasing of the invitation, for example, can help align the participant's expectations with the provided experience.

Therefore, beyond technological factors, it is worthwhile to also pay attention to the *mind of the user*. The user's mind either buys into the stimuli delivered, or doesn't. It accepts the virtual world as plausible, or it decides not to dive in. It does this despite the sure knowledge that the virtual world is not the real world [24]. Therefore, in addition to providing place illusion and plausibility illusion, the mind also needs incentives to buy into the overall delivered experience.

Providing a consistent story can be done on may levels. To give some examples that are relevant for VR research, we further discuss the factors supporting a user experience by talking about three topics that are all interrelated and help to support a consistent backstory: Priming, Transitions, and Reality-based inclusions including the Re-framing of Technology.

3.3.1   Priming

Priming is when an earlier stimulus influences the response to a later stimulus. Priming users is what we do either before users enter our lab, while they wait for their turn, while they are fitted with technology, or inside the application itself. Instead of relying on previous experiences the user may or may not have had, we can explicitly prime users prior to entering the virtual world, thereby structuring their anticipation in a way that will increase the impact of what we present. Phrasing the invitation, apologizing for things that might not work later, or giving an introduction to what will happen are all examples of priming. Indirect priming occurs, if we, for example, provide a professional looking lab, focussed only on the task to follow, or if we lead people into a very lively VR research lab with many other things going on.

3.3.1.1 Invitation

The experience actually starts way before entering a CAVE^{TM} or donning a Head-Mounted Display (HMD). Even the way in which the invitation to the CAVE is phrased will influence the experience itself. For example, people might think much more about participating in a VR experience if they have to pay five Euros, but would not even want to try it if it is free. While this may seem counterintuitive, paying for something often raises expectations and makes it appear more valuable.

Prefacing a lab visit with "I'm working on what I call the 'PlayStation 8' in my lab. Do you want to try it?" plants a seed in fertile ground in the mind of a visitor. Because the PlayStation^{TM} is usually thought of as a game system that provides a certain level of realism, and is used for gaming, the variability from user to user about what to expect is small. Simply asking "Would you like to visit my virtual reality lab?" will evoke a different set of expectations, probably with higher variation.

3.3.1.2 Waiting Line

Along the same lines, we should refrain from exposing users to supporting technology, such as cables. Disney has understood this for a long time, and masterfully implements it in its parks. Furthermore, while waiting in line for a Disney experience, visitors receive "back story" content, which puts them in a certain frame of mind, mood, and attitude [21, 29]. This then shapes their experience of what will follow. For example, consider the case that somebody is reading a scary ghost story (priming stimulus): if a cold breeze from an open window suddenly comes from behind the reader, it might evoke the feeling that the physical place is haunted and raise the fright level of the reader. If the same breeze instead blew on someone reading a newspaper, maybe it would just trigger them to get up and close the window. In each case, the material being read by the person has created very different experiences for an identical stimulus. This is what Disney does in their waiting lines [29]: shaping the expectations of visitors to support their delivered experiences. This can also be done in our VR labs by, for example, crafting the way from the entrance of our lab into the installation or by either avoiding or carefully crafting a third-persons view of the installation – watching somebody else inside the installation.

3.3.1.3 Accidental Priming

Accidental priming can also have an undesired effect. Steele and Aronson found that simply making test takers aware of race via a question on the test can have an effect on performance as found in the so called Stereotype Threat [26]. Similar findings have been reported by Young et al. for motion sickness [34]. Therefore it is highly desirable, not only in entertainment applications, to pay attention to deliberate and accidental priming. The former can be utilized to fill in gaps that our application cannot deliver, while the latter can reduce or redirect the anticipation.

3.3.2 Transitions

Users go through several transitions prior to undertaking the tasks we create for them. One has to do with moving from the real to the virtual world. This could consist of donning equipment, such as an HMD, boarding a themepark ride vehicle, or going into a CAVE. Another transition is moving from a virtual practice or waiting-room environment to the actual task area. Still, many systems simply unload the practice environment, and load the test environment, exposing the user to the terminal windows, status displays, or the windowing environment used to launch the application. The final transition is from the virtual world back to the real world.

Various projects have tried to ease the transition from the real world to the virtual world. Pierce et al. employed exaggerated cues (strobing lights) present and synchronized in both the real and HMD-based virtual worlds to allow users to more-smoothly transition between real and virtual scenes. They found users turned their heads more, felt less of a "jolt" when moving from real to virtual, and interacted more with fellow users [19].

Steinicke et al. proposed using a one-to-one virtual replica of the actual lab where the HMD is donned as the initial virtual space for a user experience. Users would incur less of a jolt when transitioning from real to virtual. Steinicke et al. also used portals between virtual environments to maintain continuity within the overall system and found good empirical support for doing so [27].

Billinghurst et al. describe the use of a physical prop-based interface metaphore (in this case, a book) to help users go from viewing the real world, to viewing the real world using a see-through HMD, to viewing an immersive VE totally occluding the real world, by flying into the pages of the MagicBook [1].

Schell and Shochet combined both physical and virtual elements of a ship, including a physical model seen by the users, purely virtual characters who would attack the ship, and group dynamics structured by the relative physical positions of each user. They found that carefully combining these elements gave the overall experience a much richer, personal feeling [21].

3.3.3 Real World Support and Re-Framing

One of the main reasons people have problems believing our virtual worlds has to do with how much better real-world experiences are. We have learned from living in our everyday "real" world some impressive features of our environment: the real world has a perfect update rate, supports a massive number of users, provides integrated multi-modal rendering, has more than convincing physics, and gives us nearly infinite fidelity, all with minimal lag; this is just the type of system we have all been chasing for decades in VR research.

Sensory fidelity does not necessarily have to come from technology and devices. One possibility is to include passive haptic elements. A deep virtual pit with a real wooden ledge corresponding to the ledge of the virtual pit greatly increased user presence (including their physiological stress responses) in the environment [17]. Real walls to match a modeled virtual training environment were another passive haptic project conducted by the University of North Carolina at Chapel Hill [10]. Indirectly, this was also used in the one-to-one virtual replica of Steinicke's lab, as the virtual walls were in fact solid by overlaying it over the real lab's walls [27].

Purposefully using and including elements of the real world wherever appropriate, therefore, could enhance the quality of VR experiences. This extends beyond simply using physical props; the idea is to tap into the real-world experiences already assembled in the mind of the user, and leverage those to improve fidelity.

Including real artifacts could also mean just taking what the technical environment requires and *re-framing* their purpose. This is especially useful if the technology is otherwise perceived as a distraction. One option is to include potential distractions into the story (giving the motion-platform a name and story, making it a buddy instead of a piece of VR technology). The experience itself is in the mind and can be guided; as Disney does so well, we also could start creating and guiding the mindset of our users.

3.4   Crafting the Experience

We as VR researchers are *technology providers, content creators*, and ultimately, *storytellers*. For too long, we have been focusing on technology, mostly neglecting the other two. What we need to learn to do is to embrace content and story, either ourselves or, better, by working with visionary experience designers. This is analogous to successful game design or theme park teams, which marry technologists, artists, and designers to craft seamless, believable, compelling experiences.

We propose to focus on *building anticipation* before a user enters the virtual world, provide a *seamless transition* from viewer to participant, promote *user engagement* in the tasks at hand, insure the *safety* of the user, *remove distractions*, and allow participants to *let go of their sense of the real world*. The key to achieving this end is rooted in harnessing the power of human imagination. Priming the user, including reality-based artifacts, re-framing technology, crafting transitions, plus including value, story, and magic into the experience are keys to establishing the experiential fidelity users draw from, helping them to buy into the (low-fidelity) virtual worlds we provide.

With the current state of technology, we feel that now is the time to pay attention to improved experience. We postulate that the ultimate experience is best achieved by providing support for the user's mind to create a platform for the experience. By carefully structuring the entire experience, we can provide a scaffold for the platform, and then align the sensory stimuli to fit with this scaffold. A fertile mind is able to effortlessly provide far greater fidelity than any technology we can conjure. The creativity and processing power of the mind must be tapped to bring virtual worlds to a level that allows us to improve user effectiveness through Experiential Fidelity, rather than striving to match the actual fidelity of the real world.

Acknowledgements The authors would like to deeply thank everyone who participated in the discussion sessions during the Dagstuhl Seminar in 2008. We particularly wish to thank Guido Brunnett, Henry Fuchs, Vicki Interrante, Michael Jenkins, Yoshifumi Kitamura, Ben Lok, Mark Mine, Betty Mohler, Anthony Steed, Greg Welch, and Mary Whitton for their passion and belief in the ideas we collectively developed.

References

1. Billinghurst, M., Kato, H., Poupyrev, I.: Magicbook: transitioning between reality and virtuality. In: CHI '01: CHI '01 extended abstracts on Human factors in computing systems, pp. 25–26. ACM, NY, USA (2001)
2. Bowman, D.A., Kruijff, E., LaViola, J.J., Poupyrev, I.: 3D User Interfaces: Theory and Practice. Addison Wesley Longman, Redwood City, CA, USA (2004)
3. Bowman, D.A., McMahan, R.P.: Virtual reality: How much immersion is enough? Computer **40**, 36–43 (2007)
4. Csikszentmihalyi, M.: Flow: The Psychology of Optimal Experience. Harper Perennial, NY, USA (1991)
5. Dede, C., Salzman, M., Loftin, B.: The development of a virtual world for learning newtonian mechanics. In: P. Brusilovsky, P. Kommers, N. Streitz (eds.) Multimedia, Hypermedia, and Virtual Reality: Models, Systems, and Application, *Lecture Notes in Computer Science*, vol. 1077. Springer, Berlin (1996)
6. Gladwell, M.: Blink: The power of thinking without thinking. Little, Brown and Co, NY, USA (2005)
7. Haselhoff, S., Beckhaus, S.: Benutzerindividuelle, tragbare Geruchsausgabe in Virtuellen Umgebungen. In: "Virtuelle und Erweiterte Realität," the 3rd Workshop of the GI working group VR/AR, pp. 83–94. Gesellschaft für Informatik, Shaker Verlag, Koblenz (2006)
8. Hodges, L.F., Watson, B.A., Kessler, G.D., Rothbaum, B.O., Opdyke, D.: Virtually conquering fear of flying. IEEE Comput. Graph. Appl. **16**, 42–49 (1996)
9. Hoffman, H., Doctor, J., Patterson, D., Carrougher, G., Furness, T.: Virtual reality as an adjunctive pain control during burn wound care in adolescent patients. Pain **85**(1-2), 305–309 (2000)
10. Insko, B., Meehan, M., Whitton, M., Brooks, F.: Passive haptics significantly enhances virtual environments. Proceedings of 4th Annual Presence Workshop (2001)
11. Interrante, V., Ries, B., Anderson, L.: Distance perception in immersive virtual environments, revisited. In: VR '06: Proceedings of the IEEE conference on Virtual Reality, pp. 3–10. IEEE Computer Society, Washington, DC, USA (2006)
12. Iwata, H., Yano, H., Uemura, T., Moriya, T.: Food simulator: A haptic interface for biting. Virtual Reality Conference, IEEE, p. 51 (2004)
13. Kotranza, A., Lok, B.: Virtual human + tangible interface = mixed reality human an initial exploration with a virtual breast exam patient. In: VR, pp. 99–106 (2008)
14. Lindeman, R.W., Beckhaus, S.: Crafting memorable VR experiences using experiential fidelity. In: VRST '09: Proceedings of the 16th ACM Symposium on Virtual Reality Software and Technology, pp. 187–190. ACM, NY, USA (2009)
15. Magnenat-Thalmann, N., Kennedy, B.O., Thalmann, D., Papagiannakis, G., Glardon, P., Joslin, C., Kim, H.: Real-Time Virtual Characters for VR/AR Applications. In: CGI 2004 (2004)
16. Mania, K., Wooldridge, D., Coxon, M., Robinson, A.: The effect of visual and interaction fidelity on spatial cognition in immersive virtual environments. IEEE Trans. Vis. Comput. Graph. **12**, 396–404 (2006)
17. Meehan, M., Insko, B., Whitton, M., Brooks, F.P.: Physiological measures of presence in stressful virtual environments. ACM Trans. Graph. **21**(3), 645–652 (2002)
18. Mori, M.: The uncanny valley (translated by karl f. macdorman and takashi minato). Energy, 7(4) **15**(6), 33 –35 (1970)

19. Pierce, J.S., Pausch, R., Sturgill, C.B., Christiansen, K.D.: Designing a successful hmd-based experience. Presence: Teleoper. Virtual Environ. **8**(4), 469–473 (1999)
20. Ruddle, R.A., Lessels, S.: Three levels of metric for evaluating wayfinding. Presence: Teleoper. Virtual Environ. **15**(6), 637–654 (2006)
21. Schell, J., Shochet, J.: Designing interactive theme park rides. IEEE Comput. Graph. Appl. **21**, 11–13 (2001)
22. Scott, R., Carroll, G., Giler, D., Powell, I.: Alien. 20th Century Fox, Century City, CA (1979)
23. Slater, M.: A note on presence terminology. http://presence-connect.com (2003)
24. Slater, M.: Place illusion and plausibility can lead to realistic behaviour in immersive virtual environments. Phil. Trans. R. Soc. B **364**(1535), 3549–3557 (2010)
25. Slater, M., Usoh, M., Steed, A.: Depth of presence in virtual environments. Presence **3**(2), 130–144 (1994)
26. Steele, C.M., Aronson, J.: Stereotype threat and the intellectual test performance of african americans. J. Pers. Soc. Psychol. **69**(5), 797–811 (1995)
27. Steinicke, F., Bruder, G., Hinrichs, K., Steed, A., Gerlach, A.L.: Does a gradual transition to the virtual world increase presence? VR '10: Proceedings of the IEEE Virtual Reality Conference, pp. 203–210 (2009)
28. Swartout, W., van Lent, M.: Making a game of system design. Commun. ACM **46**(7), 32–39 (2003)
29. Trowbridge, S., Stapleton, C.: Melting the boundaries between fantasy and reality. Computer **42**, 57–62 (2009)
30. Wenzel, E.M.: Localization in virtual acoustic displays. Presence: Teleoper. Virtual Environ. **1**(1), 80–107 (1992)
31. Whitton, M.C.: Making virtual environments compelling. Commun. ACM **46**(7), 40–47 (2003)
32. Yamada, T., Yokoyama, S., Tanikawa, T., Hirota, K., Hirose, M.: Wearable olfactory display: Using odor in outdoor environment. In: VR '06: Proceedings of the IEEE conference on Virtual Reality, pp. 199–206. IEEE Computer Society, Washington, DC, USA (2006)
33. Yanagida, Y., Kawato, S., Noma, H., Tomono, A., Tetsutani, N.: Projection-based olfactory display with nose tracking. Virtual Reality Conference, IEEE, p. 43 (2004)
34. Young, S.D., Adelstein, B.D., Ellis, S.R.: Demand characteristics in assessing motion sickness in a virtual environment: Or does taking a motion sickness questionnaire make you sick? IEEE Trans. Vis. Comput. Graph. **13**(3), 422–428 (2007)

Chapter 4
Social Gaming and Learning Applications: A Driving Force for the Future of Virtual and Augmented Reality?

Ralf Dörner, Benjamin Lok, and Wolfgang Broll

Abstract Backed by a large consumer market, entertainment and education applications have spurred developments in the fields of real-time rendering and interactive computer graphics. Relying on Computer Graphics methodologies, Virtual Reality and Augmented Reality benefited indirectly from this; however, there is no large scale demand for VR and AR in gaming and learning. What are the shortcomings of current VR/AR technology that prevent a widespread use in these application areas? What advances in VR/AR will be necessary? And what might future "VR-enhanced" gaming and learning look like? Which role can and will Virtual Humans play? Concerning these questions, this article analyzes the current situation and provides an outlook on future developments. The focus is on social gaming and learning.

4.1 Introduction

Just a little more than a decade ago, computer hardware for virtual reality set-ups such as a CAVE carried a 6-digit price tag. Today, the hardware costs have dropped by an order of magnitude while the performance of computer graphics hardware have increased dramatically. The development of graphics hardware complexity has been moving considerably faster than Moore's law [21]. A major reason for

R. Dörner (✉)
RheinMain University of Applied Sciences, D 65197 Wiesbaden, Germany
e-mail: ralf.doerner@hs-rm.de

B. Lok
University of Florida, 32611-6120, Gainesville, FL USA
e-mail: lok@cise.ufl.edu

W. Broll
Ilmenau University of Technology, D 98693 Ilmenau, Germany
e-mail: wolfgang.broll@tu-ilmenau.de

this development has nothing to do with VR, but with another application area for interactive computer graphics: computer games.

The market for computer games is huge and growing fast. According to the "Global Entertainment and Media Outlook: 2007–2011" by Price Waterhouse Coopers AG [32] a yearly business volume of 15.4 billion US$ can be expected in America, 18.8 billion US$ in Europe and Africa, and 15.4 billion US$ in Asia for the computer games market in 2011. Growing rates of 10% are predicted in the time period from 2007 to 2011. Backed by such a large consumer market, considerable resources are invested in research and development resulting in enormous progress, e.g. in computer graphics hardware. Moreover, economies of scale effects lead to price reductions.

Virtual Reality has benefited from this development since its foundations overlap with the foundations of computer games. For instance, real-time rendering of 3D imagery or high quality graphics displays are needed by many VR applications as well as entertainment applications. The VR community is well aware of this; the experience of seeing hardware prices plunging so rapidly is in the collective memory of many VR researchers and users. And there are more examples. Augmented Reality benefits greatly from the availability of low-cost Web cams and mobile devices such as smart phones that are capable of 3D rendering and equipped with cameras. The Novint Falcon haptic feedback device, marketed for usage in games such as World of Warcraft, costs with 250 US$ an order of magnitude less than existing devices meant for non-entertainment applications [29]. Also an order of magnitude less expensive is a Head-Mounted Display (HMD) for gaming applications – the eMagin Z800 [18], which sold for 550 US$. With the Virtual Boy [39], Nintendo offered a stereo display for games costing 180 US$ in 1995. The Virtual Boy bombed, however, eMagin had to increase the price for its HMD to over 1500 US$ since expected sales figures have not been met and many other attempts to bring applications of VR to a larger consumer market were not overly successful. Virtual and Augmented Reality have – in contrast to computer games – not played a major role in the consumer market. At least so far. Why?

Of course, it would be highly beneficial for the further progress of Virtual and Augmented Reality if they could benefit directly from the economies of scale and innovation pressure inherent in a large consumer market. Not only available technology but also affordable prices could make more VR and AR applications become feasible. But what are the obstacles that prevent a widespread use of VR/AR? How can we overcome current shortcomings? And what could future VR/AR consumer applications look like? This article offers some thoughts – and speculations – concerning these questions.

One approach for identifying mass markets for VR and AR methodologies is to look for ways to use them in entertainment applications. Social gaming, i.e. gaming that fosters and takes advantage of social interaction among players, is a particularly fast growing market. For example, in massive multiplayer online games such as World of Warcraft more than 40% of players state that the major aspect of the game is social interaction [10]. Social games attract people from non-traditional target groups for computer games. And they are interesting for edutainment and learning applications – given the need for lifelong learning these application areas are also good candidates for large consumer markets. With more than 17 million copies sold worldwide, Dr. Kawashima's brain training [28], one of Nintendo's most successful games, is an entertainment and training application targeted at non-traditional audiences such as the generation 50+. Since we believe that there is a potential for VR and AR especially in social gaming and learning, we focus on this in our article.

This article is organized as follows. In the next section, we will analyze current issues with VR and AR and discuss potential solutions. Because virtual humans play an important role in social gaming and learning applications, we will discuss them in greater detail in Sect. 4.3. In Sect. 4.4, we will share and illustrate our visions for VR/AR-enhanced social gaming and learning. Finally, in Sect. 4.5 we will conclude by trying to summarize answers to the questions raised in this introduction.

4.2 Deficiencies and Progress

In order to be successful in a mass market, VR and AR need to provide an added value over alternative solutions, such as 2D solutions that might be easier to use, far cheaper, or less cumbersome. Although VR and AR have proven their value in specific application fields like training and education [13] and although sophisticated technology has been developed, there still exist deficiencies in technology, authoring, behavior and simulation, standards, and privacy.

4.2.1 Technology

While for VR environments CAVE-like systems currently still present the most sophisticated solution in terms of immersion, presence, and interaction facilities, the enormous effort and space to set up such environments significantly limits their general availability and by that their suitability for a widespread use in the area of social gaming and learning applications. While CAVE-like environments present a well-established and widely-accepted tool for high-level engineering tasks (e.g. in the automobile industry), using such environments for social gaming and learning applications is typically limited to academic installations. Although one could imagine that companies successfully using CAVE-like environments may open up those environments for in-house use of such applications, major potential user groups will have to rely on access to such environments in academia and at research labs, which will actually prevent a widespread adoption. An additional major deficiency of all CAVE-like environments is their limited multi-user capability. While often used by several people at the same time, a proper stereoscopic perception and by that a higher level of immersion can only be achieved for a single person at each time (other users will see a slightly distorted view depending on the distance of their viewpoint from the position of the tracked user). In addition to the huge infrastructure costs, this fact adds to the limited scalability of such environments.

4.2.1.1   VR Displays

Simpler stereoscopic projections such as Powerwalls may be sufficient for certain application areas (although providing significantly less immersive environments and by that potentially less presence). However, the availability of such technologies is still limited to large companies and research facilities, excluding major user groups and mass adoption. This may change in the near future, if the availability and by that the dissemination of (auto-)stereoscopic TV sets as consumer devices will actually increase as predicted by some experts and expected by major industry providers.

Head-mounted displays (HMD), sometimes also referred to as head worn displays (HWD), provide an alternative to stereoscopic projections. However, except for the temporarily low-price eMagin (already mentioned in the introduction), prices are generally rather high (between 1,500US$ for low-end displays and up to several 100,000US$ for high-end displays). Beside the rather high costs, leading to similar problems as for stereo projections, quality and usability issues further reduce the overall acceptance of such displays. The quality is often rather low regarding the overall resolution (typically VGA or SVGA, only very expensive high-end displays provide higher resolutions), the brightness of the displays, and their field of view. In particular the latter one reduces the immersion and by that the presence significantly as it typically ranges between 20° and 30° for low-price displays (while high-end displays may achieve up to 45°–60° or even more when using multiple displays per eye).

4.2.1.2   AR Displays

In addition to the VR environments above, we can find AR environments augmenting the user's environment by additional virtual content. AR environments typically used either see-through HMDs or projective AR. See-through HMDs either use video see-through technology, where a video image from a camera facing into the same direction as the user is superimposed with virtual content and then displayed in a regular HMD (as used for VR), or use optical see-through displays, which e.g. use semi-transparent mirrors to combine the view of the real environment with virtual content from a display. Projective AR is based on projectors either projecting directly onto the real world object, modifying them, or by projecting on glass surfaces, achieving a similar effect as by the semi-transparent mirrors in optical see-through HMDs. While some of these technologies are used for learning applications, e.g. in science centers, these technologies generally suffer from the same obstacles as VR environments.

4.2.1.3   Tracking

Beside the projection and display technologies all of the approaches above require appropriate tracking technologies to track the user's viewpoint and viewing direction in order to adapt the displayed content accordingly. Today, a large variety of technologies applying ultra-sonic, magnetic, and optical sensors are available, ranging from ≈1,000 US$ to more than 100,000 US$ depending on the required precision and in particular the size of the space to be covered. Similar to the display and projection technologies, the setup and the costs of such systems currently prevent a widespread use.

4.2.1.4   Mobile VR/AR

Regarding the use of VR and AR technologies, we can observe a clear shift from rather complex stationary systems toward more flexible, light-weight and mobile systems. This shift also fosters a transition from pure VR systems toward more AR environments, as the actual location of the user becomes a significant part of the overall application scenario. Regarding mobile AR systems we can distinguish between systems using HMDs and those relying entirely on handheld devices. Tracking for mobile systems typically heavily relies on GPS, often combined and enhanced by computer vision – based approaches (marker or feature-based tracking) and additional orientation tracking (applying e.g. inertial sensors).

HMDs for mobile use typically are optical see-through devices and often limited to one eye (monoscopic augmentation). Beside weight aspects, the major reason are security aspects as a temporary or even complete distraction from the real environment may result in hazardous situations. Major obstacles are the brightness of the virtual content (currently no displays are available that may be used in bright sun light) as well as the obtrusiveness of the displays. However, both issues hopefully can be solved in the near future. Regarding the brilliance of the displays, OLED-based displays and laser-based retinal displays seem to be promising developments, while regarding the obtrusiveness displays applying HOE (holographic optical elements) technologies allow for a almost sun glass like appearance and by that significantly better acceptance. Another major obstacle is the necessity of one or even several tracking device to be attached to the display. This may include a web cam for computer vision – based tracking (such as marker tracking) and/or an orientation sensor with 3 degrees of freedom (DOF).

Handheld devices used for AR can be Tablet PCs, UMPCs (ultra mobile PCs), PDAs, mp3 players or smartphones. While Tablet PCs are available in configurations optimized for outdoor use (ruggedized) and in bright sunlight (using e.g. transflective displays), they are rather heavy and require additional tracking devices such as GPS receivers, web cams and orientations sensors to be attached too, limiting their overall usability. UMPCs, while providing the full functionality of a PC, are much more light-weight and typically already come along with built-in GPS and back-facing camera – some of them even with integrated inertial sensors. While graphics and processing power still limits the use of UMPCs, they currently still represent a good compromise for mobile AR. A rather new but promising field is the use of smartphones for AR. While providing similar devices (GPS, back-facing camera, inertial sensor) as UMPCs, their form factor and weight are significantly smaller, they are available to a much larger group of users, and will be carried on by their users continuously. Major deficiencies here include the limited processing and graphics power, and in particular the diversity of the software platforms including obstacles for accessing even simple functions (like getting access to the built-in camera) often differing significantly for each individual phone model. However, with the recent introduction of multi-core processors for mobile phones combined with current 3D graphics accelerators found e.g. in the Apple iPhone, the gap to UMPCs is closing pretty fast. Further, iPhoneOS from Apple and Android from the Open Handset Alliance seem to establish themselves as platforms for AR applications on smartphones. This is also reflected by an increasing number of recent AR applications available in their online application shops.

4.2.2 Authoring

Creation of content for VR/AR applications is still an issue that prevents a more widespread use of VR/AR applications in general. This is especially true for VR/AR-enhanced social gaming. Many applications in this field require that non-experts are able create or modify content. In a social learning application, for example, it is sometimes even mandatory that a trainer is able to adapt the challenges given to the students to their learning progress or to put students in situations that offer opportunities for the students to work on weaknesses identified by the trainer. And the trainer is usually proficient in pedagogy or psychology and not in computer science or even VR/AR.

Looking at the developments in the Web that are commonly referred to as Web 2.0, we can observe that major applications such as forums, blogs, podcasts, wikis, social networks, image and music sharing or massive multiplayer online role-playing games rely on user-generated content – and not on content generated by experts. A broad variety of Web users have been enabled to create content. Only this makes the wealth of interesting content found on the Web today possible, only this fosters social aspects that attract people to the Web and boosted its popularity. Similarly, we assert that VR/AR will only be able to catch the attention of a mass market if users are able to easily create content for according applications.

Naturally, VR/AR research is concerned with making VR/AR work on a conceptual and technological level in the first place. Only a few efforts have been invested in authoring aspects of VR/AR. And here the focus is on lowering the costs and making content creation more efficient for VR/AR experts. But it is the question how we enable non-experts to be productive in the content creation process that we should look into.

Why is it so hard to come up with good solutions for the authoring problem? Obviously, VR/AR authoring is more complex than say authoring text. Even for IT experts it is difficult to create content for an interactive application that meets real-time constraints. Knowledge from several disciplines such as Human-Computer-Interaction, Computer Graphics, Image Processing, Computer Networks, Parallel Programming or Computer Simulation may be needed to create VR/AR applications and according content. The necessity to use different libraries (e.g. graphics libraries, i/o specific libraries, image processing libraries) and tools (e.g. 3D modelers, compilers, calibration tools) together with a lack of appropriate standards and resulting problems with conversions, add to the burden.

Neither of the two extremes will be feasible in VR/AR authoring in the context of mass market applications: on the one hand letting the non-expert author do the complete work from scratch, on the other hand assigning experts to the author who will listen to his demands and requirements and take care of their implementation. Division of work is a strategy that has been successfully applied, e.g. in the field of computer game authoring. Here, elaborate authoring processes have been conceived over the last years together with a fine grained definition of different author roles (e.g. game designer, character artist, game engine programmer). Similar concepts are still needed in VR/AR authoring. Author roles need to be defined that non-experts are able to take over. For example, while they may not be able to model human characters they may be able to define spatial relationships between real and virtual objects in an AR application.

Each author role needs support by dedicated tools. There might be even author roles whose task is to act as a tool smith, i.e. to tailor tools to fit the individual profile of other authors. This is solution to the problem that tools may seem to be overloaded with functionality and difficult to use for author groups who have not the skills, the motivation or the time to become highly trained in using these tools. Google Sketch-Up [20] is a good example for a tool that offers far fewer features than well-known 3D modeling tools but is by far easier to use by a certain group of authors while providing sufficient functionality for their purposes.

Another issue, which needs further research, is the availability of suitable authoring metaphors. For a variety of authoring tasks it is still necessary to use scripting or even programming interfaces. Visual approaches as they are offered in tools such as Quest3D [1], Virtools [15], or Interactive Bits [7] are promising but still need improvements since they use levels of abstraction that will overstrain certain author groups. And a high level of discipline is needed if authoring tasks become a bit more complex. But even for tasks such as 3D navigation, placement and orientation of objects in virtual or augmented environments, or calibration, suitable authoring metaphors are lacking. An interesting approach here would be to research in how far VR/AR methodologies could be a basis for improvements.

Finally, equipping VR/AR software with Self-X capabilities (e.g. self-healing, self-organization, self-configuration, self-connectivity, and self-optimization) is a promising idea to free authors from tasks and simplify the set-up of authoring environments.

4.2.3 Behavior and Simulation

VR/AR applications are not only concerned with user interfaces, computer graphics and image processing but also with simulation of a wide range of behavior.

This could be the application logic of the whole environment or virtual world, the physics-based behavior of single objects, or – especially in the context of social gaming and learning – the behavior of virtual characters.

While there are methodologies available today such as semantic networks, rule engines or neural networks, the aspects and complexity of real behavior they are able to model is still limited. And there is not only the issue how to implement the simulation but also how to enable authors to express a specification of behavior that is on a suitable level for them. Good authoring metaphors are missing here. Looking at disciplines such as interactive storytelling, for example, we observe that this community is struggling with ways of how to create description of non-linear stories. Such methodologies would be highly valuable for VR/AR learning applications in order to let domain experts specify the simulation behind a training scenario. One problem in this context is that it is difficult to validate the behavior exhibited. For instance, rule-based systems are capable of creating emergent behavior – it is sometimes even impossible for an author to predict the system's behavior from reading the underlying rules. It is also difficult to visualize the inner workings of a simulation to an author. Therefore, one of the best ways to simulate character behavior is one of the simplest: to conceive a multi-user application where each user takes over a character in the application, thus simulating it.

Another issue is the coupling of different simulators. Although there are standards such as HLA available these are quite complex to use since they strive to describe large federations of simulations. And there is the issue how to connect the simulation with an according visualization in VR/AR. First successful solutions that need to be developed further have been proposed in this area. Also, because of increased computing capabilities due to parallel processing with multi-core processors or general purpose programmability of graphics hardware, there are good opportunities to have enough performance available for a more sophisticated simulation. In computer games, for example, game AI suffered because the little processing time that is allowed in real-time applications has been used almost completely for rendering the imagery.

4.2.4 Standards

A major deficiency regarding all VR and AR applications is the actual lack of standards. This significantly hinders the progress and widespread use of these technologies as applications are usually developed for an individually configured system or in case of smartphone-based solutions for an individual type of phone.

Some standards however exist in regard to 3D content. So far, most existing VR/AR systems rely on the ISO standards VRML'97 or its XML-based successor X3D. In addition to 3D geometry, those standards allow for the representation of sound, video, animation, and interactivity. VRML'97 and/or X3D are supported by a wide range of commercial and open source products, also providing a large set of tools for creating, modifying and displaying appropriate 3D content.

An emerging standard in this area is COLLADA, defining an open standard for the exchange of digital assets. While originating in games (COLLADA was once created for the PS3), it meanwhile has already established as universal exchange format for DCC tools as it has been adopted by most 3D modeling tools and several game engines. In addition to VRML/X3D it also supports physics and as such is supported by most physics engines.

The XML-based KML (the Keyhole Markup Language) schema has become popular due to its usage by Google maps and Google earth, allowing for 2D and 3D location-based visualizations and annotations. It also allows for embedding of COLLADA descriptions. It is supported by a wide range of applications, in particular as it can be easily extended by application specific content.

Further standards in this area include U3D (Universal 3D format) developed by an industry consortium and standardized by ECMA (European Computer Manufacturers Association). While aiming for similar use as COLLADA, support in existing software is rather limited. CityGML provides an XML-based common information model for the representation of 3D urban objects. It is implemented as an application schema for the Geography Markup Language 3 (GML3), which is the international standard for spatial data exchange (standardized by OGC and ISO).

In respect to 3D rendering most systems rely either on Direct3D or OpenGL as a graphic library. While OpenGL is available on basically all operating systems, Direct3D is limited to Microsoft Windows based platforms. Nevertheless, the majority of commercial gaming applications nowadays rely on Dirct3D rather than OpenGL, while most VR/AR environments and software frameworks use OpenGL. As far as mobile devices such as smartphones are concerned, with OpenGL ES and D3D Mobile, dedicated versions of the graphics libraries exist. Similar to their desktop relatives, D3D Mobile is available on Windows Mobile systems only, while all other operating systems support OpenGL ES. The use of OpenGL ES further provides the obstacle that version 2.x is not backward compatible to version 1.x.

As far as scene graph APIs, 3D (game) engines APIs, or physics engine APIs are concerned, a large variety of commercial as well as non-commercial products exist, but no standards are defined.

Another major deficiency is the lack of standards for interaction techniques and VR/AR user interfaces. While 2D desktop applications apply the well-defined WIMP-type interfaces and interaction techniques, both are entirely application specific in VR and AR environments. VRML/X3D try to apply some 3D interaction techniques, but these approaches only allow for rather simple types of interfaces and totally neglect the huge variety of individual input (and output) devices. The latter one is a major obstacle in respect to standardizing VR/AR user interfaces. While a couple of libraries and tools such as OpenTracker [34] for simplifying access to those devices through device abstraction and unified device handling exist, such approaches are far from providing a standard or even quasi standard.

4.2.5 Privacy

In order to gather necessary information about the user or the real environment every VR/AR uses one or more sensors, e.g. cameras for optical tracking. Users may be concerned who is able to read, to store or to evaluate the sensor data. For a social learning application, for example, it is a key for user acceptance that they are not afraid to reveal information about their personality that could be exploited, e.g. by their employer. While one obvious solution is to equip sensors with means to switch them off, e.g. a cover for a camera lens, this usually is not feasible as the VR/AR application will depend on the sensors. Thus, it is imperative to make transparent for the user what happens with the data and to leave no doubt about the commitment to adhere to a privacy policy.

However, privacy issues are much more concerning when it comes to mobile applications. Relying on GPS localization for user tracking, mobile VR/AR applications realize location-based services. Thus, they provide the basis for a detailed analysis of individual user movements and activities. Such user data is often recorded for debugging and evaluation purposes. Consequently, it must be ensured that it is anonymized before recording. Further, as far as head-mounted camera systems are used, those allow for recording or – in combination with tracking – reconstruction of objects, persons, etc. as observed by the individual user.

There are also privacy concerns when sensors obtain data about persons in the real-world who have not given their consent. One solution here is to make them not recognizable using image processing, e.g. exchanging their faces [6]. However, it could already be observed that AR devices applying the use of cameras (either for video see-through or for tracking) annoy passersby, as they are concerned to being intentionally filmed.

4.3 Virtual Humans and Social Aspects

4.3.1 Overview

Virtual humans are computer-generated characters with a human form. This human form is important as it appears to manifest itself as a special degree of affect with users. That is, users appear to react to virtual humans in a very compelling manner, different than with virtual cars, planes, or buildings. These virtual humans are critical for applications to present populated virtual worlds and partners for user interaction. As humans are inherently social creatures, virtual humans are critical for creating affective VR/AR experiences. Yet virtual humans, much like their human counterparts, are extremely complex to render, animate, communicate with, and automate. These are all ongoing research areas in which significant advances will need to be made as to realize compelling virtual humans.

Examples of potential applications include virtual humans as assistive tutors in educational virtual environments [14], as virtual patients with whom medical students would practice communication skills [24], and as part of crowd simulations to help in design of buildings [36]. In these applications the user sees and/or interacts with virtual humans to learn skills, practice social abilities, or observe human dynamics.

Virtual humans are composed of three main components: inputs, cognition, and outputs.

4.3.1.1   Inputs

These are the methods of transfer of information from the user to the virtual humans and can be thought of as how the user communicates to the virtual human. Common examples would include natural speech, gestures, choosing a response from a list, or typing. Research is ongoing into increasing the communication bandwidth between the user and virtual humans to make it more similar to human–human communication.

4.3.1.2   Cognition

The virtual human must incorporate the inputs from the user, consider the virtual environment, such as the location of objects, consider its goals and personality, and in turn, generate actions that it will attempt to undertake. Cognition covers many research areas including artificial intelligence, natural language processing, conversation and knowledge modeling, perception, and human psychology among others. The realization of a plausible reasoning and acting virtual human will require the integration of research from these diverse fields. While daunting, there has been some limited success in restricted-domain scenarios.

4.3.1.3   Output

The presentation of the virtual human to the user includes the rendering and display. This includes presenting to the user a 3D human with a high-level of visual, audio, and possibly haptic detail. This is complicated by the fact that humans are very sensitive to even slight deviations from expected representations, often resulting in the feeling of "something doesn't look right" or "he/she looks cartoon-like."

In this section, we will compare VR/AR virtual humans to existing video game virtual humans (Sect. 4.3.2), explore the current state of the art of virtual humans (Sect. 4.3.3), and highlight areas and application areas under active research (Sect. 4.3.4).

4.3.2 VR/AR Virtual Humans and Video Game Virtual Humans

In examining existing virtual humans in VR/AR systems, it is natural to question the significant differences between the VR/AR virtual humans and the high-quality virtual humans found in commercial video games and computer games. They share the characteristics of interactive real-time virtual humans, yet many video game characters can express significant emotion, fluidity, and expression. If the reader is unfamiliar with the quality of current video game characters, one should search popular gaming websites such as gamespot.com. A few noteworthy virtual human games to investigate includes "The Sims" by EA Maxis and "World of Warcraft" by Blizzard Software for its social constructs and goal-driven characters and "Metal Gear Solid 4" by Konami for highly-detailed, expressive virtual humans.

While certainly impressive, video game characters are only partially correlated with the VR/AR virtual humans and their requirements. Video game characters have a very restricted input set, usually consisting of button presses or joy/thumbstick control that represent commands such as "walk", "interact", or "talk". This restricted domain allows the developers to script – or at least anticipate – a large portion of the set of potential users' actions and thus generate plausible responses. In contrast, VR/AR virtual humans are being created to respond to complex gestures, natural speech, and sometimes touch within the context of a multifaceted scenario. Further, the display of the VR/AR human is often required to be life-sized (projected on a wall, using a large-screen TV, or in a head-mounted display) and be presented in stereo 3D. These additional input and output components increases the difficulty in presenting compelling virtual humans.

One area in which VR can learn and benefit from the advances of video game characters is in visual and audio fidelity. Current video game humans are the product of many man-months of work. Often, large teams of artists and animators will focus significant time in the creation, animation, and display of a few characters. As most VR/AR systems are still research endeavors, this allocation of resources is rarely possible. However, one benefit is that the video game companies have developed important character animation, rendering, networking, and artificial intelligence technologies. Further, some companies eventually release their rendering engines for academic research or as opensource libraries (e.g. the Unreal Tournament engine). VR/AR researchers benefit from building upon the significant investment of resources by the game developers.

4.3.3 Current Technologies for VR/AR Virtual Humans

One of the major challenges for computer graphics is the rendering of high-quality virtual humans. The visual complexity of the human form (and especially the human face) makes this a daunting rendering problem. This problem includes issues with computational power (current graphics systems are not capable of generating a virtual human with significant detail) and algorithms (calculating shading of skin as to realistically capture the subsurface scattering of light is still not solved). A separate, but related issue is the animation of the virtual human.

4.3.3.1 Rendering and Animation

Most virtual humans are rendered using the same graphics system as the rest of the virtual environment. In today's systems, this would include commodity PC graphics cards. The virtual humans are modeled in similar packages as the VR environment as well, including Maya, 3D Studio Max, and character specific generators such as the open source MakeHuman software, Haptek by Haptek, Inc., Poser by Smith Micro Software and Character Studio by Autodesk. These character generators allow the user to modify a base character model to more quickly generate virtual humans. There also exist commercial sites from which one can purchase pre-made virtual human models.

To animate the virtual human, developers use either motion-captured data of real humans conducting an action, animating the character by hand with the modeling software, or using a procedural animation system such as inverse kinematics. Each of these approaches has benefits and negatives that are inline with other real-time applications such as games and simulations.

4.3.3.2 Display

Unique to VR/AR virtual humans is the display of the virtual character. There are four primary methods of displaying virtual humans, desktop-monitor, large-screen TV, projector display, and head-mounted display. The last three typically present virtual humans that are perceived as life-size. That is, the virtual human takes up the appropriate field of regard within the user's visual field. This requires for the system to appropriately draw the world from the perspective of the user, skewing and sheering the virtual world as to look perspectively correct from the user's position and orientation. Even as the user might walk around in front of the screen, her tracked position will alter the perspective of the virtual human. The user's head position can also be used to reinforce social constructs, such as eye gaze, as the virtual human's eyes focus on track the user's movement. Finally, the character might be rendered in 3D using stereoscopic glasses, or a head-mounted display alongside the virtual world.

4.3.3.3 Speech

The virtual human's speech is presented using the existing speaker system. However, what the virtual human says can be quite complex and not scripted. Two common solutions are either pre-recorded speech or text-to-speech (TTS) generation. Pre-recorded speech is the easiest and most common approach with everything the virtual human speaks being recorded by voice talent. This enables significant emotion and realism, yet is typically not dynamic and logistically difficult to alter. For example, the virtual human can better portray pain or discomfort, but would not be able to address the user by their name. TTS generation systems are software that can be added to the virtual human as to enable text to be real-time processed into audio output. While the dynamic nature is a significant advantage, the realism of the voices is still 'slightly robotic' at best. Intonation and stress are still difficult to encode. Still, impressive strides in TTS quality have raised hopes that this will be an applicable solution in the near future.

4.3.3.4 Input to the Virtual Humans

In current VR/AR systems, the methods of inputs include issuing commands via button presses, typing a conversation, speaking into a microphone, and gestures (tracked with cameras, markers, or data-gloves). New work has also incorporated touch [25] and physiological measures of the user, such as brain waves, heart rate and galvanic skin response [19]. Still when considering how humans rely on a significant number of verbal and non-verbal cues in communication, the inputs to virtual humans are only beginning to be explored.

4.3.3.5 Cognitive Processing

Finally, the cognitive reasoning of the virtual human is still an area of significant research. The current approaches for how the virtual human reasons on their actions in the virtual environments include using either an a priori approach or a procedural approach. An *a priori* approach has the developers pre-generate all the actions and responses of the character and in real-time, based on the inputs, selects one to output. Procedural approaches attempt to generate in real-time the audio and animation output of the virtual human. Many different approaches are used to drive the procedural calculations, including trying to build emotion-engines that drive the virtual humans current state and motivations [38]. Again, this has the same dynamic versus realism tradeoff of the audio output discussed above.

One common solution to the virtual human's behavior is the use of Wizard of Oz interfaces (WoZ). WoZ interfaces have a real human (usually an experimenter or therapist) that is dynamically controlling the virtual human using a simplified interface, such a series of buttons that control the virtual human (e.g. "point", "speak", or "be happy"). These WoZ-ed experiences can be quite compelling if the user is unaware of the controlling mechanism and overcomes many of the issues with artificial intelligence. However, the human-in-the-loop requirement limits the large-scale application of virtual humans.

4.3.4   Ongoing Research Areas

Research into the use of virtual humans is constantly expanding. Thus, this section will cover a few fields to provide the reader with a few data points that represent the diversity of the topics that can be addressed by virtual humans. The challenge to the field is to understand the affective capabilities of virtual humans both to best apply virtual humans and not abuse their impact.

4.3.4.1   Virtual Humans for Product Design

One of the first applications of virtual humans was to understand the motion of a human. The field of ergonomics was explored with virtual humans by Norman Badler at the University of Pennsylvania with the Jack system [4]. Using Jack (which subsequently became a commercial product), designers can test the ergonomics of CAD designs of vehicles and devices. Virtual humans of different sizes, shapes, and abilities can be used to interact with yet-to-be-built interfaces as to explore design questions such as the size of people that the interface could accommodate or how much physical ability is required to operate a control. This allowed many designs to be efficiently tested and evaluated for a large group of potential users.

4.3.4.2   Virtual Humans to Simulate Large-Scale Social Situations

As researchers developed new approaches to virtual human cognition, applications began to explore modeling large-scale social situations. For example, thousands of virtual humans can be introduced to a virtual environment to explore crowd behavior. Architects can explore designs with respects to normal crowd traffic [30], emergency response behavior, or evacuation [26]. Further, they can alter their designs in real-time to visualize and quantify changes.

4.3.4.3   Virtual Humans that Simulate Interpersonal Social Situations

As interfaces to virtual humans begin to support much of the same mechanisms as those used in human-human interactions (e.g. speech, gestures, and life-size display), applications began to focus on smaller-scale social situations with virtual humans. These simulations could have profound impacts on how we educate, train, and learn from interacting with others. These interpersonal situations are prevalent in many fields, including medicine, the military, education, business, and entertainment. Provided here is only a limited list of cutting-edge projects into simulating interpersonal scenarios with virtual humans.

- Fear of public speaking – therapists have patients speaking to an audience of virtual humans (e.g. in a head-mounted display) as to help people overcome their anxiety. The therapist is able to control the number of audience members, their actions, and the scenario can be experienced at the pace of the participant's comfort. Physiological measures have validated the affective ability of the virtual human audience [37].

- Leadership training – military officers experience a virtual environment where they have to communicate with local citizens of foreign lands to achieve objectives. They speak and gesture with life-size (projector-based) virtual humans. These virtual humans reason and present emotional states. Thus, the student can practice local customs, revisit critical conversation moments, and explore alternate approaches [23].

- Cultural immersion – participants can interact with citizens of a foreign locality to practice basic communication skills. Work in this area includes teaching south Indian culture [3] and Arabic customs to soldiers [16].

- Communication skills training – participants can practice their communication skills by experiencing scenarios in which they interact with virtual humans. In the Virtual Patients project, medical students conduct ten minute interviews with virtual patients as to practice both procedural skills (e.g. conducting a breast exam) and communication skills (e.g. empathy and rapport building) [25]. These situations can augment existing training curricula which involves students role-playing with actors [24].

- Learning from virtual humans – Virtual humans are tutors in educational systems that can help students in online education systems. In these systems, students can access instructional assistance from a virtual human to augment their content exploration. For example, the AutoTutor system [14] has virtual humans play the role of teachers as students explore science learning online. As the students read about the concepts, the virtual human can be summoned to assist with explaining topics and will guide review of the concepts.

As has been highlighted by these applications, virtual humans are being used to augment information and the role played by real humans. They are being used to enhance education, provide critical training experiences, and more efficiently design around the user-experience. Known is that virtual humans appear to be capable of eliciting responses from humans at a significant level, though lower than with real people.

4.4 Visions for VR/AR-Enhanced Gaming and Learning

Given that satisfactory solutions for current deficiencies will be found – what could VR/AR gaming and learning applications that cater a mass-market look like? The next three sections will present some visions and speculation for future applications.

4.4.1   Example 1: Virtual Playing and Role Swapping

Role play is a fundamental category of playing behavior that can be observed in children as well as adults. As it is the case with social gaming in general, people perform role playing for various reasons. For example, because they enjoy social interaction, because they are curious to learn about other people's professions and workaday life or because they like challenging themselves or others [9].

One vision, where VR/AR would be the enabling technology, could be named "social role swapping". The general idea is that people can take other people's places and act if they were somebody else. In a sense, a flight simulator where one takes over the role of a pilot and is able to act accordingly is an existing example for this where the social interactions are limited and no real swapping takes place, however.

Social role swapping can not only be used for entertainment purposes. It has also serious applications. Role play is already a common methodology used for teaching and training especially of social skills such as communication skills or attitudes towards customers or co-workers. So, we can envision examples of social role swapping applications where employees of a company swap roles (e.g. a pilot swaps with an air traffic controller, a patient with a nurse, an engineer with a sales person) in order to gain a deeper understanding of other peoples' needs and motivations. Social role swapping games are also capable of conveying corporate values to employees. Another example would be applications where children or adolescents are supported in choosing their career by getting a more realistic understanding what it is like to work in a certain profession – it could also be a way of promoting jobs or educations. Museums could use social role swapping to educate people how it was like to live in a different culture or different era. Thus, the player is not the only person who has a motivation to finance such applications; there might be third parties such as companies and organizations, advertising agencies or the government who are willing to fund the creation of such applications.

Why do VR and AR methodologies enable the envisioned social gaming applications and provide a significant added value? Why is VR and AR technology fundamental to social role swapping applications? Relying on a virtual reality can even be indispensable if actions in the real world would be too dangerous (e.g. if an action could harm people or damage expensive equipment) or if the real world is not available (e.g. if it would require travel to a distant site or if it would require time travel or if the action takes place in a fantasy world). Virtual Realities are only a model of the real world and as such provide the opportunity for sensible simplification. This is a prerequisite if actions to be performed are too complex or too time consuming to learn and thus would make role swapping too difficult. AR is able to bring reality, the physical world in computer gaming – giving rise to a new genre of games often called Pervasive Games [27]. Advantages are the more realistic feel during the game, the ability to seamlessly integrate social interaction with real people, and the opportunity to physically involve the player. In case of a learning application, learning is less abstract and thus there are chances that learners can transfer results more directly to the real world. At the authoring level, AR offers the benefit that it is not necessary to model the whole environment since parts of the real environment can be used. This reduces the efforts necessary in geometric modeling and also the rendering performance needed. Moreover, the scope of what needs to be simulated is also reduced since one can rely on the behavior of the real entities. This is especially true for the simulation of humans. In some application scenarios, it might be desirable to build or improve a relationship between two humans. Thus, it would not make sense to replace one of them by a virtual human in the social game. Still, AR provides the possibility to use virtual humans when real human beings are not available or when a character has an unattractive or minor role (e.g. the roles of passengers in an airplane role play would be taken rather by virtual humans). With VR/AR, it is possible to support a player in coping with an unfamiliar role. For instance, by showing annotations, by giving hints or by drawing the players' attention to an important point.

How would a social role swapping application work? Actually, there exists a whole range of different use cases. We can distinguish broadly between online mode and offline mode. In offline mode, scenarios are prepared in advance – either by modeling a complete virtual environment or by recording videos that are augmented and where the viewpoint may be changed interactively afterwards. Also, possible interactions are provided and linked with an appropriate simulation. Players may swap roles and play simultaneously (for example, a pilot swaps the place with an air traffic controller and both act in the simulated VR/AR environment). Or the role play involves turn taking (for example, the air traffic controller takes the place of a pilot and is observed or supported by a pilot – after a while they change roles). To increase the level of social interaction, there could be some kind of replay after the actual role play where all the players discuss their experiences or rate their performances.

In online mode, there is always at least one player in a real situation, i.e. the player is acting in the real world and there is no simulation. This player can be watched by another person standing behind him using mobile devices such as PDAs or sub-notebooks that are used as a magic lens (i.e. the device records a video picture of the real scenario and uses AR methodologies to augment it and show it to the user in real-time). Alternatively, see-through glasses together with a wearable computer could be used. Annotations and explanations are shown that explain what is going on. The observer can also take actions silently; a simulation gives feedback what the result of the action would be. Or the observer can compare their actions with the actions the real persons did. Similar to offline mode, everything is recorded and discussed afterwards.

Each player has available a set of input and output devices, which could range from the typical monitor, keyboard and mouse setting to more immersive technology like large high resolution screens or projectors with stereo capabilities, 3D sound, haptic feedback devices and sensor networks that are able to track the player and determine body, finger and head position and orientation or gaze direction. It might even be possible to integrate remote sensors and actors. In the future, sophisticated set-ups might become available and will replace the tv set in the living room. There might even exist a specifically equipped "entertainment room" beside kitchen and bathroom. This room could also serve as a more general "tele presence room". Players are then able to see and to act in the role play.

Swapping of roles implies that there are at least two persons who are involved in the play. This allows for ample opportunities for social interaction – not only during the actual role play but also in a preparation phase before and a review phase afterwards. This social activity is believed to make the social role swapping application attractive. At least in highly successful online roleplay games such as World of Warcraft, the players state that interacting with other players is a major source of attraction [10]. However, it is questionable whether today's online games really foster good social interaction – or whether players are just "alone together" [17]. VR and AR could make major contribution for improving the quality of communication and social interactions. With these technologies, for instance, it is possible to substitute the loss of information (e.g. the meaning of deictic gestures, information about the atmosphere) inherent in a telephone conversation or in video conferencing. First prototypes already exist [12]. This is an opportunity for VR and AR to reach a large consumer market.

Having enough interesting content (i.e. scenarios prepared for the social role swapping game) is a critical factor for success. As we have discussed earlier, there are parties who could have an interest in financing the creation of content, e.g. for advertisements or for organizational training. If appropriate authoring tools are available, chances are high that there are people who are motivated to create content voluntarily. People have fun to supply content for others. Successful internet sites, for instance Wikipedia or YouTube, profit immensely from this. There might even be business models available where people act as guides or offer advisory services. It might even serve social work for example by fighting loneliness in an aging society.

4.4.2 Example 2: Virtual Humans and the Training of Health Professionals

Given an effective method to create effective virtual humans, we will write here about the proposed vision of a social learning curriculum that would incorporate virtual humans. This work references some of the Virtual Patients project's work at the University of Florida. In the Virtual Patients project, researchers are working to develop virtual humans that play the role of patients with whom health profession students can practice their communication skills. It is envisioned that all students working on their communication skills, including those outside of the medical field, would be able to leverage virtual human conversation partners. However, for this section, we will focus on a complete system for health profession students to learn communication skills. In doing so, the potential benefits that interaction with virtual humans could add will be enumerated.

Currently, students learn communication skills through lectures, videos, and eventually role-playing with actors (called standardized patients). While the existing system is well-tested, understood, and effective, there are significant benefits that virtual human learning interactions could add to such a curricula.

We envision a system that would present virtual humans in a mock examination room for 10 min patient-doctor conversations. These conversations are similar to standardized patient interviews in content, evaluation, and location (the current gold standard in interpersonal skills education). Students would walk up to a room, slide their ID card on a card reader on the door, and select a scenario to practice and a virtual human with whom they would practice. Then, the student would knock on the door and enter the room and see projected onto the exam room wall a life-sized virtual patient. They would walk up to the virtual human and begin conversing and gesturing as to practice their communication skills. Directional microphones and video cameras capture user behavior. The cognitive decision making of the patient is based on medical educator directed decision making, cognitive models, and educational criteria.

Given such a virtual human social learning system, the following communication skills education logistical issues can be addressed.

4.4.2.1 Frequency

Simply put, training with humans is expensive. This cost restricts the number of exposures for students. Virtual humans would provide students with an increased number of patient experiences in which to practice their skills. Students can practice basic interpersonal skills such as which questions to ask and how to ask questions with the virtual human, and thus increasing the educational efficacy of time with standardized patients.

4.4.2.2 Standardization

Virtual humans can ensure that learning experiences by all students can be similar. Virtual humans can present the same experience the fifteenth time of the day as the first, including always presenting the same information in the same manner. They also avoid being biased towards or away from the student (based on characteristics as gender and ethnicity, issues currently being grappled with by educators). Further, inter-institutional standardization is possible as students at one university can have similar educational opportunities as any other student.

4.4.2.3 Diversity

Communication skills training often requires the student to interact with a conversation partner who has a specific background, such as age, gender, ethnicity, weight, or intelligence. It is not a realistic goal to have on hand actors with the desired background and impossible when the partners include children, the elderly, or those with infrequent and dangerous conditions. This need for such cases occurs quite frequently in medical education and currently, the solution is to provide video-based examples, paper-based case studies, or lectures. Creating virtual humans with different backgrounds is straightforward and early research has shown that humans appear to socially respond to a large degree similarly to a virtual human as to real humans [5,35]. Thus educators can curricularly plan student exposure with both the medical condition and the type of patient. This will enable the educator to focus on communication skills that are currently difficult to create. For example, educators could focus on cultural competency issues as students experience a diabetes scenarios with African–American and Native American elderly male virtual human.

4.4.2.4 Feedback

Virtual human systems can be designed as to provide real-time and immediate after-action review feedback of a student's interaction with the virtual patient. Thus the system can help them review the interaction, including exploring empathetic moments, topics discussed, and non-verbal cues such as gaze and posture [33]. This enables students to self-direct review of their interview and educators to understand how students are applying class concepts.

4.4.2.5 Abnormal Findings

Human actors are – for the foreseeable future – significantly better social training tools than virtual humans. However, some conditions are not easily presented by humans. These fall under the category of abnormal findings. These are unusual conditions that are infrequently presented due to the morbidity or logistical difficulty of the scenario. An example of an abnormal finding is having students experience a cranial nerve damaged patient. For example, a patient with cranial nerve III damage would not be able to move one of their eyes past vertical when asked to follow the doctor's finger as it made a "H" motion path. Patients exhibiting such symptoms need to be examined immediately, and thus most students would experience such a condition only if such a patient arrived during their rotation. This results in most students seeing their first cranial nerve patient in practice where time to diagnose and respond is critical.

4.4.2.6 Resources

Virtual humans would provide a significant cost-benefit to the training of students. The opportunities for additional standardized experiences with feedback would provide educators with critical tools to improving communication skills. Improved communication skills in health profession students have been correlated with improved patient outcomes and lowered litigation. Thus there is a significant professional and monetary motivation towards realizing virtual humans in interpersonal skills education.

4.4.3 Example 3: AR Gaming Environments in Urban Settings

Prototypes of social gaming and learning environments applying AR technology in urban settings have been realized within various research projects [8, 11, 31]. Those applications typically enhanced the real environment by virtual content, including 3D objects, sound, etc. However, the rather sparse additional content was only registered spatially to the environment [7]. Occasionally, such as in TimeWarp [22], single existing buildings were modified or extended. Other approaches such as Epidemic Menace [26] included real world weather conditions such as wind and temperature in their game. However, a really close integration of such environments with the existing real environment has not yet been seen.

In order to attract a large number of users, future systems will have to be closely coupled to the real content of the users' environment. Thus objects of the environment will be altered or replaced according to the application content and player interactions. This will not be limited to static content such as the landscape and buildings, but will also have to extend to more temporary objects, such as parking cars or market stands. This will require quite advanced sensory capabilities allowing for detecting such content and considering it accordingly.

However, the full potential of such applications will only be achievable when including fully dynamic objects such as moving cars and in particular moving passersby. This will allow users to alter their environment entirely, e.g. replacing all cars by horse-drawn carriages or to dress other people in medieval outfits.

Of course, such applications will require advanced computer vision based tracking and recognition capabilities as well as sophisticated rendering and augmentation facilities (see Sect. 4.2). They would further be able to combine this modified real world content seamlessly with pure virtual content, making it potentially impossible for the observer to distinguish, e.g. between a virtually enhanced real passerby and a pure virtual character.

Such an approach will not only remove the clear distinction between real and virtual content, it will also seamlessly integrate non-players into the gaming environment. As those non players will have a significant influence on the overall application (e.g. the progress in the game) creating a really social game.

Another aspect of a close coupling between real and virtual content will be the extinction of real world content. While this is already done in respect to environmental sound applying noise cancellation technologies (there are even consumer head phones with built-in noise cancellation available nowadays), depending on the actual display technology used, such mechanism may also be applied for visual effects. Thus, buildings or other blocking objects may be virtually removed or partially dismantled from the user's view [2].

However, this new generation of pervasive games will not only entirely alter the way we perceive our environment and other people, or how we interact with them, it will also have implications regarding player safety. While virtual objects enhancing our real life will still be easily detected as being non real (due to their appearance, but also due to their behavior), the other way round implies potentially dangerous situations: if a real object is augmented by a virtual object and taken for virtual, while it actually is real (e.g. a car). A similar potentially dangerous situation can arise when interacting with virtually modified props.

4.5 Conclusion

So, to sum up, are social gaming and learning applications a driving force for the future of Virtual and Augmented Reality? Can they fulfill this role? The answer is yes, if we ask whether a potential exists to create a mass market. The answer is not "under no circumstances", because VR/AR are capable of providing a real added value, for example means for improved social activity even if communication is computer mediated. Also, chances are high that the costs of VR/AR can be reduced in a way that applications are marketable and reasonably priced. Suitable authoring processes and tools play a key role in cost reduction and a more widespread use.

At the moment, however, there are too many deficiencies ranging from obtrusiveness and limited fidelity of input and output devices over insufficient computer network capabilities to security concerns and lack of appropriate authoring tools and processes. Still, a lot of research work needs to be accomplished and it is questionable whether enough investments serving as "activation energy" will be made.

For most real-world applications, humans and social interactions are critical components. Thus the development of highly interactive virtual humans is a significant goal towards realizing socially relevant VR/AR experiences. Such VR/AR experiences will expand VR applicability and open up significant domains for research and development. This would be similar to the significant expansion of video games upon the development of compelling characters, online massively multi-user environments, and social-centric games.

Affective VR virtual humans would revolutionize designing for humans, interacting with humans, and training interpersonal skills. Much of this revolution is not predicated on a perfect virtual human. Thus, it is paramount for developers, researchers, and end-users to collaborate to most efficiently evolve and bring-to-market VR virtual humans. We predict this will first occur in critical interpersonal learning situations that realize a significant financial benefit if people are better communicators. This would be in three areas: medicine, the military, and business. The benefit to virtual human developers is that these areas are quite constrained and are approachable using existing technologies. As clear cost-benefit analyses of virtual humans can be constructed, a significant driving force for virtual reality will be realized.

The final answer to the question whether social gaming and learning applications provide a driving force for future VR and AR environments may be reduced to basically two aspects: Will those technologies become available on common devices such as smartphones, potentially everyone carries with her anytime, anywhere? And will the additional input and output devices (such as glasses) be unobtrusive and robust enough as well as socially accepted to be used 24/7? The answer to these two questions definitely is "yes", but it remains open, when this is actually going to happen. Based on the experiences regarding computer technology in general, it can be foreseen that the gaming applications will probably be the driving force on the technology side, while the learning applications may lead to the required broad acceptance beyond gamers.

References

1. Act-3d b.v. Product information about quest3d. URL www.quest3d.com
2. Avery, B., Sandor, C., Thomas, B.H.: Improving spatial perception for augmented reality x-ray vision. In: Proceedings of IEEE Virtual Reality (IEEE VR) 2009, pp. 79–82. IEEE Computer Society (2009)
3. Babu, S., Suma, E., Barnes, T., Hodges, L.F.: Can immersive virtual humans teach social conversational protocols? In: Proceedings of the IEEE International Conference on Virtual Reality 2007, pp. 215–218. IEEE Computer Society (2007)
4. Badler, N., Bindiganavale, R., Bourne, J., Allbeck, J., Shi, J., Palmer, M.: Real time virtual humans. In: Proceedings of International Conference on Digital Media Futures. British Computer Society (1999)
5. Baylor, A.L., Rosenberg-Kima, R.B., Plant, E.A.: Interface agents as social models: the impact of appearance on females' attitude toward engineering. In: CHI '06: CHI '06 Extended Abstracts on Human Factors in Computing Systems, pp. 526–531. ACM, NY, USA (2006). DOI http://doi.acm.org/10.1145/1125451.1125564
6. Bitouk, D., Kumar, N., Dhillon, S., Belhumeur, P., Nayar, S.K.: Face swapping: automatically replacing faces in photographs. In: SIGGRAPH '08: ACM SIGGRAPH 2008 papers, pp. 1–8. ACM, New York, NY, USA (2008). DOI http://doi.acm.org/10.1145/1399504.1360638
7. Broll, W., Lindt, I., Herbst, I., Ohlenburg, J., Braun, A.K., Wetzel, R.: Toward next-gen mobile ar games. IEEE Comput. Graph. Appl. **28**(4), 40–48 (2008)
8. Broll, W., Ohlenburg, J., Lindt, I., Herbst, I., Braun, A.K.: Meeting technology challenges of pervasive augmented reality games. In: NetGames '06: Proceedings of 5th ACM SIGCOMM Workshop on Network and System Support for Games, p. 28. ACM, NY, USA (2006). DOI http://doi.acm.org/10.1145/1230040.1230097
9. Brynskov, M., Ludvigsen, M.: Mock games: a new genre of pervasive play. In: DIS '06: Proceedings of the 6th Conference on Designing Interactive Systems, pp. 169–178. ACM, New York, NY, USA (2006). DOI http://doi.acm.org/10.1145/1142405.1142433
10. Chen, V.H.h., Duh, H.B.L.: Understanding social interaction in world of warcraft. In: ACE '07: Proceedings of the International Conference on Advances in Computer Entertainment Technology, pp. 21–24. ACM, New York, NY, USA (2007). DOI http://doi.acm.org/10.1145/1255047.1255052
11. Cheok, A., Goh, K.H., Liu, W., Farbiz, F., Fong, S.W., Teo, S.L., Li, Y., Yang, X.: Human pacman: a mobile, wide-area entertainment system based on physical, social, and ubiquitous computing. Personal Ubiquitous Computing **8**(2), 71–81 (2004)
12. Cheok, A.D., Teh, K.S., Nguyen, T.H.D., Qui, T.C.T., Lee, S.P., Liu, W., Li, C.C., Diaz, D., Boj, C.: Social and physical interactive paradigms for mixed-reality entertainment. Comput. Entertain. **4**(2), 5 (2006). DOI http://doi.acm.org/10.1145/1129006.1129015
13. Cohn, J., Schmorrow, D., Nicholson, D.: The psi handbook of virtual environments for training and education, vol. 2: Developments for the military and beyond (technology, psychology, and health). Praeger Publishers, London (2008)
14. Craig, S., Gholson, B., Driscoll, D.: Animated pedagogical agents in multimedia educational environments: Effects of agent properties, picture features, and redundancy. J. Educ. Psychol. **94**(2), 428–434 (2002)

15. Dassault systemes: Product information about virtools. URL www.virtools.com
16. Deaton, J., Barba, C., Santarelli, T., Rosenzweig, L., Souders, V., McCollum, C., Seip, J., Kerr, B., Singer, M.: Virtual environment cultural training for operational effectiveness (vector). J. Virtual. Real. **8**(3), 156–157 (2006)
17. Ducheneaut, N., Yee, N., Nickell, E., Moore, R.J.: "alone together?": exploring the social dynamics of massively multiplayer online games. In: CHI '06: Proceedings of the SIGCHI conference on Human Factors in Computing Systems, pp. 407–416. ACM, NY, USA (2006). DOI http://doi.acm.org/10.1145/1124772.1124834
18. eMagin corp. Nov. 2008. Product description of the emagin z800 visor. URL www.emagin.com/products/systems
19. Friedman, D., Leeb, R., Guger, C., Steed, A., Pfurtscheller, G., Slater, M.: Navigating virtual reality by thought: what is it like? Presence: Teleoper. Virtual Environ. **16**(1), 100–110 (2007). DOI http://dx.doi.org/10.1162/pres.16.1.100
20. Google inc. Nov. 2008. Product information about google sketchup. sketchup.google.com
21. Hanrahan, P.: Why is graphics hardware so fast? In: PPoPP '05: Proceedings of the 10th ACM SIGPLAN Symposium on Principles and Practice of Parallel Programming, pp. 1–1. ACM, New York, NY, USA (2005). DOI http://doi.acm.org/10.1145/1065944.1065945
22. Herbst, I., Braun, A.K., McCall, R., Broll, W.: Timewarp: interactive time travel with a mobile mixed reality game. In: MobileHCI '08: Proceedings of the 10th International Conference on Human Computer Interaction with Mobile Devices and Services, pp. 235–244. ACM, NY, USA (2008). DOI http://doi.acm.org/10.1145/1409240.1409266
23. Hill Jr., R.H., Gratch, J., Marsella, S., Rickel, J., Swartout, W., Traum, D.: Virtual humans in the mission rehearsal exercise system. Artif. Intell. (AI Journal) **17** (2003)
24. Johnsen, K., Dickerson, R., Raij, A., Lok, B., Jackson, J., Shin, M., Hernandez, J., Stevens, A., Lind, D.S.: Experiences in using immersive virtual characters to educate medical communication skills. In: VR '05: Proceedings of the 2005 IEEE Conference 2005 on Virtual Reality, pp. 179–186, 324. IEEE Computer Society, Washington, DC, USA (2005). DOI http://dx.doi.org/10.1109/VR.2005.33
25. Kotranza, A., Lok, B., Deladisma, A., Pugh, C.M., Lind, D.S.: Mixed reality humans: Evaluating behavior, usability, and acceptability. IEEE Transactions on Visualization and Computer Graphics (2009)
26. Lindt, I., Ohlenburg, J., Pankoke-Babatz, U., Ghellal, S.: A report on the crossmedia game epidemic menace. Comput. Entertain. **5**(1) (2007)
27. Magerkurth, C., Cheok, A.D., Mandryk, R.L., Nilsen, T.: Pervasive games: bringing computer entertainment back to the real world. Comput. Entertain. **3**(3) (2005)
28. Nintendo co., ltd. 2007. financial results briefing for the six-month period ended september 2007 (briefing date 2007/10/26), supplementary information (2007)
29. Homepage of Novint technologies, inc. URL www.novint.com
30. Paris, S., Donikian, S., Bonvalet, N.: Environmental abstraction and path planning techniques for realistic crowd simulation: Research articles. Comput. Animat. Virtual Worlds **17**(3-4), 325–335 (2006). DOI http://dx.doi.org/10.1002/cav.v17:3/4
31. Piekarski, W., Thomas, B.: Arquake: the outdoor augmented reality gaming system. Commun. ACM **45**(1), 36–38 (2002). DOI http://doi.acm.org/10.1145/502269.502291
32. Pricewaterhousecoopers International Ltd. 2007. Global entertainment and media outlook: 2007–2011 (2007)
33. Raij, A., Johnsen, K., Dickerson, R., Lok, B., Cohen, M., Duerson, M., Pauley, R., Stevens, A., Wagner, P., Lind, D.: Comparing interpersonal interactions with a virtual human to those with a real human. IEEE Transactions on Visualization and Computer Graphics **13**(3), 443–457 (2007)
34. Reitmayr, G., Schmalstieg, D.: An open software architecture for virtual reality interaction. In: VRST '01: Proceedings of the ACM symposium on Virtual reality software and technology, pp. 47–54. ACM, NY, USA (2001). DOI http://doi.acm.org/10.1145/505008.505018
35. Rossen, B., Johnsen, K., Deladisma, A., Lind, S., Lok, B.: Virtual humans elicit skin-tone bias consistent with real-world skin-tone biases. In: IVA '08: Proceedings of the 8th international

conference on Intelligent Virtual Agents, pp. 237–244. Springer, Berlin (2008). DOI http://dx.
doi.org/10.1007/978-3-540-85483-824
36. Shao, W., Terzopoulos, D.: Autonomous pedestrians. Graph. Models **69**(5–6), 246–274 (2007).
DOI http://dx.doi.org/10.1016/j.gmod.2007.09.001
37. Slater, M., Guger, C., Edlinger, G., Leeb, R., Pfurtscheller, G., Antley, A., Garau, M., Brogni,
A., Friedman, D.: Analysis of physiological responses to a social situation in an immersive
virtual environment. Presence: Teleoper. Virtual Environ. **15**(5), 553–569 (2006). DOI http:
//dx.doi.org/10.1162/pres.15.5.553
38. Swartout, W., Gratch, J., Hill, R.W., Hovy, E., Arsella, S.M., Rickel, J., Traum, D.: Toward
virtual humans. AI Mag. **27**(2), 96–108 (2006)
39. Virtual boy infopage: Independent database with info about the nintendo virtual boy. URL
www.virtual-boy.org

Chapter 5
[Virtual + 1] * Reality
Blending "Virtual" and "Normal" Reality to Enrich Our Experience

Steffi Beckhaus

Abstract Virtual Reality aims at creating an artificial environment that can be perceived as a substitute to a real setting. Much effort in research and development goes into the creation of virtual environments that in their majority are perceivable only by eyes and hands. The multisensory nature of our perception, however, allows and, arguably, also expects more than that. As long as we are not able to simulate and deliver a fully sensory believable virtual environment to a user, we could make use of the fully sensory, multi-modal nature of real objects to fill in for this deficiency. The idea is to purposefully integrate real artifacts into the application and interaction, instead of dismissing anything real as hindering the virtual experience. The term virtual reality – denoting the goal, not the technology – shifts from a core virtual reality to an "enriched" reality, technologically encompassing both the computer generated and the real, physical artifacts. Together, either simultaneously or in a hybrid way, real and virtual jointly provide stimuli that are perceived by users through their senses and are later formed into an experience by the user's mind.

5.1 The Human, the Interface and the Virtual World

Interfaces that enable a human being to get in touch with a virtual environment, or more generally a computer, nowadays have mostly been standardized. Virtual worlds are mainly visually presented, and interaction with them is typically realized with a hand manipulated input device. This is the case for most application contexts, regardless of whether they are 2D window applications or 3D representations of the real world or if they are in an automotive, educational or cultural context. Also, regarding their input and output modalities, desktop systems (PCs) do not differ fundamentally from the majority of systems delivering immersive virtual

S. Beckhaus
im.ve, Department of Informatics, University of Hamburg, Vogt-Kölln-Str. 30,
22767 Hamburg, Germany
e-mail: steffi.beckhaus@uni-hamburg.de

S. Coquillart et al. (eds.), *Virtual Realities*, DOI 10.1007/978-3-211-99178-7_5,
© Springer-Verlag/Wien 2011

environments (iVE). As a standard, most of the virtual worlds with PCs as well as iVEs are only perceived with the eye and manipulated by the fingers or hand [26].

The human being, who is recipient and actor in the real as well as virtual world, however, is a multisensory being with manifold capabilities to perceive and act.

This view informs our current research of the im.ve lab at the University of Hamburg. We aim at advancing possibilities to create true interactive experiences within virtual environments, using Virtual Reality (VR) technology and, for that reason, develop basic system technologies. We also explore fundamentally new interfaces that, apart from functionality, enable people to have an extensive, enjoyable and rich experience. We believe that this is one of the keys for the acceptance and efficiency of virtual environments. With current technological possibilities and thinking further than just into technology-only approaches, we feel that this area offers exciting new possibilities and challenges. In the pursuit of this vision, we not only develop core VR systems and technology, but also take a "reality-based" approach to interaction, a term recently coined by Jacob et al. [15].

This chapter firstly provides motivation for taking this viewpoint and approach. It starts by comparing the human perception of the real world with our experience of virtual worlds and discusses the role of interfaces that connect both these worlds. It then introduces the user's perspective, challenging the idea that, on the core perceptual level, the real world and the technology mediated world are in any way different and discussing the major role of mind for experience. Following this, two projects are presented that purposefully include reality-based components into the virtual environment, in pursuit of developing rich interfaces that ultimately also aim at being more intuitive, enjoyable, and rich. The first example deals with the ChairIO, a chair-based interface for the navigation through virtual worlds. The second example demonstrates options for multisensory control by way of an installation using granules on an interactive table. We conclude by encouraging to take the above described approach, discussing its potential to "enrich" reality and experiences.

5.1.1 Our Perception of the World

The world around us provides us with extensive, rich sensory impressions. We see, hear, feel, smell and taste.

Mostly our consciousness is focussed only on a part of this extensive offer from outside. While reading a book, for example, we mainly concentrate on the written words, sentences and their meaning. We visually perceive the letters and mentally immerse into the story. Nevertheless, the physical book has an impact on our experience, we feel the size of the book, the cover, its weight. We smell the paper, know if it is an old or new book, and hear the rustling while turning the pages. At the same time we subconsciously notice how and on what we sit or stand, whether the air around us is warm or cool and which environment we are in. On the other hand, we ignore that an airplane is flying over our house or that dinner time has passed and our body signals being hungry. We are also subconsciously influenced by what we have met before we started reading and by our cumulated experiences. Together with many other sensory, contextual, and emotional components, those impressions influence our perception, even if some or most of this information is not relevant to a current goal we might have.

To understand how we can aid the development of extensive, enjoyable and rich experiences, we first have to look at this process and the nature of experience. Figures 5.1 and 5.2 show an overview of the general ingredients of a user experience that will be discussed in the following. We start with the programmed virtual world, followed by its mediation through VR technology – the only interface to the virtual world – together forming the virtual environment. Then, we talk about how those contribute to a user experience, especially describing the capabilities of our mind.

5.1.2   The Programmed Virtual World

Contrary to the real world the virtual world is just a programmed digital product. In its description it is not physical and it remains a vision, an idea, until it is displayed. In itself, it cannot be physically experienced, it needs a mediator for display and interaction.

This mediator, the display and interface, however, can only react on whatever is programmed. In order for virtual objects come to life, that they become touchable, seizable, movable, modifiable, these aspects first have to be explicitly programmed. Each object, each material property, each physical law has to be described. For a virtual experience, the diversity that we are used to in the real world: firstly, has to be collected, processed and prepared into a technical description; secondly, adjusted for the current situation in the virtual world; and, finally, submitted to the human being. If it is not programmed in the first place, no high fidelity system will be able to deliver it.

This sounds trivial at first, but if we consider what makes virtual worlds work, then this is the part that is distinctively different to any real artifact. If we take a "real" object, it has all those mentioned features already built in and those are delivered in the highest possible fidelity.

5.1.3   The Interface as (Exclusive) Contact with the Virtual World

The virtual description that exists in the computer has to be made accessible and perceivable by a mediator. Regardless of how perfectly the virtual world may be conceptualized and modeled, its presentation can only be as good as the mediator, the technical systems employed for the presentation. The result depends on the kind, quality and condition of the transmitting display, the interaction devices and the interaction techniques that jointly form the technical interface (TI), as shown in Fig. 5.1. In desktop systems, for example, those technical interfaces consist of a

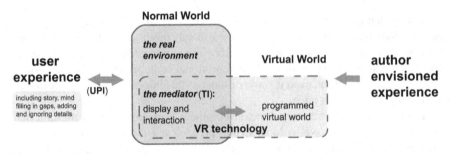

Fig. 5.1 VR technology always needs the "normal" physical world as a mediator to present the idea of the virtual world. The mediator is the technical interface (TI). The user's perceptual interface (UPI), the body sensors, perceive the whole "normal" physical world which also includes the TI

monitor for the visual presentation and mouse plus keyboard for the control. Even technologically advanced variations of immersive stereo-projected displays such as CAVE™, i-Cone™, or other installations focus mostly on visual displays. The immersive systems are navigated by standardized hand-manipulated input devices such as a flying joystick or wand. Acoustic or haptic displays exist, but are not widely used.

Technical limits in the mediation, for example, restrictions of quality, resolution, display frequency, visual field, the interaction space or the supported modalities, dominate how we perceive the virtual world. When only visual information is made available, the virtual world can only be experienced with the visual sensory system. The physical hardware of the displays and interaction devices, however, delivers a fully sensory experience: they are noticed by their sounds, warmth, and vibrations, adding to what users perceive and therefore providing real world stimuli, unintended to support the envisioned virtual world. In order to fully concentrate one's attention only on the presented virtual world, those dominant disturbances would have to be ignored.

It can safely be said that the current state of technology cannot provide us with a real solution for the technical only (TI) presentation of fully sensory interactive virtual worlds yet. A vision of StarTrek's Holodeck is out of reach and, for the time being, not practicable and the focus of current research in the area of iVE and VR technology does not promise quick improvement. It is questionable anyway, whether the Holodeck vision should be the only final goal in the development of virtual worlds.

For the time being, computer with current technical possibilities only allow for a very limited reproduction of the world. The "normal", physical world, however, shows all its capabilities and beauty without anyone having to lift a finger: everything material around us directly, completely, and richly presents itself to us, while everything virtual has to be programmed and displayed first, by potentially adding new undesired stimuli to the experience, like clumsy interaction devices or noise from machines.

5.1.4   The User Experience

Any stimulus from outside, regardless if delivered by the "normal" world or from VR technology, is processed by our senses – so to say the user's perceptual interface (UPI) to the world as shown in Fig. 5.2. The body has sensors for visual, auditory and many more stimuli, transforming the external in information for stem and brain [18].

A human being, however, is more than just its body components. At any moment, it is our mind that decides, consciously or subconsciously, which aspect out of the multitude of information we focus our attention on, depending on the range of aspects offered from outside and inside and depending on our current interest: the book's story, the layout, the images, or the people that have just entered the room. In this way, the mind works like a *multidimensional flexible lens* which is constantly refocussing based on many internal factors, like values, expectations, prior experience, prior stimuli and so on, as shown in Fig. 5.2.

5.1.4.1   Our Mind: The Multidimensional Flexible Lens

Mind has manifold capabilities, developed to support us in various situations. It has the extraordinary ability to ignore external stimuli or interpret them in different ways, plus to create its own inner world. Mind is capable of extremely slowing down the perception of time and can focus on a specific aspect of what is happening outside [10]. It can accidentally or purposefully focus on some parts and ignore other parts, as change blindness and inattentional blindness phenomena show [28, 29,31]. Training of mind can change emotional responses to emotional and stressful situations, shown by Davidson and Lutz [7]. Mind can ignore (or amplify) outer stimuli like pain either by focussing on alternative stimuli from outside like in VR pain treatment [13] or by focussing on itself as in meditation [11, 16]. It creates its

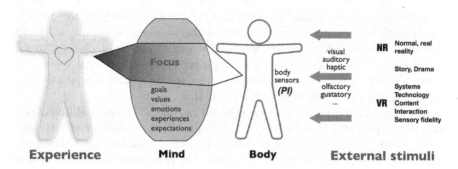

Fig. 5.2 From "Normal, Real" Reality (NR) and "Virtual" Reality (VR) Stimuli to Experience. The mind's focus is the key transformer of stimuli into experience based on its internal state, e.g. on goals, expectations and prior experiences

own inner world, when we think or dream. Furthermore, mind is known to be able to change its host, the body, as recent studies on neuroplasticity show [7].

5.1.4.2 The Factors of Experience

The experience of outer or inner stimuli is, thus, significantly defined of the current state of mind which in turn is a product of mind itself. We could – theoretically and after a lot of training – be in control. However, the truth is that mind mostly works unconscious to us. This in fact is also a big advantage, as otherwise we would not be able to walk while absorbed in talking or, even after years of practicing, would drive a car like a beginner.

What makes the mind focus in one way and not the other in a particular situation, consciously or subconsciously? Some relevant aspects are:

- *Intention*: The pursuit of a goal makes us fail in the change blindness test to see a gorilla [29]. The goal to win or experience a game distracts from physical pain [13]. And the goal to meet a publication deadline distracts from being hungry.
- *Expectations* [23]: A recent VR paper, for example, describes the role of expectation in smell detection, explaining that not the correct olfactory stimulus is of importance, but the match between expectation and rough stimulus [24]. Expectations come from prior stimuli and prior experiences and they are colored by the current goal of a person.
- *Prior and built-in experience*: We have numerous intuitive and trained skills that can be tapped into by using appropriate metaphors. Jacob et al. [15] list some general areas of those like naive physics, body awareness and skills, environmental awareness and skills, and social awareness and skills. But also *priming* effects on users are well known and fundamentally change the outcome of tests like demonstrated, for example, in the Stereotype test [30].

There is much more as known from user experience research on products. Aesthetics, values, pragmatic qualities (functionality and usability), hedonic qualities of stimulation, identification, and evocation, all are contributing factors to how users experience a product or an application in this or another way. Also, story and characters strongly influence the experience. We often found that including "small, innocent, cute looking" creatures that are in danger immediately resonates with participants (see Sect. 5.3.3.3 for an example). There is a lot to learn from storytelling about that, tapping into the mind of the user [21].

In summary, our experience is very personal and depends on many different factors, mostly tempered by the current state of mind. Mind is selective and its inner world distorts the outer world. To mind there is nothing objective, as it filters, modifies, colors all outer stimuli, for example, based on past experiences. By focussing on itself, mind is also capable of experiencing without sensing. In that very moment, experiences have nothing to do with an outside stimulus; therefore, creating stimuli does not necessary lead to creating an experience.

5.1.4.3 Authoring an Experience

An author attempts to control this variability and freedom of mind by targeting content and presentation of a virtual world in a specific way, but he cannot fully control it. Being active participants of the real and the virtual world, we theoretically may choose what we wish to focus on, out of the multitude of stimuli, even though, arguably, conscious control is only possible with a trained, focussed mind.

Nevertheless, building on those factors described in Sect. 5.1.4.2 it is possible to aid users to have a more rich and deep experience. Currently, much of VR research focusses on developing the technical interface (TI), the VR stimuli in Fig. 5.2. As an example, in Sects. 5.2 and 5.3 we give two examples that use built-in knowledge and body awareness skills, and deliver a full sensory experience, purposefully adding real and technical components, jointly presenting rich physical stimuli to the user's perceptual interface (UPI).

5.1.5 Perspectives for the User Experience

It seems that with the emergence of technological assisted environments, we, as human beings, more and more fit ourselves to comply to the technology and not vice versa. Current interfaces are far from capable of providing people with the range of information they are used to in the real world. The limited range of interfaces and the quality of experience they deliver is not questioned by most of the currently developed applications. Developers and users alike tolerate that the experience and control of the virtual world is only from a distance and more a mental exercise, as we have to trick our mind that we are able to believe what is presented.

David Rokeby, author and developer of "Very Nervous System", a famous early interactive installation, describes this by way of an experienced aftereffect of having been in a VR installation; one hour after he left the installation, he suddenly felt as if he was off the floor and at a certain angle. He explains this in the way that, while he was in the installation, he "desensitized his responses to the balancing mechanisms in the inner ear in order to sustain the motion in a purely visually defined 3D space", but failed to reinstall it afterwards. When stimulated by the design of sharply angled lines on the wall, his mind changed its idea about the body's orientation in space and lifted him up and around, despite of the ears correctly reporting that he was standing upright – which caused a wave of nausea [27].

This shows, on the one hand, the capabilities of mind to support the suspense of disbelief. On the other hand, it shows what we impart on people, if we rely on them adapting to our installations need. Computer work is omnipresent, both at work and leisure, and more and more, virtual environments are utilized to support training, work, and therapy. Therefore it seems worthwhile to look for ways to "enrich" the otherwise limited experience of the currently delivered virtual worlds and to aid the development of extensive, enjoyable and rich experiences.

The previous paragraphs point to several ways how to "enrich" the otherwise limited experience of the currently delivered virtual worlds. Storytelling would be one of the options, leveraging the users mind to buy into the provided experience. Many possibilities exist that use perceptual illusions, characters, and story to guide the users mind into a rich experience. As we as VR researchers are not mainly storytellers, the remainder of this chapter will focus on another possibility, the idea of deliberately integrating objects from the real world into the installation and interaction.

The underlying idea is to regard the technical environment not only as a medium and as potential obstacle, but to actively integrate technology and real, existing, material objects into the experience of the virtual world. By this the definition of the interface to virtual worlds is extended from the "mediator" in Fig. 5.2 (TI) to include all aspects of the "normal", physical world, supporting the whole perceptual interface (UPI) of users. With movement sensors in mobile devices and other advancing technologies, nowadays, we have vast potential to overcome those limitations that human computer interaction used to have because of the reduction of the multi-sensory human being to a person with eyes and hands only. By actively and "naturally" stimulating using all senses and composing them to a holistic experience, it will become possible to mediate multisensory and multimodal information, without having to model them in the virtual world. This potentially also fosters the discovery of more intuitive interfaces, tapping into mind's vast treasures.

The following examples demonstrate two possibilities in this direction. The first one is about the navigation of virtual worlds; The second one demonstrates new possible interaction paradigms on interactive tables.

5.2   The ChairIO: Navigation in Virtual Worlds

An example of a computer interface that allows the intuitive control of movements through virtual worlds and, at the same time, delivers a rich emotional experience to the user is the ChairIO. The ChairIO is a chair-based computer interface consisting of a flexible office stool with sensors. The sensors record the stool's movements transmitting them to the computer. The computer translates this information in movements through a 3D world or in games, GoogleEarth or GUI environments. The ChairIO can equally be employed for desktop systems as well as for large projections. An extensive summary of the ChairIO is in [3].

5.2.1   The Navigation of Virtual Worlds with a Chair

The chair we use is the Swopper™ by [1], illustrated in Fig. 5.3. This office chair has a flexible central column that is a spring-and-damper system. The Swopper's base supports the single legged stool at a single, centred point. The seat of the

Fig. 5.3 The ChairIO's DOFs using the Swopper™ as underlying chair

chair is connected to the base via a complex linkage. The connection at the base allows the seat to pivot freely in all directions, to a maximal angle of about 30 °. The pivot's flexibility is adjustable, making the tilting movement easier or harder. Above the pivot joint is a suspension system – a shock and coil spring. The spring stiffness is adjustable to account for users of different weight. The shock length is also adjustable, controlling the height of the seat at rest. The suspension system allows the Swopper seat to move up and down approximately 20 cm. The piston of the shock forms the connection to the seat and allows the seat to rotate freely on the linkage.

The Swopper can be moved and rotated along the degrees of freedom (DOF) shown in Fig. 5.3. The chair allows control on 4 axes: tilt left/right, tilt front/back, move up/down and rotate left/right. The two tilt axes can be either considered as rotational or translational axes. The movement of the seat on the linkage forms a rotational DOF. The up/down axis is slightly limited in its usability, as changing the height requires placing more or less weight on the chair. Short rapid movements, such as bouncing, are performed easily, however, even small up/down shifts are physically difficult to produce for more than a few seconds. Alternatively, the up/down axis can be used as a discrete, button like, input.

Such a chair is an ideal candidate to navigate virtual worlds. Two features are needed for navigation in virtual environments: first, the view around, which changes the orientation, and second, the relocation in all directions. For free navigation, a user needs control of theses two modes.

The ChairIO based on the Swopper seat supports these navigation features by deflecting the stool and controlling the rotation of the seat. If the chair's seat is tilted slightly forwards or backwards, the view in the virtual world moves accordingly. If it is tilted slightly to the left or to the right, the view moves sideways. All analog directions in-between also work. If the seat is rotated in one or the other direction, the virtual world turns (i.e. virtual rotation) around the current position until the chair is returned into the straightforward position. This works with minimal movements

Fig. 5.4 The ChairIO mapping in a virtual world

of the chair, as well as with drastic ones. The wider the tilt or rotation the faster becomes the movement. The chair is controlled by the movements of the hips, based in the legs. It is not necessary, but possible, to use the whole body and dynamically follow the chair's movements with chest and arms also.

All of the described movements can also be combined. Riding in a fast curving motion, a sliding like motion is produced by moving the chair by 45° forwards and sidewards while rotating the seat. Physically speaking, the hip is moved tangentially to the movement's direction, similar to skiing. Sliding through the virtual world is comparable to a similar movement in the real world caused by the centrifugal force in this direction (Fig. 5.4).

5.2.2   The Experience

Apart from the technical aspects, the user's experience is influenced by the below mentioned points while navigating through the virtual world:

- The chair's current position and the user's body itself inform the user about his physical position in space, providing passive feedback.
- The user seated on the chair controls the chair's movement with his body and through this merges with the interface and interaction to a harmonious ensemble.
- The chair's movement activates the whole body down to the toes and boosts the body's mobility. This kind of movement is realized by the Swopper™ itself. The combination of this with a computer to control an application enhances and encourages those kinds of movements actively. Instead of slouching in front of the computer screen for hours and just moving the fingers, the whole human being is actively engaged and inspired to move.

Operating the chair, users merge with the movement through virtual space. They are part of the installation and receive immediate passive feedback.

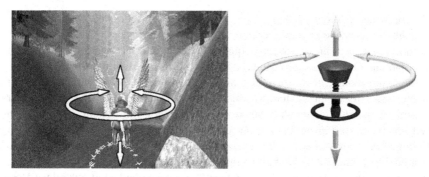

Fig. 5.5 Bird flight controlled with the ChairIO. The *left image* shows the game with the indicated ways of navigation: orientation and wing beat. The *right image* shows the corresponding illustration of the parameters on the ChairIO

We employed the ChairIO in different navigation applications of virtual worlds and games [4]. An example that describes well one aspect of possible experiences is the simulation of flying a bird. To do this, we used one of the mini-games of "Harry Potter and the Prisoner of Azkaban" (EA Games), in which the user normally controls the wing beat of a "Hippogriff" and its orientation by striking keys on the keyboard. Harry, in this case representing the user himself, is seated on the Hippogriff and has to navigate through rings placed along a path through the air above the environment. The beating of the wings has to be initiated at just the right moment, when the bird is ready to beat its wings. High frequency input leads, at the best, to erratic behaviour and usually, the wing beat commands get lost completely. As long as the previous beat is not finished, no click can produce new wing beats. If the wings are not beat, the bird will slowly glide to the ground. Therefore, it is necessary to find the right timing and the right rhythm in order to let the bird reach the proper altitude to glide through the rings.

In our ChairIO version, shown in Fig. 5.5, a wing beat is performed by bouncing once on the stool. The direction is controlled by rotating the seat slightly. Therefore, a user physically bounces on the chair to make the wings beat. She experiences the same flapping and gliding motion by passive, implicit feedback triggered through controlling the bird, as if sitting on the bird themselves. The users swing together with the bird, receiving the full sensory experience of the motion. This can be amplified by spreading the arms as wings. In this way, the user immerses into a flow-like, harmonic, rich experience, maybe even inducing the experience of being the bird.

5.2.3 Usability

The previous example implemented with the ChairIO showed the potential for rich experiences by purposefully including the "normal" and physical world into our interaction with the computer. Physical, passive and implicit feedback, enaction, plus purposeful, directed body movement greatly enriches the experience and, through that, provide an intuitive, rich and joyful experience.

Implicitly, such an experiential quality of user interfaces is motivated in the International Organization for Standardization norm for usability: the ISO 9241-11 "Ergonomic requirements for office work with visual display terminals (VDTs)" defines usability as the "extent to which a product can be used by specified users to achieve specified goals with *effectiveness, efficiency* and *satisfaction* in a specified context of use." From this we can conclude that user satisfaction, defined as "the feeling of pleasure that comes when a need or desire is fulfilled," should be regarded as a goal as important to Human-Computer Interaction (HCI) and VR research as effectivity and efficiency are. For the ChairIO, we have conducted several user tests that evaluate all three aspects [2, 3, 6]. We showed that the interface is immediately usable, without explanation even for novice users, and that users could travel easily, performing complex tasks, like moving around a column while keeping it in view. The body seems to know in an intuitive way how to move the chair, tapping into its body awareness skills. This intuitive knowledge is used control the virtual movement but at the same time to enrich the user experience in the real world. Users also like the experience very much, making it a satisfying interface not only in the "just usable" sense.

5.2.4 Conclusion

The ChairIO is a good example to demonstrate that it is possible to successfully combine precise and intuitive navigation in the virtual world with a rich experience of users in the real world. The survey as well as comments of many highly experienced VR users indicate that this kind of interface could be one of the most intuitive possibilities to navigate in 3D worlds – if a seated control is appropriate.

This inspires further exploration of sensory rich interfaces with real components that are not pushed to the background, but are deliberately employed. Those might have a high potential of being intuitive, user friendly and ultimately making users more happy, just because of their full sensory richness, their metaphorical value to mind and body, and their matching affordance (See [9,25], and [15]). The richness of the delivered stimulus, both the active involvement and the passive feedback through the body, can add a lot to the user experience itself.

5.3 The GranulatSynthese: Modeling Space on an Interactive Table

Virtual worlds are mainly discussed on the basis of desktop systems, immersive projection systems, or head-mounted displays (HMDs). Current developments in computer science increasingly use interactive tables that were first introduced as the "Responsive Workbench" for virtual realities in the 1990s [20]. Nowadays, they are more and more used as monographic multi-touch tables, for example in [12]. Although the possibility of interaction with a touchscreen seems to be dynamic and intuitive, it follows the trend described before that reduces humans and their activities to their eyes and fingertips as seen by the computer [26]. Therefore, the question is: how can this reduction be overcome when using interactive tables? Many solutions exist that use marker-based tangible interaction methods, employing tools like reacTIVision and ARToolkit, the latter well known from Augmented Reality [17, 19]. The advantages of tangible, graspable markers with an individual identifier made from thick cardboard or plastic pucks are that they are intuitive to control and have clear affordances. The drawback is the lack of expression in these tools. Markers have a specific form and function. They can change their meaning, can be (re-)applied to specific data, but are only a stand-in for a specific information, which can then be moved through space.

The artistic project GranulatSynthese [5, 8] presented in the following offers a different approach to work with physical space, in this case modeling space. Its potential is to control form and function by the form of shapes that are built by material on the table, either implicitly or explicitly (Fig. 5.6).

5.3.1 The Installation

The current installation of GranulatSynthese is a box occupying about one cubic meter, containing a glass plate covered with a thin semi-transparent layer, a mirror, a projector, a camera, speakers, and the controlling PC. A layer of granules, approximately 0.5 cm thick, covers the table surface. The installation is either situated in a

Fig. 5.6 The GranulatSynthese, a meditative audio-visual-haptic installation and a colorful, interactive, musical sandbox

darkened or semi-lit room, flooded by overhead infrared lighting or the infrared light source is placed inside the box. Underneath the table, an infrared camera observes the table surface. From these images, the software detects the shape of granule covered area and the exposed space in between (the "hills" and "lakes" of the landscape). From the shades of the infrared light filtered by the semi-transparent material, it is possible to calculate the shape of the granules landscape and any open space on the table. In contrast to the Sandscape installation of Ishii et al. [14], who use a laser range scanner to calculate the three-dimensional shape of a rolling landscape, covering the full table surface, we use less material to allow for partly freed table surface. Our current installation uses the position, size, orientation, and shape of the resulting open spaces on the table as control parameters.

Visually, the forms of the opened areas are filled with color and waves flow out from these forms through the covered areas, like waves flow around an island. The waves are reflected from the boundaries of the installation, but lose energy over time. Acoustically, depending on position, orientation, size, and shape, sound samples are selected and adjusted in volume and pitch, to conform to the "selected" parameters. Instead of having immediate effect, changes to parameters gradually lead to changes in the generated audio and visuals.

5.3.2 The Experience

Working with granules is a well-known experience. Probably everybody played with sand as a child. Even though just building something may have been the apparent motivation to do so, the haptic, tactile sensation itself likely contributed to the appeal of sand boxes. Furthermore, the tactile stimulation is known to have positive effects on learning and the development of the brain in childhood. The appeal of the flexible, semi-liquid but still formable, haptic matter makes sand and other more course-grained materials enjoyable to work with. Today, the authors still find themselves enjoying the feel of sand trickling through their fingers on a beach or using the granules on the table.

One of the main features of the interface is the joy of interacting with the granules. Touching the granules is a very haptic experience similar to touching rice or coffee beans. It also has very similar acoustic features. The material is hard enough, to make clear and distinctive sounds when dropped on the table, but it is also warm and pleasant to the touch. It encourages moving one's hands through the granules to shape hills or free spaces, making noises by moving the material. Users enjoy rummaging through the material. We have observed many visitors to our lab playing absent-mindedly with the granules, even when the installation was not switched on. With a working system, visitors often just step back to watch their or other users' audio-visual creation evolve.

The interface is rich in both the real and virtual domains; the granules are both an interface with sonic, haptic, and playful features and a three-dimensional projection area. Additionally, the interface creates sound, both in the computer-generated and real domains. Rummaging through the material, flattening the landscape by patting it, or letting the material flow in a stream on the table will contribute distinctive real acoustic and haptic information to the experience.

5.3.3 Applications and Interaction Metaphors

The GranulatSynthese installation is an art composition. It sets the frame for the user to explore and create compositions. Most flavours of the current installation have a very meditative character, the visitor is invited to pause in order to take in the sound images. The installation has a potential for other areas of implementation: as playful and explorative interface with interactive storytelling content, as a real music and sound producing device that physically produces sounds with the employed material as well as electronically through the navigated parameters, or as a modulation tool of continued parameters on a surface. In combination with an HMD, it can be also used in immersive virtual environments, matching virtual images to the real world sand sculpture on the table. Then, three components merge: its use an interface, the visual virtual world and the haptic real landscape presentation. The discussed interface was designed and presented by means of an art installation to test new interactive ideas, to examine their accessibility and appeal, and to test the controllability of digital and continuous parameters. In doing so, three new tangible interaction paradigms have been realized: shape-based, amount-based and area-based interaction.

5.3.3.1 Shape-Based Interaction

The shape-based interaction has already been employed in the GranulatSynthese installation. The shape of a "lake" is meaningful to the application. Position and size of the shape is meaningful, too. Shapes can be predefined or implemented freely. Figure 5.7 demonstrates six possible forms, from a wavelike line, to an upright, triangular, flat, round and unregular shape. The GranulatSynthese installation used a subset of those.

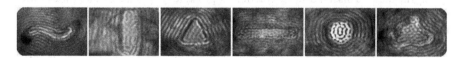

Fig. 5.7 Shape-based interaction: six examples of shapes

Fig. 5.8 Amount-based interaction: controller values correspond to the degree of coverage, here, from *left* to *right* 0, 50, and 100%

5.3.3.2 Amount-Based Interaction

For the amount-based interaction, the value of a traditional GUI control is controlled by the amount of granules lying on top them and covering 0–100% of it. With the example of a slider, Fig. 5.8 demonstrates the concept that can be utilized in two ways: the maximum value is either shown with a completely uncovered slider or a completely covered slider. The figure demonstrates the first case. Using the semi-transparent granules, the slider control is still visible, however blurred.

5.3.3.3 Area-Based Interaction: Granulinge: The Game

A particular instance of the "shape-based interaction" in Sect. 5.3.3.1 has been employed on a table top in the interactive game "Granulinge": the area-based interaction. In shape-based interaction, different shapes have different meanings. In area-based interaction, one or more shapes together define one or more areas. In the game, the uncovered areas of the table top define the game area and those areas covered with granules define its boundaries.

"Granulinge", small lemming-like creatures, have to move from their starting point to a predefined target, passing over the uncovered areas on the table. They stubbornly move straight forward and change their direction only when getting to the edges of the area. Then, they are diverted like a ray of light on a mirror. Randomly, monsters appear at several points of the game area and feed on the passing granulinges. The users themselves create the playing field and influence the granulinges' direction, taking advantage of the borders of the uncovered areas to divert the little creatures in order to create a free route toward the target. At the same time, these uncovered areas can be reached by the monsters as well. The players' task is to dynamical redesign the playing field, such that the granulinges reach the goal without being eaten by the monsters. Players try to cover monsters with granulate to disarm them. This kind of interaction is possible as all users can work at the same time, collaboratively and in a simple, intuitive way on the representation of the playing field.

What makes the game interesting is the fact that as many players as fit around the table together can participate in the game and take an active part in saving the granulinge. At several public demonstrations, we repeatedly witnessed that, because of its accessibility and simplicity, this kind of interaction would inspire uninvolved spectators, who are passively watching from the second row, to engage in dynamic rescue operations.

5.3.4   Conclusion

With the GranulatSynthese art application and our subsequent developments, we were able to develop new possibilities of interaction with the computer and to imply new paradigms for intuitive control of computer parameters based on a haptic, granules covered table display. Spacial parameters like shape and landscape can easily be created. The possibilities for controlling parameters presented here do not have the precision that is normal for classical input devices, but they provide new dimensions of parameter control and experience and a much more intuitive, fast and easy way to input spacial parameters. They transport the computer control into the real space and offer new impulses for the current development of the tactile, touchable interfaces.

It is not likely that a granule covered table will be a useful interaction device in an immersive projection environment like a CAVE^{TM}. This method, however, in limits might work together with a stereoscopic workbench. We are currently exploring the possibilities of merging the table surface with 3D content and a stereo projection. Including the Sandscape metaphor of sculpting landscape [14], the granulate covered table is a suitable 3D interaction method to creating landscapes that can include virtual stereoscopic content delivered with an HMD.

This project provides insight in two ways: first, tactile input is rewarding, accessible and provides for a rich experience. This project shows ideas that might inspire new ways of thinking about interaction with computers. As more and more table and touch computers evolve that bring user and display device closer together, the chance for richer interaction methods arise, than simple finger gestures or external devices can provide. These possibilities are also relevant to VR research, as VR often is about managing spacial context. The presented installation provides first steps into the general direction of modelling 2D and 3D space with simple material and a real-time link to the computer that enables merging real and virtual to control and enrich the virtual environment.

5.4   "Enriched" Reality and "Enriched" Experience

Commonly, computer interfaces are supposed to disappear behind the task. They are meant to support the user's activity within the digital domain and are not supposed to be visible or recognizable. Research is focussing on the development of purely virtual worlds and navigation with functional but extremely reduced input devices which themselves often add unwanted effects to the experience of the virtual environment (VE).

From a human perspective, we suggest providing a richer mapping of the virtual world and actively integrating the real world to a larger extent into the interface of the virtual world. Thus, virtual reality + "real, normal" reality. To mind, everything is just another stimulus anyway, as argued in Sect. 5.1.

Latest progress in human computer interaction has enriched the interaction space through the integration of input and output. In augmented reality, table top and tangible interface approaches, the visual projection surface and the interacting space are merging, by forging close links with one another. We propose to use similar approaches in virtual environment applications with regard to the interfaces employed. Instead of forcing people to view the virtual world through a sensory keyhole, we propose to use the multisensory features of real objects to offer people a more comprehensive and enjoyable experience in their daily work and their exploration of virtual worlds. We believe that out of this approach many new possibilities for most intuitive human-computer interfaces will effortless arise, which are one of the basic requirements to foster a wider acceptance and distribution of virtual environments.

What is proposed is not Augmented Reality (AR) that adds virtual content to the real world. It is also not Augmented Virtuality that includes images of the real world into the virtual world. It is seeing both parts, real and virtual as two jointly contributing factors to a user experience, giving up on the idea of separating virtual reality from "normal', real" reality. The user experiences both parts at the same time through their senses (no matter whether this is purposefully modeled or a by-product) and the user's mind forms an experience from it. In terms of experience, the body's perceptual system and mind do not make the artificial differentiation between real and virtual and specific points in between. There is only one experience! This discrimination is only good for discussing the amount and relation of technology (TI) and "normal world" used in an application, as done in the Taxonomy of the Mixed Reality Spectrum [22]; but it is not useful for discussing the user experience.

It can be argued that, if the term "virtual" reality denotes the presentation of virtual worlds, delivered by VR technology in a (arguably today mostly) notable way, this in fact only denotes a badly working alternate reality. If the Holodeck vision would come true, then the reality it presents would be indistinguishable from the "real" reality. Therefore, it seems more appropriate to talk about computer *"enriched" reality*, providing a computer *"enriched" experience*, and taking a holistic approach to creating VR experiences. This approach does not strive for the Holodeck vision, but sees what we now call VEs and VR technology as what it is: something we deliver to our users, arm in arm with the physical world.

In this approach, Human-Computer Interaction and VR merge, as we allow real artifacts into our virtual worlds (and still claim to work in VR), purposefully enriching our experienced reality with whatever is appropriate with current technology. We do this to help the user's minds fill in the gaps that we leave open, as long as we do not have the high fidelity technology and algorithms to fully copy the real world.

Acknowledgements The author would like to deeply thank all her collaborators: Martin Berghoff, Kristopher J. Blom, Jan Brauer, Matthias Haringer, Roland Schröder-Kroll and all of her students who worked on advancing the GranulatSynthese project in WS 2007/2008.

References

1. aeris-Impulsmöbel GmbH: The Swopper™. http://www.aeris.de
2. Beckhaus, S., Blom, K.J., Haringer, M.: Intuitive, hands-free travel interfaces for virtual environments. In: New Directions in 3D User Interfaces Workshop of IEEE VR 2005, pp. 57–60 (2005)
3. Beckhaus, S., Blom, K.J., Haringer, M.: A new gaming device and interaction method for a First-Person-Shooter. In: Computer Science and Magic 2005, GC Developer Science Track. Leipzig, Germany (2005)
4. Beckhaus, S., Blom, K.J., Haringer, M.: ChairIO – the Chair-Based Interface. In: C. Magerkurth, C. Röcker (eds.) Concepts and Technologies for Pervasive Games: A Reader for Pervasive Gaming Research vol. 1, chap. 10, pp. 231–264. Shaker (2007)
5. Beckhaus, S., Schröder-Kroll, R., Berghoff, M.: Back to the sandbox: playful interaction with granules landscapes. In: TEI '08: Proceedings of the 2nd international conference on Tangible and embedded interaction, pp. 141–144. ACM, NY, USA (2008)
6. Brauer, J., Beckhaus, S.: Sitzbasierte Steuerung von Desktopapplikationen und eine ergonomische Bewertung. In: Dokumentation des 56. Arbeitswissenschaftlichen Kongresses in Darmstadt, pp. 243–248. GfA-Press, Dortmund, Germany (2010)
7. Davidson, R.J., Lutz, A.: Buddha's brain: Neuroplasticity and meditation [in the spotlight]. Signal Processing Magazine, IEEE 25(1), 176 –174 (2008)
8. Duce, D.: The John Lansdown Award 2007. Computer Graphics Forum 26(4), 858–859 (2007)
9. Gibson, J.J.: The theory of affordances. In: R. Shaw, J. Bransford (eds.) Perceiving, acting and knowing: toward an ecological psychology, pp. 67–82. Erlbaum, Hillsdale, NJ, USA (1977)
10. Gladwell, M.: Blink: The power of thinking without thinking. Little, Brown and Co, NY, USA (2005)
11. Grant, J.A., Rainville, P.: Pain sensitivity and analgesic effects of mindful states in zen meditators: A cross-sectional study. Psychosomatic Medicine 71, 106–114 (2009)
12. Han, J.Y.: Low-cost multi-touch sensing through frustrated total internal reflection. In: UIST '05: Proceedings of the 18th annual ACM symposium on User interface software and technology, pp. 115–118. ACM, NY, USA (2005)
13. Hoffman, H., Doctor, J., Patterson, D., Carrougher, G., Furness, T.: Virtual reality as an adjunctive pain control during burn wound care in adolescent patients. Pain 85(1–2), 305–309 (2000)
14. Ishii, H., Ratti, C., Piper, B., Wang, Y., Biderman, A., Ben-Joseph, E.: Bringing clay and sand into digital design – continuous tangible user interfaces. BT Technology Journal 22(4), 287–299 (2004)
15. Jacob, R.J.K., Girouard, A., Hirshfield, L.M., Horn, M.S., Shaer, O., Solovey, E.T., Zigelbaum, J.: Reality-based interaction: unifying the new generation of interaction styles. In: CHI '07: CHI '07 extended abstracts on Human factors in computing systems, pp. 2465–2470. ACM, NY, USA (2007)
16. Kabat-Zinn, J., Lipworth, L., Burney, R.: The clinical use of mindfulness meditation for the self-regulation of chronic pain. Journal of Behavioral Medicine 8(2), 163–190 (1985)
17. Kaltenbrunner, M., Bencina, R.: reactivision: A computer-vision framework for table-based tangible interaction. In: TEI '07: Proceedings of Tangible and Embedded Interaction, pp. 69–74. ACM, NY, USA (2007)
18. Kandel, E.R., Schwartz, J.H., Jessell, T.M.: Principles of Neural Science, 4rd Ed. McGraw-Hill, NY, USA (2000)
19. Kato, H., Billinghurst, M.: Marker tracking and hmd calibration for a video-based augmented reality conferencing system. In: IWAR '99: Proceedings of the 2nd IEEE and ACM International Workshop on Augmented Reality, p. 85. IEEE Computer Society, Washington, DC, USA (1999)
20. Krüger, W., Fröhlich, B.: The Responsive Workbench. IEEE Computer Graphics & Applications 14(3), 12–15 (1994)

21. Lindeman, R.W., Beckhaus, S.: Crafting memorable vr experiences using experiential fidelity. In: VRST '09: Proceedings of the 16th ACM Symposium on Virtual Reality Software and Technology, pp. 187–190. ACM, New York, NY, USA (2009)
22. Milgram, P., Kishino, F.: Taxonomy of mixed reality visual displays. IEICE Transactions on Information and Systems **E77-D**(12), 1321–1329 (1994)
23. Most, S.B., Scholl, B.J., Clifford, E.R., Simons, D.J.: What you see is what you set: Sustained inattentional blindness and the capture of awareness. Psychological Review **112**(1), 217–242 (2005)
24. Nambu, A., Narum, T., Nishimura, K., Tanikawa, T., Hirose, M.: Visual-olfactory display using olfactory sensory map. In: VR '10: Proceedings of the IEEE Virtual Reality. IEEE Computer Society, Los Alamitos, CA, USA (2010)
25. Norman, D.A.: Affordance, conventions, and design. Interactions **6**(3), 38–43 (1999)
26. O'Sullivan, D., Igoe, T.: Physical computing: sensing and controlling the physical world with computers. Thomson, Boston, MA, USA (2004)
27. Rokeby, D.: The construction of experience: interface as content, pp. 27–47. ACM Press/Addison-Wesley Publishing Co., NY, USA (1998)
28. Simons, D.J., Chabris, C.F.: Gorillas in our midst: Sustained inattentional blindness for dynamic events. Perception **28**, 1059–1074 (1999)
29. Simons, D.J., Levin, D.T.: Change blindness. Trends in Cognitive Science **1**, 261–267 (1997)
30. Steele, C.M., Aronson, J.: Stereotype threat and the intellectual test performance of african americans. Journal of personality and social psychology **69**(5), 797–811 (1995)
31. Steinicke, F., Bruder, G., Hinrichs, K., Willemsen, P.: Change blindness phenomena for stereoscopic projection systems. In: VR '10: Proceedings of the IEEE Virtual Reality. IEEE Computer Society, Los Alamitos, CA, USA (2010)

Chapter 6
Action Capture: A VR-Based Method for Character Animation

Bernhard Jung, Heni Ben Amor, Guido Heumer, and Arnd Vitzthum

Abstract This contribution describes a Virtual Reality (VR) based method for character animation that extends conventional motion capture by not only tracking an actor's movements but also his or her interactions with the objects of a virtual environment. Rather than merely replaying the actor's movements, the idea is that virtual characters learn to imitate the actor's goal-directed behavior while interacting with the virtual scene. Following Arbib's equation action = movement + goal we call this approach Action Capture. For this, the VR user's body movements are analyzed and transformed into a multi-layered action representation. Behavioral animation techniques are then applied to synthesize animations which closely resemble the demonstrated action sequences. As an advantage, captured actions can often be naturally applied to virtual characters of different sizes and body proportions, thus avoiding retargeting problems of motion capture.

6.1 Introduction

6.1.1 Motivation and Basic Idea

Supporting the analysis of the interaction between a user and a technical product in early phases of the product's design is an important application area for 3D computer graphics and Virtual Reality (VR). Consider the problem of evaluating the ergonomics of a virtual prototype, e.g. a car interior. One approach for analyzing the user-friendliness of the prototype's operation is the application of immersive

B. Jung (✉), H.B. Amor, G. Heumer, and A. Vitzthum
VR and Multimedia Group, Institute of Informatics, TU Bergakademie Freiberg, Freiberg, Germany,
e-mail: jung@informatik.tu-freiberg.de, amor@informatik.tu-freiberg.de, guido.heumer@informatik.tu-freiberg.de, vitzthum@informatik.tu-freiberg.de
http://vr.tu-freiberg.de

Virtual Reality (VR) where a VR user performs various operation procedures on the prototype. An advantage of this approach is that the user interaction is highly natural, as it involves the same movements as would be used on a real prototype or final product. However, a disadvantage of the approach results from the evaluation setup which relies on the subjective experience of a single or a few VR users only. The limited group of test users could be a cause that some crucial insights are missed in the analysis of the prototype.

In order to gain more general insights on the usability aspects of virtual prototypes, ergonomic analyses nowadays often make use of virtual humans. As an advantage, virtual humans can come in many sizes and body proportions to serve as arbitrarily large group of test persons. Further, with virtual humans, the simulated procedures can be repeated many times, in many variations, and without much effort. Ergonomic analyses can become much more objective this way. However, difficulties arise from specifying life-like animations of virtual humans in desktop settings. When animating complex, articulated 3D models such as virtual humans via desktop GUIs, subtle details of human movements might be missed and, as consequence, the resulting ergonomic analyses might be rendered less meaningful.

Our idea is to combine the advantages of the two approaches: First, a VR user simulates the operation of a virtual prototype using immersive VR technology, such as 6 DOF tracking devices and data gloves. Then, by exploiting the interaction protocols of the VR user's performance, animations of a variety of virtual humans repeating the demonstrated operating procedures are generated. We call this approach *action capture*. Action capture extends conventional motion capture as it not only records an actor's movements in 3D space but also the goal-directed actions he or she performs on the objects of a virtual environment (Fig. 6.1).

6.1.2 Challenges

The goal of action capture is to synthesize natural-looking animations of virtual humans from example interactions of a Virtual Reality user. While this idea may appear simple at first glance, its realization faces several non-trivial challenges:

Fig. 6.1 *Left*: A VR user interacts with the virtual prototype of a car. *Right*: The user actions are repeated by a virtual character

1. Motion capture is not enough: Today, motion capture is a standard method for generating natural looking animations in games and movie productions. However, when applying recorded motion data to virtual characters of different body sizes, the resulting animations will be slightly different in each case. The problem becomes particularly evident when the animation involves interactions with virtual objects, i.e. the retargeting problem [Gle98]. Implementing action capture should instead comprise techniques for automatic animation retargeting. We tackle this challenge by employing procedural animation techniques that enable the virtual humans of displaying situationally adjustable, goal-directed behavior.

2. Inaccuracies of VR input devices: VR input devices such as position trackers and data gloves are sometimes hard to calibrate. Even when sufficiently calibrated, the delivered sensor readings often do not perfectly match the user's body and hand movements. One way of coping with these slight, yet possibly troublesome inaccuracies of VR input devices is to abstract from raw motion data and to represent actions at a higher level instead. For example, instead of resynthesizing hand shapes during grasping from recorded joint angles directly, we first classify hand shapes w.r.t. a grasp taxonomy and then animate the grasp from this symbolic description. In doing so, we can also optimize contact conditions between the virtual human's hand and the virtual object.

3. Unnaturalness of the user interaction in VR: Due to the slight inaccuracies of VR input devices and, even more important, the lack of convincing haptic feedback in typical immersive VR settings, VR users often interact with virtual objects in a somewhat cautious or even unnatural manner. When animating virtual humans, we do not want to replicate jitters in the VR user's movements while interacting with a virtual prototype. Instead, the resulting animations should appear natural and life-like. This challenge can be tackled, e.g. by training the system with statistical models of natural reach motions and hand shapes. Animation synthesis is then a mixed data- and model-driven process to ensure that the generated animations are both natural-looking and goal-directed, quite possibly exceeding the original interactions of the VR user in these respects.

6.1.3   Related Work

The problem of animating goal-directed actions of virtual humans on the objects of a virtual environment is highly relevant not only for virtual prototyping applications and has been the topic of various other research (see e.g. [BPW93, MTT04]). The main contribution of action capture is that it provides novel answers to the questions of what actions to animate and how to parameterize these actions (e.g. how far to turn the steering wheel). In previous approaches, action sequences were specified using scripting languages (e.g. [BBA$^+$00]), predefined task models [JR97], or sometimes natural language instructions (e.g. [BWKE91]) which make the specification of subtle details of human movements hard to impossible. By using immersive

Virtual Reality as frontend in which desired actions are demonstrated first by means of full body 3D interaction and natural grasping, action capture provides an intuitive way for rapid specification of the animation. Further, whereas some other approaches rely on certain "intelligent agent" capabilities such as path planning, (e.g. [KL00, YKH04]), action capture can generate plausible animations simply by using the demonstrated actions of a VR user as a resource to inform the animation generation process. The action capture method combines work in the fields of VR-based grasping interaction, object and action representation, and animation of goal-directed behavior; related work on these subtopics will be addressed in the respective sections of this contribution. Generally, the action capture approach builds on research in imitation learning and applications in robotics.

6.1.4 Background: Imitation Learning

Action capture is a method for synthesizing animations of virtual humans from interactions of a human VR user in a virtual environment. To put this in slightly different, more anthropomorphic terms: Action capture is a method that equips virtual humans with the ability to *imitate*[1] the behavior of a VR user.

Learning by imitation is a powerful ability of humans (and higher animals), which enables them to acquire new skills by observing actions of others. An instructive distinction between different stages of imitative abilities during child development is proposed by Meltzoff and coworkers (see [Mel96] and [RSM04]). After the initial body babbling phase, the imitative abilities progress as follows:

1. *Imitation of Body Movements:* The infant uses its body parts to imitate observed body movements or facial acts.
2. *Imitation of Actions on Objects:* Later, infants learn to imitate the manipulation of objects which are external to their body.
3. *Inferring Intentions:* In an even higher form of imitative learning, a demonstrator's goals and intentions are inferred from his observed behavior. In such a case, even an unsuccessful act can be correctly imitated.

The name 'action capture' owes to this distinction which is also expressed in the formula of neuroscientist Arbib: action = movement + goal, i.e. actions are always associated with a target object [Arb02]. Thus, whereas motion capture serves to reproduce an actor's body movements, action capture aims to reproduce a VR-user's actions on objects in the virtual environment. Imitation at the even higher level of intentions could possibly be implemented by means of Artificial Intelligence techniques but is beyond the action capture framework presented here.

Recent years have seen a growing interest in technical implementations of imitation learning, mainly in the field of robotics as a method of 'Programming by Demonstration (PbD)'; the edited collections of Dautenhahn and Nehaniv [DN02, ND07] and Billard and Siegwart [BS04] provide general overviews. Technical

---

[1] According to Thorndike [Tho98] imitation is: "from an act witnessed learn to do an act."

implementations of imitation learning generally provide solutions for three subtasks (cf. [BK96]):

1. *Observation:* The demonstrator's actions are observed, segmented, and abstracted into suitable action primitives.
2. *Representation:* The actions are represented through an internal model.
3. *Reproduction:* Based on the internal model, the actions are adapted to the current situation to reproduce an appropriate variant of the actions.

As VR-based instantiation of imitation learning, the technical realization of action capture implements these subtasks, as will be described in the following sections.

6.1.5   Overview of This Contribution

Section 6.2 presents a general framework for action capture including its setting and a system architecture for its implementation. Also, we briefly describe our approach adding interaction capabilities to virtual worlds, including a method for direct object manipulation. Section 6.3 describes techniques for analyzing the VR user's movements and manipulations of scene objects. In Sect. 6.4, we introduce the XSAMPL3D description language for representing action sequences extracted from user interactions. Section 6.5 describes a method for generating animations of virtual characters from action representations using behavioral animation techniques. Finally, we discuss the proposed action capture method in Sect. 6.6.

6.2   Action Capture Framework

6.2.1   Action Capture: The Concept

Action capture is a VR-based method for recording the actions of a human VR user and later reproducing these actions by virtual characters. Similar to motion capture, the user's movements are recorded by means of position trackers and data-gloves. However, not only the user's movements are tracked but also his or her interactions with scene objects. User movements and interactions are then abstracted to higher level action representations which, among other parameters but different from motion capture data formats, contain references to the scene objects involved in the respective actions. In the playback phase, such action sequences are reproduced by virtual characters using behavioral animation techniques (cf. e.g. [Tom05]). By re-synthesizing complete actions on objects rather than mere movements, valid animations can be reproduced for virtual characters of different sizes and body proportions as well as in situations where the task environment slightly differs from the original recording situation, e.g. in the case of repositioned control elements.

The *setting* for action capture thus consists of:

- Immersive virtual environment: which supports its interactive manipulation by means of natural 3D interaction techniques. I.e. the virtual environment contains interactive objects which, e.g. can be picked up and displaced, buttons that can be pushed, knobs for turning etc.
- Human demonstrator (teacher): who performs an action or a sequence of actions in the virtual environment. The human teacher's actions are tracked using typical VR input devices such as position trackers and data gloves.
- Virtual character (learner): who observes the teacher's actions and learns to repeat them. The virtual character's body is assumed to be similar to the teacher's body, i.e. humanoid. This assumption ensures a more or less straightforward mapping of the teacher's body parts to the virtual character's body, thus simplifying the solution of the so-called correspondence problem (cf. [ND02]). The virtual character's body size and proportions may however differ from the human VR user.

6.2.2 Action Capture: A Prototypical Implementation

The action capture concept presented above has been implemented in a prototypical VR system. Figure 6.2 illustrates the main functional components of the system:

1. Action observation and analysis: during which the demonstrator's movements and interactions with scene objects are tracked, segmented, and classified as interaction events (see Sect. 6.3).

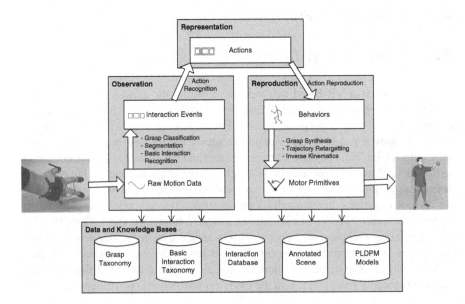

Fig. 6.2 Components of a system architecture for action capture

2. Action representation: Observed interaction events are combined to high-level representations of the action or action sequence. Actions are represented in symbolic form and are thus amenable to manual post-processing by a human editor (see Sect. 6.4).

3. Action reproduction: where the action's representation is mapped to goal-directed behaviors of the virtual character. Behaviors are responsible for calculating contact conditions between the virtual character's hand and scene objects for the animation of object manipulations. They are executed by calling the lower-level motor programs which serve to animate the virtual character (see Sect. 6.5).

All components in the architecture have access to several shared data and knowledge bases, including a grasp taxonomy, interaction databases, semantic object annotations, statistical motion models etc.

6.2.2.1 Annotated Object Model

Although the action capture method has interesting applications in static virtual environments, e.g. reach and visibility analyses, it becomes even more interesting when dynamic virtual worlds with interactively manipulable objects are considered. The kind of actions supported in our prototype system include, e.g. 6DOF displacement (pick and place) and manipulations on control actuators such as pushing/pulling levers, pressing buttons, turning knobs, moving sliders, etc. This exceeds the possibilities that a purely graphical object representation offers by far. To implement the functionalities of these objects, several functional components need to be integrated into the VR application. Besides graphical rendering there is a need for collision detection, dynamics simulation, interaction support etc. These different functional components also have different demands on object representations, e.g. geometric, physical, etc., and databases such as scenegraph vs. flat object collections.

To facilitate the design and management of virtual reality scenes and as a unified form for the declaration of higher-level interaction information for scene objects, the concept of *annotated objects* has been introduced [WHAJ06]. Annotated objects (AOs) are akin to the concept of *smart objects* (SOs) by Kallmann and Thalmann [KT99, KT02] in the sense that in both cases the object description is enriched with *interaction features*.[2] In contrast to SOs, however, AOs do not contain any form of behavior description, neither for object nor for actor behavior. For SOs, behavioral features are specified using pre-defined plans which are merely triggered by a user or virtual actor. SOs are thus rather fixed in their specific form of execution and also limited in their outcome to certain specified goal states. The object behavior of AOs, however, is determined fully only at runtime. i.e., the user or a virtual actor is able to influence the object's state through direct object manipulation (see below), allowing for an infinite number of intermediate states within the specified constraints

---

[2] According to their definition in [KT02] as: "all parts, movements and descriptions of an object that have some important role when interacting with an actor."

and degrees of freedom. Although our current implementation of object behavior is physics-based, pseudo-physical implementations as in [MF10] are also compatible with the annotated object model.

The need for explicitly modeling actor behavior, as present in the smart objects model, does not arise for annotated objects. Indeed, this is exactly the goal of the action capture method, i.e. for the user to demonstrate possible actions on the objects in an intuitive and easy to use way using the VR setup. Whereas, e.g. in the smart object behavior modeling technique, the hand posture for a specific action has to be explicitly modeled joint angle by joint angle in a time-consuming process, in the action capture method the desired hand posture is demonstrated by the user by just assuming it with his/her real hand.

Additionally, for the use case of hand-coding animations by directly specifying animation plans for the virtual character, certain parameters can be annotated that provide the animation algorithms with the necessary information to generate the desired animation of the behavior. Examples for such parameters are, e.g., the approach vector (or corridor of approach vectors) for the hand for grasping the object with a certain grasp type or a certain area of interest to aim for during the reach motion.

Annotated objects are declared and managed in an XML-based representation structure. This structure incorporates all information about types of scene objects in a common database. Such information includes the associated graphics model, type information, component references, physical parameters, collision proxies, joint definitions, the aforementioned animation parameters, etc. A central annotated objects management component handles the instantiation and destruction of objects and provides each functional component of the VR application with the information relevant to its specific functionality.

In addition to rigid bodies, a system for defining and simulating articulated control elements (buttons, sliders, knobs, etc.) has been implemented. Such objects normally consist of a fixed fitting and one or more actuator components. The actuators are attached to the fitting by joints of varying degrees of freedom, joint constraints and with the support for discrete lock states. The actuators' behavior is fully simulated by a dynamics engine and thus reacts realistically to forces exerted by the user's virtual hand model as well as to environment influences such as object-object collisions, gravity, etc. This object model forms a solid and versatile basis for direct object manipulation in realistic virtual prototyping scenarios [GHJV09].

6.2.2.2 Direct Object Manipulation

User interaction in action capture settings relies on direct manual manipulation of scene objects. Here we briefly describe how this interaction technique is implemented in our prototype system. A virtual hand model forms the bridge between the real world and the virtual scene and is driven by input from a data glove or similar hand posture measuring devices. The hand model has several functions to fulfill:

- *Represent the real hands of the user as accurately as possible.* This is done by employing a skeletal model with bone lengths adjusted to the respective bone lengths of the VR user's real hands. The joint rotations of the VR user's fingers can be tracked with different devices, e.g. Immersion Cybergloves or A.R.T. Fingertrackers. The user's wrists are tracked via 6DOF trackers to determine translation and orientation of the hand models in the virtual environment.

- *Detect collisions between the virtual hand model and the virtual objects.* For this purpose we employ collision sensors which are attached to key locations on the bones of the virtual hand model. These sensors consist of geometric primitives (spheres, boxes, cylinders etc.) and thus facilitate efficient collision detection. Each sensor is assigned to a specific position on a specific finger or palm segment. Thus, when a collision of a sensor and a scene object occurs it is clear which part of the hand model touched the object. This provides further cues for grasp classification, c.f. Sect. 6.3.2, and drives the grasping heuristics. The grasping heuristics determines when an object is completely grasped by the user and thus is attached to the user hand movements. The release of objects is determined similarly.

- *Determine the outcome of hand-object collisions.* In grasped state, the grasped object just follows the hand motions. For all other hand-object collisions, forces are determined based on contact points, contact normals and intersection depth of the collision. These forces are applied to the object and allow slight manipulations of objects even in ungrasped state, such as pushing, or manipulations of the articulated control actuators.

For the description of the bone structure of the hand model we use the Cal3D format and a model that adheres to the HANIM standard for humanoid models. For the description of the collision sensors and their placement on the hand model a custom XML formalism has been developed. Figure 6.3 shows a screenshot of the hand model with sensors and an excerpt of the XML sensor definition file. The figure illustrates the close approximation of the hand shape by our sensor model.

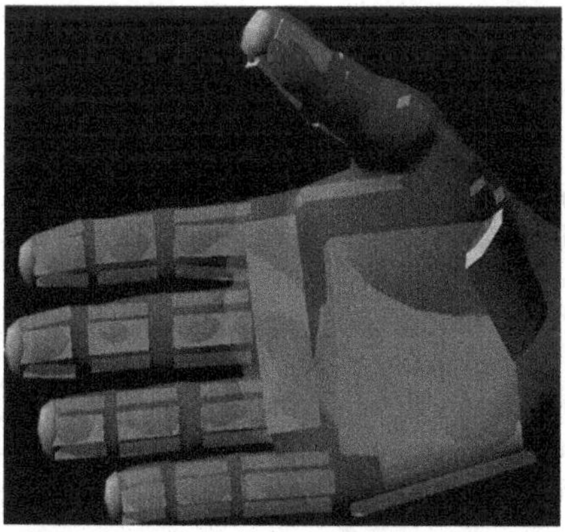

```
<sensor name="right-thumb-sensor3-volar">
    <bone>r_thumb3</bone>
    <rel-translation>0.0 0.0 -1.25</rel-translation>
    <in-between-next-bone>r_thumb_distal_tip
    </in-between-next-bone>
    <geometry>
        <primitive>cube</primitive>
        <scale>3.0 1.5 1.5</scale>
        <rotation-angles>0 -10 0</rotation-angles>
    </geometry>
    <sensor-segment-info>
        <segment>thumb_distal</segment>
        <location>volar</location>
    </sensor-segment-info>
</sensor>

<sensor name="right-hand-back">
    <bone>r_middle0</bone>
    <rel-translation>8.0 -2.0 1.8</rel-translation>
    <geometry>
        <primitive>cylinder</primitive>
        <scale>5.0 5.0 0.6</scale>
```

Fig. 6.3 *Left*: Virtual hand model with collision sensors. *Right*: Example sensor definition in XML

6.3   Observation: Interaction Analysis

The analysis process of user interactions works through several levels of abstraction. It starts with the raw data collected from the input devices tracking the user. From this raw data atomic basic interactions are extracted by a segmentation and classification process. Information about these basic interactions is passed on in the form of *interaction events* to higher levels of the application, such as the action recognition component.

6.3.1   Motion Capture Level

At the motion capture level, data from the various tracking devices is collected in a continuous fashion. In a typical scenario, the user is head tracked via markers attached to stereo vision goggles. The arms are tracked at several key locations, such as shoulders, elbows and wrists through 6DOF-markers. Finger movements are tracked through either data gloves or optical fingertracking systems. From all the collected data, a virtual representation of the user's posture over time is generated (in the current implementation limited to the upper body).

All input devices together produce a continuous and extensive stream of heterogeneous data. To enable persistence and to facilitate the recording and playback process, an interaction database module has been implemented. This database collects all data created in the motion capture process in the form of various channels and stores it in a central data store. All data is explicitly assigned to its specific recording session. These recording sessions can further be annotated with meta information, such as the interacting user, the virtual scene, optional video footage, etc. This allows for reproduction of individual recording sessions as well as analysis on a larger scale, across session boundaries, such as training data collection for classification algorithms, principal component analysis, etc.

6.3.2   Basic Interaction Level

The goal of this level is to recognize instances of a taxonomy of *basic interactions* from the continuous stream of motion and interaction data. A basic interaction is the smallest distinguishable unit of interaction within this stream. All basic interactions are characterized by one specific aspect that is modified by the respective type of interaction, such as hand-object distance, hand-object contact, forces, prehension, and object position or orientation. Besides its distinct type or category, a basic interaction is further qualified by a type-specific set of parameters. Figure 6.4 shows the different types of basic interactions that are currently distinguished. The individual types are explained in detail below:

- *Reach:* The movement of the user hand towards a scene object. This can be along a relatively straight line as well as via a complex approach trajectory. The

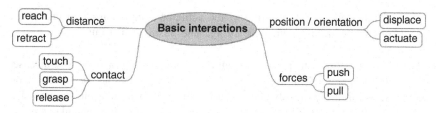

Fig. 6.4 Taxonomy of basic interactions

modified aspect is the distance between the user hand and the object and the outcome is that the user hand is able to touch the object.

- *Retract:* This is the counterpart to *reach*, increasing the distance between hand and object. The hand movement can be directed towards a rest position or towards the next target object. In the latter case, one half of the movement has to be considered as retract while the other half is considered as reach. A prerequisite for *retract* is that object manipulation occurred before.
- *Grasp:* Refers to the full prehensile enclosure of the object by the user hand. Grasping can happen by various different grasp types which are detected through a classification process w.r.t. a given grasp taxonomy. The modified aspect is the contact between the user hand and the object with the outcome that the user firmly holds the object and is able to move it to another location, or, in the case of control actuators, manipulate the actuator components according to its degrees of freedom.
- *Touch:* The same as grasp, but does not result in object prehension. Also modifies contact between the user hand and the object with the outcome that a non-prehensile contact has been established that allows loose manipulation, e.g., pushing.
- *Release:* The counterpart to *grasp* and *touch*. Also modifies hand-object contact with the outcome that the object is released from prehension by the user hand. In the non-prehensile case, all contact between hand and object is dissolved with the result that no further control over the object through the hand persists.
- *Displace:* Refers to the movement of the object as a whole and is thus restricted to freely movable rigid bodies. Also requires object prehension. The modified aspect is the object's location and orientation in space.
- *Actuate:* This is the counterpart of *displace* but with respect to control actuators. In contrast to displace, object manipulation is restricted to movements possible within the constraints and degrees of freedom of an actuator relative to its fitting. This basic interaction is further restricted to control actuators which are not dynamically simulated, i.e. not based on exertion of forces. For the case of dynamically simulated parts, see *push* and *pull* below.
- *Push:* This includes any exertion of forces on the object in a non-prehensile state. The outcome of the forces depends on the nature of the object. In the case of a freely movable rigid body it normally leads to a position change. In the case of articulated objects it depends on the specific degrees of freedom of the actuator.

Normally it leads to a translation of the actuator component along one of the actuator axes without moving its fitting. The pushing of a button is a typical example.

- *Pull:* This is similar to push but requires a prehensile grasp or special cases like the hook grasp. This basic interaction is only applicable for control actuators since for freely movable objects all prehensile manipulation is regarded as *displace.* The pulling of a lever or the opening of a drawer is a typical example.

6.3.2.1 Basic Interaction Recognition

A first step in the detection of basic interactions is the segmentation of hand movement data. Hand trajectories are recorded and segmented when pauses in movement occur. These pauses normally denote the end of one interaction and the possible beginning of a new one. Another step is the reaction to collision information from the hand sensors. Whenever a collision of a hand sensor with an annotated object is detected, contact has been made with the object and possibly a prehensile grasp has occurred. A grasp heuristics is applied to determine this, based on which points of the hand make contact with the object. For example, contact with the thumb and the index finger at their palmar sides are a strong indicator for a prehensile grasp. When a grasp occurs, its grasp type is classified based on the hand posture information from the tracking devices; see [HBAJ08] or [HBAWJ07] for details on the classification process.

In case a dynamics simulation is used, forces are calculated based on the intersection depth of the hand sensors with the objects in direction of their contact normals. These forces can lead to either pushes or pulls, depending on the type of grasp and the type of object involved. Displacement occurs when the whole hand is moved while an object is grasped.

6.3.2.2 Interaction Events

Another important functionality of this layer is to make the information about detected basic interactions available to other components of the application in a flexible way. For this reason, the concept of *interaction events* has been introduced. These events are posted via a dispatcher/subscriber system (observer pattern). Some system components can send interaction events to the dispatcher, e.g. when one of the basic interactions has been detected or when interaction sessions are played back from the database. The dispatcher in turn passes the events on to the registered listener components which can react accordingly based on their respective functionality. Example functionalities for event receivers are visualization, persistence (to file or to database) and most importantly action recognition.

Interaction events have a type, based on the basic interaction encapsulated. In terms of structure, interaction events consist of a type independent header and type dependent contents. The header contains type and timing information (start time and duration). Additionally, each event is assigned a universally unique identifier

(UUID) so that events can be non-ambiguously referenced by higher-level formalisms such as the action representation (see Sect. 6.4). The type dependent part contains details about the basic interactions described in the event. A *grasp* event, for instance, contains hand configuration, hand position, an identifier of the grasped object, contact points between hand and object, detected grasp type, etc. A *reach* event contains the hand motion trajectory, end position, etc.

In addition to the hand-related interaction events, control actuators send information about changes of their internal state. These can be of varying degree of detail and reach from just the final state via discrete intermediate states to a complete state history for every frame. The latter allows for an exact in-effect reproduction of the performed manipulation even when the playback component does not have a dynamics simulation.

For persistence and to allow for manual analysis, an XML format for interaction events has been developed. This format can be stored and retrieved to file or database and contains all details in human-readable form. See Fig. 6.5 for an example *grasp* event.

```
<event type="grasp" start-time="1.84234" duration="2.10739"
       id="IE-9cf9ae8a-1012-11df-91b5-00142225ef0d">
  <low-level-features>
    <hand-side>right</hand-side>
    <start-data>
      ...
    </start-data>
    <goal-data>
      <hand-posture>
        <joint-angle joint-id="r_index1">30.21 -0.09 0.92 0.37</joint-angle>
        ...
        <joint-angle joint-id="r_thumb3">14.59 0 1 0</joint-angle>
      </hand-posture>
      <hand-transform-wcs> 0.2139 -0.1972 -0.9567 0
                          -0.2443  0.9374 -0.2479 0
                           0.9457  0.2868  0.1524 0
                          -0.4025 -0.1120  0.9957 1
      </hand-transform-wcs>
      <contact-points object-id="Bottle-1">
        <contact-point sensor-id="right-pinky-sensor3 distal">
          <pos-ocs>-0.4824 0.0058 0.9047</pos-ocs>
          <normal-ocs>1 0.9047 0.0058</normal-ocs>
        </contact-point>
        ...
      </contact-points>
    </goal-data>
  </low-level-features>
  <medium-level-features>
    <pca-coordinates space-id="Schlesinger::cylindrical"
                     pca-space="pca/schlesinger/cylindrical.pldpm"
                     dimensions="3">-2.7379 -1.70609 0.114498
    </pca-coordinates>
  </medium-level-features>
  <high-level-features>
    <target-object>Bottle-1</target-object>
    <grasp-type taxonomy="Schlesinger">cylindrical</grasp-type>
  </high-level-features>
</event>
```

Fig. 6.5 Example XML representation of an interaction event (grasp)

6.4   Representation of Actions

One possibility to animate a virtual human would be to directly use interaction events generated from raw tracking data as animation input. However, it should also be possible to author an animation description quickly with an appropriate editor, e.g., an XML editor. A basic interaction description would not be a good choice to solve this task since it tends to become too complex to be human-readable for long interaction event sequences. For this reason, an abstraction from the interaction event level is called for. We provide this abstraction in the form of the language XSAMPL3D (XML Synchronized Action MarkuP Language for 3D). The language additionally offers the possibility to easily rework or change recorded interaction event sequences after transforming them (automatically) into the XSAMPL3D format.

Regarding the fact that we want to automatically generate natural-looking animations from an action description, XSAMPL3D allows the inclusion of references to underlying interaction event sequences (see Sect. 6.3). In this way, basic interaction data can also directly be used by an animation synthesis tool. However, the action description must retain the power to enable the derivation of plausible animations even if links to the underlying interaction description layer are not present.

XSAMPL3D is defined by an XML-schema. This schema includes different aspects, such as (manipulated) objects, different action types, action composition, synchronization and timing. In contrast to related approaches such as [BBA+00], XSAMPL3D descriptions contain more details (e.g. concerning the definition of target object positions, orientations, timing values, grasp types, etc.) in order to enable a mostly faithful reproduction if the XSAMPL3D code was generated from captured action data.

The transformation of interaction events into actions was implemented with XSLT and Java. Single actions are derived from interaction events by using pattern matching and machine learning techniques. In order to generate animations from actions, a second XSLT-based transformation tool was realized. This allows mapping actions to the set of behaviors implemented by the underlying animation framework. In the following, individual aspects of XSAMPL3D will be explained in more detail.

Objects

Objects can be divided into several classes: *fixed objects*, *movable objects* and *articulated objects* (e.g., control actuators). Although fixed objects cannot be moved, they can be touched. Movable objects can be moved arbitrarily (e.g., a ball). Articulated objects have specific movement constraints. For example, a *slidable object* is an articulated object which can only be moved along one axis and has a maximum and a minimum position. Another special kind of an articulated object is a so called *discrete state object*, which represents an articulated object with defined discrete states (e.g., a gearshift lever).

Properties, constraints and discrete states of objects (such as the minimum and maximum position of a slider or the *ON* and *OFF* states of a toggle button) can be defined in annotated object documents (see Sect. 6.2.2.1) which are referenced by the corresponding objects. The XML code below shows two example object definitions.

```
<MovableObject id="Hammer" annotation="hammer.xso"/>
<DiscreteStateObject id="CarRadioOnOffButton" annotation="button.xso"/>
```

Actions

An *action* describes the interaction between the user's hand and a particular object. Conceptually, an action consists of different phases: *reaching* (approaching the object), *grasping* or *touching*, *object contact/manipulation* and *releasing* the object. Different action types can be distinguished: *constrained movements*, *manipulate* actions and actions which don't result in an object displacement (*touch actions*). Some action types can be only performed using a special kind of object. For instance, the *constrained movement* subtype *slide* can be only performed using a *slidable object*. Manipulate actions normally result in a change of the position and/or orientation of a *movable object*. A manipulate action consists of one or more interaction phases (or *interactions* for short), such as *turn*, *shift*, *place* and *pause* (for pauses before or after interactions). By combining interactions, different manipulate actions can be specified.

The XSAMPL3D code fragment in Fig. 6.6 defines the action "PlaceHammer". In this example, the hammer object is picked (using one of the grasp types defined by Schlesinger [Sch19]) and then placed on the workbench (if no grasp type is specified, then the animation player has to decide which grasp type can be applied in order to generate a plausible animation). After that, the hammer is shifted parallel to the X-Y-plane to a second position on the workbench's surface. The target positions of the hammer are specified in local coordinates of the workbench object. It is also possible to define global coordinates by omitting the *posRelTo* attribute of the corresponding interaction. As the example shows, an action is always performed on a particular object (in that case, the hammer).

```
<Manipulate ID="PlaceHammer" graspType="schlesinger:cylindrical"
    object="Hammer" reachDuration="0.5">
    <Place duration="1.0" position="0.5 0.5 0.2" posRelTo="workbench">
    <Shift duration="0.5" position="0.2 0.3" posRelTo="workbench"
        locked="Z_AXIS">
</Manipulate>
```

Fig. 6.6 XSAMPL3D definition of the *manipulate* action "PlaceHammer"

```
<RightHand startTime="2" relaxDuration="2">
    <Touch object="CarRadioOnOffButton"
           reachDuration="1" duration="0.5"
           graspType="schlesinger:tip"/>
    <Touch targetObject="CarRadioChannelSeekButton"
           reachDuration="0.5" duration="1"
           graspType="schlesinger:tip"/>
</RightHand>
```

Fig. 6.7 Example XML representation of an *action unit* containing two consecutive actions

Action Composition

Actions can be grouped together using an *action unit*. An action unit contains a sequence of actions which are executed with a single hand or two hands cooperatively. In order to enable an appropriate description of action units, three different kinds of action units were predefined: *right hand*, *left hand* and *bimanual*. The term action unit was inspired by Kendon [Ken04] who analogously uses the term *gesture unit* to describe a sequence of gestures.

A right hand type action unit containing a sequence of two *touch* actions is described by the XML example code in Fig. 6.7.

Synchronization

Synchronization aspects in XSAMPL3D were inspired by the Synchronized Multimedia Integration Language [Wor08]. Several action units can be grouped together using an *action unit composite*. There are two different types of action unit composites: *parallel* and *sequential*. In contrast to the execution of action units contained in a sequential composite, in a parallel composite all units are concurrently executed. The processing of a unit composite ends if the last (in sequential composites) or longest action unit (in parallel composites) is completed.

Timing

Actions and interactions, action units and unit composites are so called *time containers*. Each time container has its own internal timeline starting from zero. Time-related container property values mark events on this timeline (e.g., the start of an action). By default, duration and time values are specified in seconds.

The duration of an action consists of the *reach duration* and – depending on the action type – the *contact* or *manipulation duration*. The *reach duration* represents the time required to position the hand on the target object (reaching phase). During the reaching phase, the hand is preshaped to perform a non-prehensile touch or a prehensile grasp. The reaching phase has finished if a touch or a stable grasp has been established. Afterwards, the *contact phase* (for touch actions) or *manipulation phase* (for other actions) starts. This phase ends with releasing the object. Usually, duration values are directly set via respective attributes. However, there is one exception: For *manipulate* actions, the overall interaction duration is derived from the durations of all contained interactions. For instance, in the "PlaceHammer" example above, the overall interaction duration is 1.5 s, i.e. the sum of the place (1.0 s) and the shift (0.5 s) interaction durations.

Time-related properties of an action unit are *start time* and *relaxation duration*. The *start time* is the point in time when the first action of the unit starts after the unit was entered. All actions of the unit are then executed consecutively in the order defined in the corresponding XSAMPL3D instance document. After the last action has completed, the unit enters the relaxation phase. The *relaxation duration* of an action unit describes the time required to return to the hand's relaxation position.

In this section we discussed several aspects of XSAMPL3D, an XML-based language which provides a compact representation of actions performed on objects. A more detailed description of XSAMPL3D can be found in [VAHB09].

6.5   Reproduction of Actions

So far, we described how interactions of a real human are analyzed and how the performed actions are stored in an XML-representation. For the intended application, it is vital that stored actions can also be replayed by virtual humans. This calls for animation synthesis algorithms which can generate convincing human-like animations. Synthesis algorithms need to take the environmental context into account in which a particular action in performed. For example, if the position of a button to be pressed has changed since recording the data, then, of course, the animation needs to be adapted to the new position of the button. The approach for animation synthesis in Action Capture also follows the imitation learning methodology introduced earlier. Grasp shapes, kinematic configurations or trajectories recorded from the human user are taken as input data to machine learning algorithms resulting in statistical models of postures and motions. The learning algorithms can be trained on-line using the data of the current user, or off-line by querying the data of various users from the interaction database. Models are later used to control the virtual humans by imitating the learned behavior. In the following we summarize the main results from [BAHJV08, BAWHJ07].

6.5.1   Learning Behaviors with PLDPM

Creating a repertoire of motor skills for a virtual human is a challenging and often labor intensive task. Modern machine learning techniques can help to overcome this problem. In Action Capture, machine learning is used to extract important information about kinematic synergies and constraints of the human body, which are stored in a so-called *Probabilistic Low-Dimensional Posture Model* (PLDPM). Figure 6.8 shows an example of PLDPM-Learning of a grasping behavior. First, data about human grasping is acquired using an optical fingertracking system. The hand poses are stored as rotations of finger joints (three ball joints per finger, i.e. 45° of freedom in total). This dataset Q of postures is then processed by a manifold learning technique, such as PCA, ISOMAP [TdSL00] or LLE [RS00]. Manifold learning refers to a set of dimensionality reduction techniques that can project high-dimensional data onto low-dimensional manifolds. This is particularly helpful when working with human postures, due to the high number of degrees of freedom and the interdependency between joints. Application of manifold learning on dataset Q results in a low-dimensional subspace with dimensionality d which represents the recorded grasps. The process additionally produces the set of projected points $\widetilde{Q}$. Each point in a low-dimensional manifold represents a human grasp and can, hence, be projected back into the original space of joint rotations. Note that a finite set of demonstrated postures allows us to extract a continuous space with an unlimited number of possible interpolations and extrapolations.

In addition to dimensionality reduction, we need a model of the anatomical constraints of the human hand. As can be seen in Fig 6.8, some hand shapes in the low-dimensional space are anatomically infeasible. Therefore, some method for discriminating between anatomically feasible and infeasible postures is needed. This can be achieved by learning a Gaussian Mixture Model (GMM) [DLR77] based on the projected grasps in the low-dimensional manifold. The GMM estimates the probability density function of the grasps. This is done by performing the GMM learning rules, more specifically the expectation-maximization algorithm, on the set $\widetilde{Q}$.

After dimensionality reduction and probability density estimation are finished, a grasp for an arbitrary 3D object can be synthesized. Since a grasp is represented as a point in the low-dimensional space, the problem of finding a suitable grasp can be expressed as an optimization problem. More precisely, finding a suitable grasp can be found by searching for a point in the lower-dimensional posture model, which optimizes a provided *grasp metric*. The goal of grasp optimization is to find a natural looking hand shape leading to a stable grasp on a user-provided 3D object. Various metrics and quality measures for grasps have been proposed in the robotics

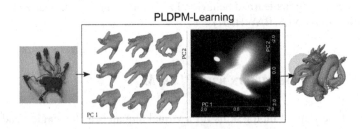

Fig. 6.8 Fingertracking data is used to learn a probabilistic low-dimensional posture model for grasping. The learned model can later be used to synthesize realistic grasps for arbitrary 3D objects

literature [MF96], many of which are based on physical properties of the object and the performed grasp. In contrast, the following simple grasp metric is specifically designed for computer graphics applications and is therefore focused on the realistic appearance.

As a first component in our metric we use the distance between each finger sensor and the object. This distance needs to be minimized to ensure that the fingers touch the object. The second component, the stability measure, follows the definition of a stable grasp found in [MI94]. In particular, we adopted the concept of *cone of friction*. According to MacKenzie and Iberall, the cone of friction is a geometric interpretation of the maximally allowed angle ϕ between the surface normal and the applied force vector. If the applied force at the contact point makes an angle α with $|\alpha| < \phi$, then no slip will be produced at the fingertip. The angle ϕ is determined by the coefficient of friction of the grasped object. To determine if a grasp induced by two fingers is stable, we first compute the contact points of the fingers with the object. Then we compute the connecting line. If this line lies within both cones of friction at the intersection points with the object surface, we regard the grasp as stable. In other words, for achieving a stable grasp with two fingers we need to minimize the angles α_1 and α_2 between the connecting line and the contact normals (see Fig. 6.9), until both are smaller than ϕ. Finally, as a last component to our grasp metric, we also incorporated a penalty term v (violation) for every finger sensor that penetrates the object:

$$v_i = \begin{cases} V & : \quad \text{sensor } i \text{ penetrates object} \\ 0 & : \quad \text{sensor } i \text{ does not penetrate object} \end{cases} \qquad (6.1)$$

This ensures that no finger unrealistically enters the object during the grasp. In our case a value of $V = 100$ produced satisfactory results. For every pair of opposite finger sensors we compute the above components and combine them into one metric

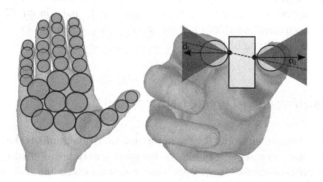

Fig. 6.9 *Left*: Position and size of sensors in the hand. *Right*: Visualization of the calculations during the estimation of the grasp stability. The angles α_1 and α_2 between the connecting line and the contact normals need to be inside the cone of friction (visualized by *triangles*) for a stable grasp

according to the formula:

$$M = \sum_{i=0}^{SP}(d_{i,1} + \alpha_{i,1} + v_{i,1}) + (d_{i,2} + \alpha_{i,2} + v_{i,2}) \tag{6.2}$$

where SP is the number of antagonistic sensor pairs, $d_{i,1}$ and $d_{i,2}$ are the distances of each respective sensor to the object surface, $\alpha_{i,1}$ and $\alpha_{i,2}$ are the angles between the connecting line and the contact normals and values $v_{i,j}$ are the penalty terms. Lower values for M indicate better grasps.

To synthesize a new grasp, an optimization algorithm such as an evolutionary algorithm can be used to search for a set of low-dimensional coordinates which correspond to a hand configuration minimizing the above metric. To ensure that the synthesized grasp is anatomically plausible, we add a constraint to the optimization process. For this, during optimization, we compute the probability of each solution candidate with respect to probability density function modelled by the GMM. If the probability of a solution candidate, that is a possible hand configuration, is below a given threshold, then the candidate is discarded from the optimization process. The result of the optimization process is a hand configuration, which best fits the provided 3D object. In contrast to other work on grasping, such as the work in [PZ05], our focus is not the optimization of physical parameters of a given grasp. Instead, the shape and configuration of the grasp are subject to optimization. Hence, grasps for new objects can be efficiently synthesized without human intervention.

PLDPMs are not confined to the synthesis of single hand postures, but can also synthesize full animations. For this, it is important to notice, that an animation corresponds to a trajectory in a PLDPM. Therefore, for synthesizing animations for virtual humans, we need to specify a trajectory in a PLDPM and project each point along the trajectory back into the original space of joint rotations. This procedure can, for instance, be used to dynamically synthesize a grasping motion for a new object. After a realistic grasp is optimized using the technique described above, a trajectory is created starting at the current position of the hand in the PLDPM and ending at the optimized position. Each point along this trajectory corresponds to a hand shape at a given time of the animation.

6.5.2 Learning Goal-Directed Trajectories

Trajectories are important tools for the animation of virtual humans. For example, they can be used to represent the motion of the agent's wrist position during a reaching task. But how should the trajectory be changed, if the object the agent is trying to reach is displaced? Also, can we dynamically add slight changes to the trajectories, so they always look a little bit different and thus more lifelike?

A computationally efficient way to tackle this problem is the use of a dynamic coordinate system which is spanned between the hand of the virtual human and the position of the target. The idea is based on behavioral and neurophysiological findings which suggest that humans make use of different coordinate systems (CS) for planning and executing goal-directed behaviors, such as reaching for an object [HS98]. Although the nature of such CS transformations is not yet fully understood, there is empirical support for the critical role of eye-centered, shoulder-centered and hand-centered CS. These are used for transforming a sensory stimulus into motor commands (visuomotor transformations). For retargeting, we use a hand-centered CS which is oriented towards the target object. The basis of this CS is denoted by $B(\mathbf{h}, \mathbf{o}, \mathbf{up})$, where $\mathbf{h}$ is hand position at the beginning of the animation, $\mathbf{o}$ is the target (object) position, and $\mathbf{up}$ is an up-vector (typically $(0/0/1)$).

$$B(\mathbf{h}, \mathbf{o}, \mathbf{up}) = \begin{bmatrix} | & | & | \\ \mathbf{x} & \mathbf{y} & \mathbf{z} \\ | & | & | \end{bmatrix}, \quad \mathbf{y} = \mathbf{o} - \mathbf{h}, \quad \mathbf{x} = \frac{\mathbf{y} \times \mathbf{up}}{|\mathbf{y} \times \mathbf{up}|}, \quad \mathbf{z} = \frac{\mathbf{x} \times \mathbf{y}}{|\mathbf{x} \times \mathbf{y}|} \quad (6.3)$$

To do so we compute for each trajectory a matrix $T_j^{to\,local}$ which transforms the trajectory into a local space. The origin of this space is centered at the hand position, while the target position is located at $(0, 1, 0)^T$ on the y-axis

$$T_j^{to\,local} = \begin{bmatrix} B(\mathbf{x}_j^0, \mathbf{x}_j^n, \mathbf{up})^{-1} & 0 \\ 0 & 1 \end{bmatrix} \begin{bmatrix} I & -\mathbf{x}_j^0 \\ 0 & 1 \end{bmatrix} \quad (6.4)$$

$$T^{to\,global} = \begin{bmatrix} I & \mathbf{h}' \\ 0 & 1 \end{bmatrix} \begin{bmatrix} B(\mathbf{h}', \mathbf{o}', \mathbf{up}) & 0 \\ 0 & 1 \end{bmatrix}. \quad (6.5)$$

In Fig. 6.10 we see the effect of transforming all trajectories into a hand-object CS. The variance which is due to different goal positions of the reach motion was removed and the projected trajectories have higher similarity. The new space can be regarded as an end-position invariant space of trajectories. Applying the synthesis algorithm in this space is likely to produce better results than with global-space trajectories. Next, a statistical model of the trajectories is learned. This is done using Gaussian Mixture Regression (GMR). The learned GMR model can be queried for a new trajectory having similar shape to the training trajectories. Finally, the synthesized trajectory can be retargeted to a new start- and end-position $\mathbf{h}'$ and $\mathbf{o}'$ by computing $T^{to\,global}$ and multiplying the resulting matrix with all trajectory points. The above algorithm can be used to synthesize a large number of slightly different trajectories, which at the same time share a common structure. The changes in the trajectory avoid repetitiveness and, hence, increase the naturalness of the animation. In addition, the user can specify arbitrary start and end positions for the trajectories, such that adaptation to a changed environment becomes possible.

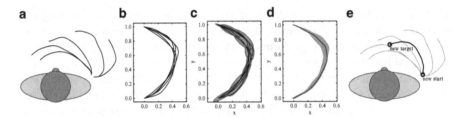

Fig. 6.10 (**a**) Trajectories in global-space recorded from a human demonstrator. (**b**) Trajectories in local-space after coordinate system transformation. (**c**) A GMM is learned by fitting a set of Gaussians. (**d**) A GMR is learned and new trajectory is synthesized (*black*). The synthesized trajectory is retargeted based on the new start- and end-position

6.5.3 Generating Animations from Actions

For animating virtual humans, we need to translate the high-level actions into motions (cf. Fig. 6.2). This is done by translating each action into a sequence of behaviors from the virtual human's repertoire of skills. In turn, each behavior uses one or several motor primitives. Motor primitives are low-level programs, which modify the joint parameters of a virtual human. Basic behaviors include:

- *Turn head:* Turns the head towards a given position or object.
- *Follow trajectory:* Moves the wrist along a recorded or synthesized trajectory.
- *Grasp close:* Grasps an object by closing the hand.
- *Grasp open:* Opens the hand and brings it into an idle position.

In addition, secondary behaviors such as an 'idle motion' behavior are used, in order to increase the believability of the virtual human. All behaviors can be combined to create complex motions, where, for instance, the virtual human fixates the object and opens his hand while reaching for it. Motion trajectories and hand shapes are synthesized according to the environmental configuration. For example, if an object to be grasped has been displaced, a new reach-trajectory is synthesized using GMR, which takes the new position into account. Further, a new hand shape for grasping the object is optimized using a learned PLDPM. Figure 6.11 shows the reproduction of actions under different environmental configurations. During the recording of actions (left), a real user grasped the gear-shift, the steering wheel and later a radio button. The action reproduction subsystem translates these actions into a set of 'follow trajectory', 'grasp open' and 'grasp close' behaviors. The synthesized animations are robust against changes in the environment. As can be seen in Fig. 6.11 (right), the recorded actions can be reproduced in VR, even if the position of the gear-shift and the body proportions of the virtual human change.

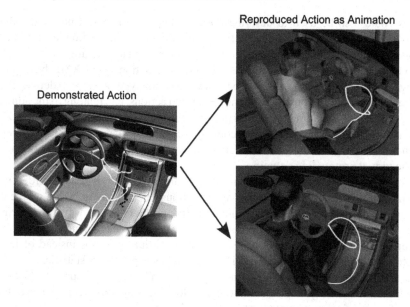

Fig. 6.11 *Left*: A user performs several actions in a cockpit scenario. The motion is shown as a *white* trajectory. *Right*: Recorded action files are used to animate virtual humans of different size and body proportions. Animations are robust against changes in the virtual prototype; e.g. in the *lower image*, the gear-shift has been repositioned. *White lines* indicate the trajectories of the right hand's wrist while interaction with several control elements in a car

6.6   Conclusion

Action capture is a VR-based extension of motion capture that takes advantage of interactive virtual environments: Whereas traditional motion capture just aims to replay the body movements of an actor, action capture further aims to replicate the actor's interactions with the objects of a virtual environment. As an advantage, animations are automatically adapted to varying task conditions, e.g. when virtual characters of different body sizes and proportions are used or when the virtual environment is slightly modified between action recording and replay.

In our prototype action capture system, the interactions of the VR user are recorded and analyzed on three, increasingly abstract levels: on the motion capture level, essentially the output of tracking devices is recorded, i.e. raw sensor data and joint angles. Next, on the basic interaction level, the continuous motion data are segmented and classified into discrete interaction events. Nine types of basic interactions were identified that describe the various phases during the manipulation of scene objects. In particular, the identified basic interactions cover the handling of control elements during the simulated operation of virtual prototypes. In the current implementation, the set of possible interactions is restricted to the manipulation of scene objects performed with the upper limbs, which reflects the typical interaction setting in immersive virtual environments. However, the introduced basic interaction types could also be used to describe object manipulations performed with other body parts, such as the pushing of a foot pedal. Finally, on the action level, typical sequences of basic interactions, such as reach-grasp-displace-release, are combined into high-level action descriptions. As action representation, a new XML-based language XSAMPL3D has been developed. Several action types have been defined that correspond to various constraints of the performed actions, e.g. relating to the admissible degrees of freedom of a virtual prototype's control elements. XSAMPL3D is defined in an extensible manner to account for the domain-dependent nature of these high-level actions, allowing the definition of further action types beyond those found in the virtual prototyping domain.

A potential drawback of generating virtual human animations from recorded VR interactions results from the often overly cautious interactions in VR, e.g. due to missing haptic feedback. We have addressed this problem in two ways: (a) During analysis of the interaction, observed movements are generalized to action representations that rely, e.g. on hand shape classifications during grasps instead of joint angle recordings. And (b), during animation synthesis, pre-learnt statistical models of arm trajectories and hand shapes are applied and adapted to the current situation. From these models, goal-directed yet natural looking animations can be generated even if the original movement in VR is somewhat jittery.

Recorded actions can be reproduced using virtual humans of different sizes and body proportions. The resulting animations give us important insights about various aspects of a virtual prototype, such as design or ergonomics. We believe that action capture will prove particularly beneficial in virtual prototyping settings that require the automated generation of animations for many variants of prototypes and virtual humans.

Finally, the action capture method can be conceptualized as an instance of imitation learning. In analogy to a distinction made in developmental psychology between the stages of movement and action imitation, action capture can be seen as a next stage in the synthesis of life-like character animations, accomplished by placing the actor in an interactive VR environment.

Acknowledgements The research described in this contribution was supported by the DFG (Deutsche Forschungsgemeinschaft) in the Virtual Workers project.

References

[Arb02] M. A. Arbib. The mirror system, imitation, and the evolution of language. In Dautenhahn and Nehaniv *Imitation in Animals and Artifacts*. MIT, Cambridge, 2002.

[BAHJV08] H. B. Amor, G. Heumer, B. Jung, and A. Vitzthum. Grasp synthesis from low-dimensional probabilistic grasp models. *Computer Animation and Virtual Worlds*, 19(3–4):445–454, 2008.

[BAWHJ07] H. B. Amor, M. Weber, G. Heumer, and B. Jung. Coordinate system transformations for imitation of goal-directed trajectories in virtual humans. In *Virtual Environments 2007. IPT EGVE 2007. 13th Eurographics Symposium on Virtual Environments. Short Papers and Posters*, 2007.

[BBA+00]   N. I. Badler, R. Bindiganavale, J. Allbeck, W. Schuler, L. Zhao, and M. Palmer. Parameterized action representation for virtual human agents. In *Embodied conversational agents*, pages 256–284. MIT Press, Cambridge, 2000.

[BK96]   P. Bakker and Y. Kuniyoshi. Robot see, Robot do: An Overview of Robot Imitation. In *AISB96 Workshop: Learning in Robots and Animals*, pages 3–11, 1996.

[BPW93]   N. I. Badler, C. B. Phillips, and B. L. Webber. *Simulating Humans: Computer Graphics and Animation and Control*. Oxford University Press, New York, 1993.

[BS04]   A. Billard and R. Siegwart, editors. *Special Issue on Robot Learning from Demonstration*, volume 47 of *Robotics and Autonomous Systems*, 2004.

[BWKE91]   N. I. Badler, B. L. Webber, J. Kalita, and J. Esakov. Animation from instructions. In *Making them move: mechanics, control, and animation of articulated figures*, pages 51–93. Morgan Kaufmann, San Francisco, 1991.

[DLR77]   A. P. Dempster, N. M. Laird, and D. B. Rubin. Maximum likelihood from incomplete data via the EM algorithm. *Journal of the Royal Statistical Society. Series B (Methodological)*, 39(1):1–38, 1977.

[DN02]   K. Dautenhahn and C. Nehaniv, editors. *Imitation in Animals and Artifacts*. MIT, Cambridge, 2002.

[GHJV09]   F. Gommlich, G. Heumer, B. Jung, and A. Vitzthum. Simulation of Articulated Standard Control Actuators in Dynamic Virtual Environments. In *Proceedings of IEEE Virtual Reality 2009*, pages 269–270. IEEE, 2009.

[Gle98]   M. Gleicher. Retargetting Motion to New Characters. In *SIGGRAPH'98 Conference Proceedings*, Computer Graphics Annual Conference Series, pages 33–42. ACM, 1998.

[HBAJ08]   G. Heumer, H. B. Amor, and B. Jung. Grasp recognition for uncalibrated data gloves: A machine learning approach. *Presence: Teleoperators & Virtual Environments*, 17(2):121–142, 2008.

[HBAWJ07]   G. Heumer, H. B. Amor, M. Weber, and B. Jung. Grasp Recognition with Uncalibrated Data Gloves – A Comparison Of Classification Methods. In *Proceedings of IEEE Virtual Reality Conference, VR '07*, pages 19–26, March 2007.

[HS98]   H. Heuer and J. Sangals. Task-dependent mixtures of coordinate systems in visuomotor transformations. *Experimental Brain Research*, 119(2):224-236, 1998.

[JR97]   W. L. Johnson and J. Rickel. Steve: an animated pedagogical agent for procedural training in virtual environments. *SIGART Bulletin*, 8(1–4):16–21, 1997.

[Ken04]   A. Kendon. *Gesture: Visible Action as Utterance*. Cambridge University Press, Cambridge, 2004.

[KL00]   J. Kuffner and J. Latombe. Interactive Manipulation Planning for Animated Characters. In *Proceedings of Pacific Graphics, 2000*,

[KT99]   M. Kallmann and D. Thalmann. Direct 3D Interaction with Smart Objects. In *Proceedings ACM VRST 99*, London, 1999.

[KT02]   M. Kallmann and D. Thalmann. Modeling behaviors of interactive objects for realtime virtual environments. *Journal of Visual Languages and Computing*, 13(2):177–195, 2002.

[Mel96]   A. N. Meltzoff. The human infant as imitative generalist: a 20-year progress report on infant imitation with implications for comparative psychology. In *Social Learning in Animals: The Roots of Culture*, pages 347–370, 1996.

[MF96]   A. Moon and M. Farsi. Grasp Quality Measures in the Control of Dextrous Robot Hands. *Physical Modelling as a Basis for Control (Digest No: 1996/042), IEE Colloquium on*, pages 6/1–6/4, 1996.

[MF10]   M. Möhring and B. Fröhlich. Enabling Functional Validation of Virtual Cars through Natural Interaction Metaphors. In *Proceedings of IEEE Virtual Reality Conference, VR 2010*, 2010.

[MI94]   C. L. MacKenzie and T. Iberall. *The Grasping Hand*. Elsevier-North Holland, 1994.

[MTT04]   N. Magnenat-Thalmann and D. Thalmann, editors. *Handbook of Virtual Humans*. Wiley, 2004.

[ND02]   C. Nehaniv and K. Dautenhahn. The Correspondence Problem. In Dautenhahn and Nehaniv [DN02], pages 41–61.

[ND07]   C. Nehaniv and K. Dautenhahn, editors. *Imitation and Social Learning in Robots, Humans and Animals: Behavioural, Social and Communicative Dimensions*. Cambridge University Press, Cambridge, 2007.

[PZ05]   N. S. Pollard and V. B. Zordan. Physically based Grasping Control from Example. In *SCA '05: Proceedings of the 2005 ACM SIGGRAPH/Eurographics symposium on Computer animation*, pages 311–318. ACM, New York, 2005.

[RS00]   S. T. Roweis and L. K. Saul. Nonlinear dimensionality reduction by locally linear embedding. *Science*, 290(5500):2323–2326, 2000.

[RSM04] R. Rao, A. P. Shon, and A. N. Meltzoff. A Bayesian model of imitation in infants and robots. In *Imitation and Social Learning in Robots, Humans and Animals: Behavioural, Social and Communicative Dimensions*, Cambridge University Press, Cambridge, 2004.

[Sch19] G. Schlesinger. Der Mechanische Aufbau der Künstlichen Glieder. In M. Borchardt et al., editors, *Ersatzglieder und Arbeitshilfen für Kriegsbeschädigte und Unfallverletzte*, pages 321–661. Springer, Berlin, 1919.

[TdSL00] J. B. Tenenbaum, V. de Silva, and J. C. Langford. A global geometric framework for nonlinear dimensionality reduction. *Science*, 290(5500):2319–2323, 2000.

[Tho98] E. L. Thorndike. Animal intelligence: an experimental study of the associative processes in animals. *Psychological Review Monographs*, 8, 1898.

[Tom05] B. Tomlinson. From linear to interactive animation: how autonomous characters change the process and product of animating. *ACM Computers in Entertainment*, 3(1), 2005.

[VAHB09] A. Vitzthum, H. B. Amor, G. Heumer, and B. Jung. Action description for animation of virtual characters. In *6. Workshop Virtuelle und Erweiterte Realität*. GI-Fachgruppe VR/AR, 2009.

[WHAJ06] M. Weber, G. Heumer, H. B. Amor, and B. Jung. An animation system for imitation of object grasping in virtual reality. In *ICAT*, pages 65–76, 2006.

[Wor08] World Wide Web Consortium. *Synchronized Multimedia Integration Language (SMIL 3.0)*, 2008.

[YKH04] K. Yamane, J. J. Kuffner, and J. K. Hodgins. Synthesizing animations of human manipulation tasks. *ACM Trans. Graph.*, 23(3):532–539, 2004.

Chapter 7
Cloth Simulation Based Motion Capture of Dressed Humans

Nils Hasler, Bodo Rosenhahn, and Hans-Peter Seidel

Abstract Commonly marker based as well as markerless motion capture systems assume that the tracked person is wearing tightly fitting clothes. Unfortunately, this restriction cannot be satisfied in many situations and most preexisting video data does not adhere to it either. In this work we propose a graphics based vision approach for tracking humans markerlessly without making this assumption. Instead a physically based simulation of the clothing the tracked person is wearing is used to guide the tracking algorithm.

7.1 Introduction

In the last years motion capture has gained significant importance in the entertainment industry as well as in medical and sports sciences based motion analysis. All of the available marker or vision based motion capture systems, however, make the assumption that tracked persons are wearing tightly fitting clothes. Marker based systems try to avoid unnecessary marker occlusions by this restriction and ensure that the markers closely follow the motion of the tracked person. Most vision based systems, however, are unable to handle the arbitrary deformations loose fitting clothes introduce during motion.

N. Hasler (✉)
Weta Digital, Wellington, New Zealand
e-mail: nhasler@wetafx.co.nz
and
MPI Informatik, Saarbrücken, Germany

B. Rosenhahn
Institut für Informationsverarbeitung, Hannover University, Hannover, Germany
e-mail: rosenhahn@tnt.uni-hannover.de

H.-P. Seidel
MPI Informatik, Saarbrücken, Germany
e-mail: hpseidel@mpi-inf.mpg.de

S. Coquillart et al. (eds.), *Virtual Realities*, DOI 10.1007/978-3-211-99178-7_7,
© Springer-Verlag/Wien 2011

In this work we present a procedure that applies the well-studied computer graphics method for simulating textiles to a vision problem. Namely, we attempt to overcome the tight-fitting clothing restriction for vision based algorithms by embracing an analysis-by-synthesis approach. The method is founded on a silhouette based motion capture technique which assumes initial knowledge of a model representing the tracked person. The algorithm is augmented with a physically based cloth simulation as is commonly used in today's feature films. The combined silhouettes of both the humanoid model and the clothing draped over the model are then used to explain the video data.

Results are verified visually as well as by comparison with a commercial marker based motion capture systems that was run in parallel with our algorithm.

The paper is structured as follows: Section 7.2 introduces the state of the art of the involved areas of research, Sect. 7.3 details our cloth simulation based approach for motion capturing dressed humans markerlessly. In Sect. 7.4 the performed experiments and results are presented. We conclude with a brief summary in Sect. 7.5.

7.1.1 Contributions

We present a graphics driven computer vision approach to tracking of loosely dressed humans. A physically based cloth simulation system as commonly encountered in the computer graphics community is coupled in an analysis-by-synthesis manner with a state-of-the-art motion capture method to allow tracking and animation of subjects wearing unrestrained garments.

7.2 Previous Work

As our approach touches upon two areas of research, namely, vision based motion capture systems and physically based cloth simulation a brief overview of both fields is given in the following.

Muybridge is commonly credited for being the first to do motion analysis. His famous experiments published in 1887 [23] comprise sequences of photographics depicting the locomotion of humans and some animals. The footage was shot using arrays of synchronised cameras.

Vision based motion capture, however, was pioneered by Hogg [15] and Rohr [27] who were both able to track a person walking parallel to the viewing plane of a single camera. By using an a priori model of the human gait they effectively reduced the problem to one-dimension. Both authors used skeleton-based models of the tracked human made up of cylinders which are deformed to best fit the edges of observed person and model.

Gavrila and Davis [14] introduced an approach that matches tapered superquadrics to multi-view video frames and then employs an analysis-by-synthesis technique to match a high degrees of freedom skeleton-based model to the observed data. The similarity of model and video data is also evaluated using an edge-based metric. Tracked persons are required to wear colour coded clothing.

The approach presented by Wren et al. [35] employs a statistical colour-based model for segmenting foreground blobs from the background. The models are updated during tracking compensating for slow changes in the background. The model of the person, commonly consisting of several blobs with different colours, is generated automatically. As the system is based on a single camera and uses simple texture analysis algorithms significantly less information can be recovered by their approach than by modern motion capture algorithms. Yet, it has to be pointed out that they were able to perform simple gesture analysis and that the proposed system works robustly even in cluttered environments.

Only a short time later Bregler and Malik [4] introduced a new mathematical method for tracking articulate bodies. By using products of exponential maps and twist motions only a simple linear system has to be solved to update the kinematic chain. This allows more sophisticated, hierarchically organised bodies with more degrees of freedom to be tracked efficiently. While their approach models humans as a hierarchy of cylinders and spheres triangular mesh models can just as well be used. An extension to the work was published by Bregler et al. [5] proposing a technique that also allows the automatic extraction of the kinematic chain.

Probably the work most closely related to our current was presented by Rosenhahn et al. [28]. They also base their system on exponential maps and twists but enhance the approach with a geometric cloth model. This allows them to track loosely dressed humans. However, as they employ a geometric cloth model a new procedure has to be developed for every new type of garment that is to be tracked. In contrast, the model we propose here only requires the generation of a new pattern of the garment.

For more in-depth surveys on the subject area we refer the interested reader to Gavrilla [13] and Moeslund and Granum [21].

Besides motion capture algorithms a brief overview of the cloth simulation area has to be given. Despite strong interest has been shown in cloth simulation on the one hand and cloth tracking and reconstruction on the other only little effort has been put into combining the efforts by employing analysis-by-synthesis approaches to cloth tracking.

One algorithm was presented by Jojic and Huang [16] which estimates the hidden points a cloth is resting on. They do require 3D-range data of the real cloth to achieve this goal and the two-phased nature of their algorithm allows it to be applied to static situations only.

An analysis-by-synthesis approach was also employed by Bhat et al. [3] but their goal was fundamentally different. Instead of striving to detect the motion of the fabric they assumed prior knowledge of the motion which was conducted by a robot and attempted to extract the static and dynamic fabric parameters from video images. A simulated annealing optimiser was used to demonstrate that a wide variety of cloth types could be reconstructed. Their research, however, lacks verification with a mechanical cloth property extraction method such as the Kawabata Evaluation

System (KES) [18]. The method has also been criticised because it is apparently unable to accurately estimate the bend resistance parameter [24].

Other cloth tracking and reconstruction approaches do not make use of a cloth simulation to guide the reconstruction. The algorithm by Pritchard and Heidrich [24] can be divided into three stages. First, stereo correspondences are used to reconstruct most of the textured cloth. Secondly, holes are interpolated and Lowe's SIFT descriptor [19] is employed to map points on the world-space cloth to points on the two-dimensional reference cloth. Identified points are then connected by a seed-and-grow algorithm, rejecting spurious points in the process.

Several other algorithms to recover the three-dimensional layout of a cloth were published. Scholz and Magnor [29] presented an approach that used optical flow to calculate the three-dimensional scene flow. Holes in the model are not interpolated as in Pritchard's approach. Instead a deformable cloth model is matched to the surface, minimising the deformation energy of the patch. Drift is countered by constraining the edge of the simulation to the silhouette of the real cloth. Unfortunately, their algorithm was only demonstrated on synthetic data. Their work was continued with a publication on tracking cloth marked with a pseudo random coloured dots pattern [30]. The proposed algorithm detects coloured ellipses using colour and brightness information and identifies the exact position on the cloth by examining their local neighbourhood. The identified locations are connected in a way similar to Pritchard's approach. Three-dimensional coordinates are reconstructed by using a multi-camera setup. As a last step holes are filled by means of a thin-plate spline interpolation technique. Recently, an extension to the approach was presented by White et al. [34] who proposed a stereo-setup to reconstruct a random pattern of coloured triangles printed on a cloth. Their principal contributions are an extension to the seed-and-grow algorithm introduced by Pritchard and a strain minimisation technique that allows them to reconstruct points that are visible in one camera only.

Physically based cloth simulation as used in this paper was pioneered by Terzopoulos et al. [32]. In their work a number of techniques that are common now such as semi-implicit integration, hierarchical bounding boxes, and adaptive time-step control were proposed. Until [2] reintroduced semi-implicit integration explicit integration techniques were common.

In the last few years two major strands of development can be made out in the cloth simulation community. One, aiming for real-time simulation, focusses on computation speed alone, sacrificing expressiveness and accuracy if necessary. Desbrun et al. [11] simplified the equation system that needs to be solved every step by precomputing parts of it. Kang and Cho [17] used a coarse mass-spring discretisation and added wrinkles in a post-processing step by interpolating with a cubic spline.

The other strand attempts to simulate cloth as realistically as possible. The use of nonlinear and hysteretic cloth properties has been introduced by Eberhardt et al. [12]. Simplified nonlinearities have since been integrated into a number of systems such as [6, 10]. Impressive results were presented by Volino and Magnenat-Thalmann [33].

7.3 Approach

The overall tracking procedure is summarised in Fig. 7.1. It can globally be segmented into two modules: segmentation and pose estimation. The purpose of the
segmentation algorithm is to detect the silhouette of the tracked person. This can
become arbitrarily difficult due to noise, shading, occlusion or texture transitions
between the object and the background. Our approach is based on level set image
segmentation [8]. The pose estimation module then tries to recreate the observed
silhouette by applying a rigid body motion and a deformation to the model of the
tracked person.

7.3.1 Segmentation

A level set function $\Phi \in \Omega \mapsto \mathbb{R}$ splits the image domain Ω into two regions Ω_1
and Ω_2 with $\Phi(x) > 0$ if $x \in \Omega_1$ and $\Phi(x) < 0$ if $x \in \Omega_2$. The zero-level line thus
marks the boundary between both regions. On a discrete image, the level set func-
tions are modeled through a distance transform from the contour line to the inner and
outer region with negative and positive distance values, respectively. Both regions
are analysed with respect to the probabilities of image features (e.g. gray value
distributions, colour or texture channels). Now the key idea is to evolve the contour line, to maximise the probability density functions with respect to each other.
Furthermore, the boundary between both regions should be as small as possible.
This can be expressed by adding a smoothness term. For an optimum partitioning,
we minimise the following energy functional, which is an extended version of the

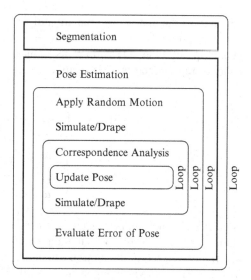

Fig. 7.1 The overall
structure of the tracking
approach is split into two
major blocks: segmentation
and pose estimation

Chan–Vese model [9]:

$$E(\Phi, p_1, p_2) = -\int_\Omega H(\Phi(x)) \log p_1$$
$$+(1 - H(\Phi(x))) \log p_2 + v|\nabla H(\Phi(x))| \, dx$$

where $v > 0$ is a weighting parameter and $H(s)$ is a regularised version of the Heaviside function, e.g. the error function. The probability densities p_i are estimated according to the expectation-maximisation principle. Having the level set function initialised with some contour, the probability densities within the two regions are estimated by the feature histograms smoothed with a Gaussian kernel K_σ and its standard deviation σ.

7.3.2 Twist Based Pose Estimation

Assuming an extracted image contour and the silhouette of the projected surface mesh, the closest point correspondences between both contours are used to define a set of corresponding 3D lines and 3D points. Then a 3D point-line based pose estimation algorithm for kinematic chains is applied to minimise the spatial distance between both contours: For point based pose estimation each line is modeled as a 3D Plücker line $L_i = (n_i, m_i)$, with a (unit) direction n_i and moment m_i [22]. The 3D rigid motion is expressed as exponential form

$$\mathbf{M} = \exp(\theta\hat{\xi}) = \exp\begin{pmatrix} \hat{\omega} & \mathbf{v} \\ 0_{1\times3} & 0 \end{pmatrix},$$

where $\theta\hat{\xi}$ is the matrix representation of a twist $\xi \in se(3) = \{(\mathbf{v}, \hat{\omega})|\mathbf{v} \in \mathbb{R}^3, \hat{\omega} \in so(3)\}$, with $so(3) = \{\mathbf{A} \in \mathbb{R}^{3\times3}|\mathbf{A} = -\mathbf{A}^T\}$. The Lie algebra $so(3)$ is the tangential space of the 3D rotations. Its elements are (scaled) rotation axes, which can either be represented as a 3D vector or a screw symmetric matrix,

$$\theta\omega = \theta\begin{pmatrix} \omega_1 \\ \omega_2 \\ \omega_3 \end{pmatrix}, \text{ with } \|\omega\|_2 = 1,$$

$$\theta\hat{\omega} = \theta\begin{pmatrix} 0 & -\omega_3 & \omega_2 \\ \omega_3 & 0 & -\omega_1 \\ -\omega_2 & \omega_1 & 0 \end{pmatrix}.$$

A twist ξ contains six parameters and can be scaled to $\theta\xi$ for a unit vector ω. The parameter $\theta \in \mathbb{R}$ corresponds to the motion velocity (i.e., the rotation velocity and pitch). For varying θ, the motion can be identified as screw motion around an axis in space. The six twist components can either be represented as a 6D vector or as a

4×4 matrix,

$$\theta\xi = \theta(\omega_1, \omega_2, \omega_3, v_1, v_2, v_3)^T, \|\omega\|_2 = 1,$$

$$\theta\hat{\xi} = \theta \begin{pmatrix} 0 & -\omega_3 & \omega_2 & v_1 \\ \omega_3 & 0 & -\omega_1 & v_2 \\ -\omega_2 & \omega_1 & 0 & v_3 \\ 0 & 0 & 0 & 0 \end{pmatrix}.$$

To reconstruct a group action $\mathbf{M} \in SE(3)$ from a given twist, the exponential function $\exp(\theta\hat{\xi}) = \mathbf{M} \in SE(3)$ must be computed. This can be done efficiently by using the Rodriguez formula [22].

For pose estimation the reconstructed Plücker lines are combined with the screw representation for rigid motions: Incidence of the transformed 3D point $\mathbf{x_i}$ with the 3D ray $L_i = (\mathbf{n_i}, \mathbf{m_i})$ can be expressed as

$$\left(\exp(\theta\hat{\xi})\mathbf{x_i}\right)_{3\times 1} \times \mathbf{n_i} - \mathbf{m_i} = 0.$$

Since $\exp(\theta\hat{\xi})\mathbf{x_i}$ is a 4D vector, the homogeneous component (which is 1) is neglected to evaluate the cross product with $\mathbf{n_i}$. Then the equation is linearised and iterated.

Joints are expressed as special screws with no pitch of the form $\theta_j\hat{\xi}_j$ with known $\hat{\xi}_j$ (the location of the rotation axes is part of the model) and unknown joint angle θ_j. The constraint equation of an ith point on a jth joint has the form

$$\left(\exp(\theta\hat{\xi})\exp(\theta_1\hat{\xi}_1)\dots\exp(\theta_j\hat{\xi}_j)\mathbf{x_i}\right)_{3\times 1} \times \mathbf{n_i} - \mathbf{m_i} = 0,$$

which is linearised in the same way as the rigid body motion itself. It leads to three linear equations with the six unknown pose parameters and j unknown joint angles.

7.3.3 Cloth Simulation

The new part of the pose estimation module is the physically based cloth simulation framework. Our procedure is a mélange of previously published techniques. The basic cloth model is fashioned after the system described by Volino and Magnenat-Thalmann [33] which is based on triangles instead of on the more commonly used edges (springs). Even though the implementation is more complex it could be found that this model is not only more accurate but also significantly faster. The idea is to model the stress in three independent directions (warp uu, weft vv, and shearing uv) according to physical measurements of real fabrics as a function of the observed strain in these directions and its derivatives.

$$\sigma_{uu}(\epsilon_{uu}, \epsilon_{vv}, \epsilon_{uv}, \epsilon'_{uu}, \epsilon'_{vv}, \epsilon'_{uv})$$
$$\sigma_{vv}(\epsilon_{uu}, \epsilon_{vv}, \epsilon_{uv}, \epsilon'_{uu}, \epsilon'_{vv}, \epsilon'_{uv})$$
$$\sigma_{uv}(\epsilon_{uu}, \epsilon_{vv}, \epsilon_{uv}, \epsilon'_{uu}, \epsilon'_{vv}, \epsilon'_{uv})$$

The deformation of a triangle is computed using its two-dimensional warp-weft coordinates. Then the strain-stress relationship can be used to compute forces acting on the masses at the corners of the triangles. The relative warp-weft coordinates of the corners of a triangle (Ru_i, Rv_i) can be precomputed using their warp-weft coordinates (u_i, v_i)

$$Ru_1 = (v_2 - v_3)/d \quad Rv_1 = (u_2 - u_3)/d$$
$$Ru_2 = (v_1 - v_3)/d \quad Rv_2 = (u_1 - u_3)/d$$
$$Ru_3 = (v_1 - v_2)/d \quad Rv_3 = (u_1 - u_2)/d$$

where

$$d = u_1(v_2 - v_3) + u_2(v_3 - v_1) + u_3(v_1 - v_2).$$

During simulation the warp and weft directions $\mathbf{u}$ and $\mathbf{v}$ are computed using the three-dimensional coordinates of the triangle vertices $\mathbf{x_i}$.

$$\mathbf{u} = \sum_i Ru_i \mathbf{x_i}, \quad \mathbf{v} = \sum_i Rv_i \mathbf{x_i}, \text{ with } i \in [1, 3].$$

The in-plain strains ϵ can then be computed using

$$\epsilon_{uu} = |\mathbf{u}| - 1 \quad \epsilon_{vv} = |\mathbf{v}| - 1 \quad \epsilon_{uv} = \frac{|\mathbf{u} + \mathbf{v}|}{\sqrt{2}} - \frac{|\mathbf{u} - \mathbf{v}|}{\sqrt{2}}$$

and the force on vertex i is defined as

$$\mathbf{f_i} = -\frac{d}{2}\left((Ru_i\sigma_{uu} + Rv_i\sigma_{uv})\frac{\mathbf{u}}{|\mathbf{u}|} + (Ru_i\sigma_{uv} + Rv_i\sigma_{vv})\frac{\mathbf{v}}{|\mathbf{v}|}\right).$$

Bending resistance is computed using a model introduced by Bridson et al. [7]. As a single triangle cannot bend in itself neighbouring triangles are combined to form bending units. The given equations are guaranteed to damp neither motion nor rotation or in-plane deformation of the triangles defined by $(\mathbf{x_1}, \mathbf{x_3}, \mathbf{x_4})$ and $(\mathbf{x_2}, \mathbf{x_3}, \mathbf{x_4})$ respectively. The bending resistance is defined as

$$\mathbf{f_{bend}} = k_b \frac{|\mathbf{e}|^2}{|\mathbf{n_1}| + |\mathbf{n_2}|} \sin(\theta/2)\mathbf{u_i}, \quad i \in [1, 4],$$

where $\mathbf{n_1} = (\mathbf{x_1} - \mathbf{x_3}) \times (\mathbf{x_1} - \mathbf{x_4})$ and $\mathbf{n_2} = (\mathbf{x_2} - \mathbf{x_4}) \times (\mathbf{x_2} - \mathbf{x_3})$ are the non-unit length normals of the adjacent triangles, $\mathbf{e} = \mathbf{x_4} - \mathbf{x_3}$ is the shared edge vector, k_b is the bending resistance constant, and θ the dihedral angle. Since

$$\sin(\theta/2) = \frac{\mathbf{n}_1}{|\mathbf{n}_1|} \times \frac{\mathbf{n}_2}{|\mathbf{n}_2|} \cdot \frac{\mathbf{e}}{|\mathbf{e}|} \sqrt{\frac{1}{2} - \frac{\mathbf{n}_1 \cdot \mathbf{n}_2}{2\,|\mathbf{n}_1|\,|\mathbf{n}_2|}},$$

the expression for $\mathbf{f}_i$ can be expressed in linear algebra terms. The $\mathbf{u}_i$ define the direction and scale of bending resistance forces. Their definition is simple for the two vertices opposite to the shared edge.

$$\mathbf{u}_1 = |\mathbf{e}|\,\frac{\mathbf{n}_1}{|\mathbf{n}_1|^2} \qquad \mathbf{u}_2 = |\mathbf{e}|\,\frac{\mathbf{n}_2}{|\mathbf{n}_2|^2}$$

However, the factors for the shared vertices are more complicated.

$$\mathbf{u}_3 = \frac{(\mathbf{x}_1 - \mathbf{x}_4) \cdot \mathbf{e}}{|\mathbf{e}|}\,\frac{\mathbf{n}_1}{|\mathbf{n}_1|^2} + \frac{(\mathbf{x}_2 - \mathbf{x}_4) \cdot \mathbf{e}}{|\mathbf{e}|}\,\frac{\mathbf{n}_2}{|\mathbf{n}_2|^2}$$

$$\mathbf{u}_4 = -\frac{(\mathbf{x}_1 - \mathbf{x}_3) \cdot \mathbf{e}}{|\mathbf{e}|}\,\frac{\mathbf{n}_1}{|\mathbf{n}_1|^2} - \frac{(\mathbf{x}_2 - \mathbf{x}_3) \cdot \mathbf{e}}{|\mathbf{e}|}\,\frac{\mathbf{n}_2}{|\mathbf{n}_2|^2}$$

In addition to these internal forces gravity which is trivial to implement and a sophisticated airdrag model that was suggested by Bhat et al. [3] are defined

$$\mathbf{f}_{\mathrm{air}} = -A\left(\frac{k_n\,|\mathbf{v_n}|^2}{1 + k_f\,|\mathbf{v_n}|^2}\,\frac{\mathbf{v_n}}{|\mathbf{v_n}|} + k_t \mathbf{v_t}\right).$$

Here $\mathbf{v_n}$ and $\mathbf{v_t}$ are the normal and tangential velocities of a triangle, A is its area and k_n, k_f, and k_t are damping constants.

Collision detection and response are modeled according to Provot [25] who explicitly states conditions for continuous collision detection and gives a nice heuristic for reducing the number of self-collision tests. We also took the advice about k-DOP (discrete oriented polytope) based bounding volume hierarchies from [20]. That is we use bounding volume trees of 14-DOPs with order 4. Collision response is done as suggested by Bridson [6] applying cancelling impulses to colliding particles, triangles and edges.

The model is integrated using a semi-implicit backward Euler integrator based on the improved preconditioned conjugate gradient solver that was introduced by Ascher and Boxerman [1].

7.3.4 System Integration

The cloth simulation is integrated into the tracking framework as shown in Fig. 7.1. During pose estimation, a gradient descent type optimisation is used to iteratively approach the real pose of the tracked person. Unfortunately, if the dynamics of the

Fig. 7.2 Determining the configuration of the skirt-model compound in the first frame is split into three steps. The initial configuration is manually determined on the undeformed model, the model is deformed, and the cloth is draped on the legs

cloth are to be preserved the fabric has to be resimulated starting from the previous frame's pose for every iteration. Yet, since this property is one of the primary advantages of the physically based cloth model over the geometric approach and the system is not aimed at real-time operation, this option is pursued.

The cloth simulation has to operate at a significantly higher frame-rate than the rest of the pose estimation algorithm which runs at video refresh rate. Intermediate poses of the model are obtained by linearly interpolating the time varying positions of the model's mesh nodes.

The first frame is assumed to be a static configuration. So a slightly different procedure for determining the cloth configuration is performed. As visualised in Fig. 7.2 the flat pattern of the skirt is first placed on the undeformed model. Then the model is moved and deformed according to the rigid body motion and angular parameters the pose estimation procedure chooses to evaluate. The cloth is at this stage assumed to be attached to the root node of the model. That is, it is only affected by the rigid body motion. At last, a variation of the classical cloth simulation is used to generate a resting pose of the cloth on the model. This configuration is then evaluated using the silhouette based correspondence analysis as described in Sect. 7.3.2.

7.4 Experiments

Three sequences of a subject performing different actions are analysed. Exemplary frames from these sequences are shown in Fig. 7.3. The first sequence consists of simple walking, in the second a complex pattern of walking sideways and turning is performed, while in the third sequence a knee bending exercise is executed. The sequences were chosen due to their importance in medical motion analysis on the one hand and their inherently challenging properties for the algorithm in general and the cloth simulation in particular on the other. The sequences were captured by a synchronised setup of four cameras. In order to allow accuracy evaluation of our approach a commercial marker based motion capture system was run in parallel. The markers were attached to the hips, knees, shins, and feet so that they could not interfere with the skirt (Fig. 7.4). In [28] a geometric cloth model was presented that allows tracking of persons wearing skirts. We compare our results with their findings.

The model of the cloth was manually created using a photography of the real skirt (Fig. 7.5) as a template. The constructed straight line graph was Delaunay-tessellated and a refinement algorithm [31] that was modified to allow stitching different parts together was then used to create the final tessellation with around 1,300 triangles.

Fig. 7.3 The analysed sequences include a simple walking sequence (*left*) and side stepping (*middle*) and knee bending (*right*) exercises

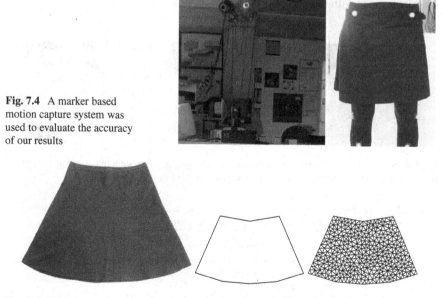

Fig. 7.4 A marker based motion capture system was used to evaluate the accuracy of our results

Fig. 7.5 The skirt pattern was manually created using the photography of the real skirt as a template. The resulting *straight line graph* was then tesselated using a Delaunay algorithm

7.4.1 Results

The motion capture results obtained with our framework are evaluated visually by
overlaying the wireframe of the model with the captured scene (Fig. 7.6) as well
as by reanimating the captured model in a different scene (Fig. 7.11). In addition,
selected angles are compared to the motion capture data obtained with the marker
based system and the geometric cloth modelling technique.

Mean error and standard deviation of the left knee joint angle compared to the
marker based motion captured data are given in Table 7.1. As the errors are in the
same range as the error of the marker based system which is around 3° [26] we are
unable to evaluate the precision of our approach more accurately. Yet, our findings
are consistently closer to the marker based system and the variance is in all but
the knee bending sequence smaller than that of the geometric model. For the knee
bending sequence the results proved hard to improve because the estimation of the
geometric model are fairly accurate already.

In one of the frames of the knee bending sequence a grabbing error occurred. Yet,
since the segmentation algorithm uses a strong prior which introduces the tracking
assumption into the algorithm the procedure is able to handle the difficulty smoothly.
Figure 7.7 shows the broken frame and the consecutive frame with the overlaid
wireframe model in the estimated pose.

Knee angles as a function of time as estimated by the marker based system, our
algorithm, and the geometric algorithm previously published by Rosenhahn et al.
[28] are displayed in Figs. 7.8, 7.9, and 7.10. In these plots it becomes apparent
that our measurements are in comparison significantly smoother. This observation
is confirmed by the lower variance exhibited in Table 7.1. This is also the reason
why animations with these measurements look more appealing.

Fig. 7.6 Selected frames of the three sequences (walking – *left*, side stepping – *middle*, and knee
bending – *right*) are shown overlaid with the wireframe model used for tracking

Table 7.1 Mean error μ and standard deviation σ of the knee joint angles in ° for the different
sequences using the marker based motion capture data as ground truth

	Our system		Geometric model	
	μ	σ	μ	σ
Walking	1.62	1.44	2.72	8.21
Side stepping	2.64	5.45	3.43	7.3
Knee bending	3.03	4.25	3.33	4.18

Fig. 7.7 A grabbing error occurred in one frame of the knee bending sequence. On the *left* the faulty and on the *right* the consecutive frame is shown

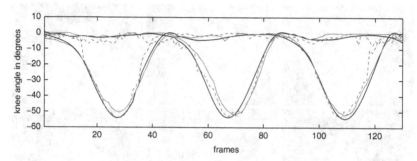

Fig. 7.8 The knee angles as estimated by our system (*gray*), by the geometric model (*dashed*), and the marker based motion capture system (*black*)

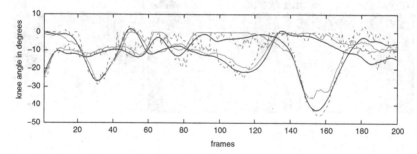

Fig. 7.9 The knee angles as estimated by our system (*gray*), by the geometric model (*dashed*), and the marker based motion capture system (*black*)

7.5 Summary

We have presented a versatile approach for tracking loosely dressed humans. The analysis-by-synthesis tracking algorithm incorporates a generic cloth simulation system as is commonly used in animation and rendering. This allows us to track and reanimate sequences of loosely dressed humans that would otherwise be hard

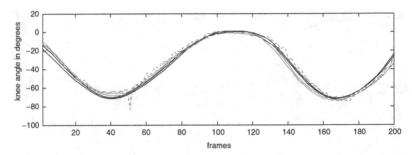

Fig. 7.10 The knee angles as estimated by our system (*gray*), by the geometric model (*dashed*), and the marker based motion capture system (*black*)

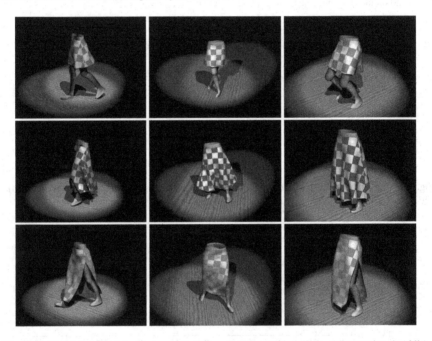

Fig. 7.11 Reanimation of the scenes with different skirts walking (*left*), side stepping (*middle*), and knee bending (*right*)

or impossible to track using a model based approach. In comparison to a previous technique our approach is significantly more flexible as the system is able to handle arbitrary textiles instead of being restricted to one type of garment. The same cloth simulation system can, as this is the primary application of textile simulations, also be used to produce animations of loose garments as demonstrated in Fig. 7.11.

Acknowledgements We gratefully acknowledge funding by the Max-Planck Center for Visual Computing and Communication.

References

1. Ascher, U., Boxerman, E.: On the modified conjugate gradient method in cloth simulation. The Visual Computer **19**(7–8), 523–531 (2003)
2. Baraff, D., Witkin, A.: Large steps in cloth simulation. In: Proceedings of ACM SIGGRAPH 98, pp. 43–54. ACM (1998)
3. Bhat, K., Twigg, C., Hodgins, J., Khosla, P., Popović, Z., Seitz, S.: Estimating cloth simulation parameters from video. In: Proceedings of ACM SIGGRAPH/Eurographics Symposium on Computer Animation (SCA 2003), pp. 37–51. ACM (2003)
4. Bregler, C., Malik, J.: Tracking people with twists and exponential maps. In: CVPR '98: Proceedings of the IEEE Computer Society Conference on Computer Vision and Pattern Recognition, p. 8. IEEE Computer Society, Washington, DC, USA (1998)
5. Bregler, C., Malik, J., Pullen, K.: Twist based acquisition and tracking of animal and human kinematics. International Journal of Computer Vision **56**(3), 179–194 (2004). DOI http://dx. doi.org/10.1023/B:VISI.0000011203.00237.9b
6. Bridson, R.: Computational aspects of dynamic surfaces. Ph.D. thesis, Stanford University (2003)
7. Bridson, R., Fedkiw, R., Anderson, J.: Robust treatment of collisions, contact and friction for cloth animation. ACM Transactions on Graphics (ACM SIGGRAPH 2002) **21**(3), 594–603 (2002)
8. Brox, T., Rousson, M., Deriche, R., Weickert, J.: Unsupervised segmentation incorporating colour, texture, and motion. In: N. Petkov, M.A. Westenberg (eds.) Computer Analysis of Images and Patterns, *LNCS*, vol. 2756, pp. 353–360. Springer, Groningen, (2003)
9. Chan, T., Vese, L.: Active contours without edges. In: IEEE Transactions on Image Processing, vol. 10, pp. 266–277. Los Angeles, CA, USA (2001)
10. Choi, K.J., Ko, H.S.: Stable but responsive cloth. ACM Transactions on Graphics (ACM SIGGRAPH 2002) **21**(3), 604–611 (2002)
11. Desbrun, M., Schröder, P., Barr, A.: Interactive animation of structured deformable objects. In: Proceedings of Graphics Interface (GI 1999), pp. 1–8. Canadian Computer-Human Communications Society (1999)
12. Eberhardt, B., Weber, A., Straßer, W.: A fast, flexible, particle-system model for cloth draping. IEEE Computer Graphics and Applications **16**(5), 52–59 (1996)
13. Gavrila, D.M.: The visual analysis of human movement: A survey. Computer Vision and Image Understanding **73**(1), 82–98 (1999)
14. Gavrila, D.M., Davis, L.S.: 3-d model-based tracking of humans in action: a multi-view approach. In: CVPR '96: Proceedings of the 1996 Conference on Computer Vision and Pattern Recognition (CVPR '96), p. 73. IEEE Computer Society, Washington, DC, USA (1996)
15. Hogg, D.: Model-based vision: a program to see a walking person. Image and Vision Computing **1**(1), 5–20 (1983)
16. Jojic, N., Huang, T.: On analysis of cloth drape range data. In: ACCV '98: Proceedings of the Third Asian Conference on Computer Vision-Volume II, pp. 463–470. Springer, London (1997)
17. Kang, Y.M., Cho, H.G.: Bilayered approximate integration for rapid and plausible animation of virtual cloth with realistic wrinkles. In: Proceedings of Computer Animation, pp. 203–214. IEEE Computer Society (2002)
18. Kawabata, S.: The standardization and analysis of hand evaluation. The Textile Machinery Society of Japan (1980)
19. Lowe, D.: Object recognition from local scale-invariant features. In: International Conference on Computer Vision, pp. 1150–1157 (1999)
20. Mezger, J., Kimmerle, S., Etzmuß, O.: Progress in collision detection and response techniques for cloth animation. In: Proceedings of 10th Pacific Conference on Computer Graphics and Applications (PG 2002), pp. 444–445. IEEE Computer Society (2002)
21. Moeslund, T., Granum, E.: A survey of computer vision-based human motion capture. Computer Vision and Image Understanding: CVIU **81**(3), 231–268 (2001)

22. Murray, R.M., Sastry, S.S., Zexiang, L.: A Mathematical Introduction to Robotic Manipulation. CRC, Boca Raton (1994)
23. Muybridge, E.: Animal Locomotion (1887)
24. Pritchard, D., Heidrich, W.: Cloth motion capture. Computer Graphics Forum (Eurographics 2003) **22**(3), 263–271 (2003)
25. Provot, X.: Collision and self-collision handling in cloth model dedicated to design garments. In: Proceedings of the Eurographics Workshop on Computer Animation and Simulation (CAS 1997), pp. 177–189. Springer (1997)
26. Richards, J.G.: The measurement of human motion: A comparison of commercially available systems. Human Movement Science **18**(5), 589–602 (1999)
27. Rohr, K.: Incremental recognition of pedestrians from image sequences. In: Computer Vision and Pattern Recognition, 1993. Proceedings CVPR '93., 1993 IEEE Computer Society Conference on, pp. 8–13. New York (1993)
28. Rosenhahn, B., Kersting, U., Powell, K., Klette, R., Klette, G., Seidel, H.P.: A system for articulated tracking incorporating a clothing model. Machine Vision and Applications (2006). DOI 10.1007/s00138-006-0046-y
29. Scholz, V., Magnor, M.: Cloth motion from optical flow. In: B. Girod, M. Magnor, H.P. Seidel (eds.) Proc. Vision, Modeling and Visualization 2004, pp. 117–124. Akademische Verlagsgesellschaft Aka GmbH, Stanford (2004)
30. Scholz, V., Stich, T., Keckeisen, M., Wacker, M., Magnor, M.: Garment motion capture using color-coded patterns. Computer Graphics Forum (Proc. Eurographics EG'05) **24**(3), 439–448 (2005)
31. Shewchuk, J.R.: Triangle: Engineering a 2D Quality Mesh Generator and Delaunay Triangulator. In: M.C. Lin, D. Manocha (eds.) Applied Computational Geometry: Towards Geometric Engineering, *Lecture Notes in Computer Science*, vol. 1148, pp. 203–222. Springer, Berlin (1996)
32. Terzopoulos, D., Platt, J., Barr, A., Fleischer, K.: Elastically deformable models. In: Computer Graphics (Proceedings of ACM SIGGRAPH 87), pp. 205–214. ACM (1987)
33. Volino, P., Magnenat-Thalmann, N.: Accurate garment prototyping and simulation. Computer-Aided Design Applications **2**(5), 645–654 (2005)
34. White, R., Forsyth, D., Vasanth, J.: Capturing real folds in cloth. Tech. Rep. UCB/EECS-2006-10, EECS Department, University of California, Berkeley (2006)
35. Wren, C.R., Azarbayejani, A., Darrell, T., Pentland, A.P.: Pfinder: Real-time tracking of the human body. IEEE Trans. Pattern Analysis and Machine Intelligence **19**(7), 780–785 (1997). DOI http://dx.doi.org/10.1109/34.598236

Chapter 8
Remote 3D Medical Consultation

**Greg Welch, Diane H. Sonnenwald, Henry Fuchs, Bruce Cairns, M.D.,
Ketan Mayer-Patel, Ruigang Yang, Andrei State, Herman Towles,
Adrian Ilie, Srinivas Krishnan, and Hanna M. Söderholm**

Abstract Two-dimensional (2D) video-based telemedical consultation has been
explored widely in the past 15–20 years. Two issues that seem to arise in most
relevant case studies are the difficulty associated with obtaining the desired 2D camera views, and poor depth perception. To address these problems we are exploring
the use of a small array of cameras to synthesize a spatially continuous range of
dynamic three-dimensional (3D) views of a remote environment and events. The
3D views can be sent across wired or wireless networks to remote viewers with
fixed displays or mobile devices such as a personal digital assistant (PDA). The
viewpoints could be specified manually or automatically via user head or PDA
tracking, giving the remote viewer virtual head- or hand-slaved (PDA-based) remote
cameras for mono or stereo viewing. We call this idea remote 3D medical consultation (3DMC). In this article we motivate and explain the vision for 3D medical

G. Welch (✉), H. Fuchs, K.M.-Patel, A. State, H. Towles, A. Ilie, and S. Krishnan
The Department of Computer Science, The University of North Carolina at Chapel Hill, Campus
Box 3175, Chapel Hill, North Carolina 27599-3175, USA
e-mail: welch@cs.unc.edu, fuchs@cs.unc.edu, kmp@cs.unc.edu, andrei@cs.unc.edu,
herman@cs.unc.edu, adyilie@cs.unc.edu, krishnan@cs.unc.edu

D.H. Sonnenwald
School of Information and Library Studies, University College Dublin, Belfeild, Dublin 4, Ireland
e-mail: Diane.Sonnenwald@ucd.ie

B. Cairns, M.D.
The Department of Surgery, The University of North Carolina at Chapel Hill, Campus Box 7228,
Chapel Hill, North Carolina 27599-7228, USA
e-mail: bruce_cairns@med.unc.edu

R. Yang
The Department of Computer Science, The University of Kentucky, 232 Hardymon Building,
Lexington, Kentucky 40506-0195, USA
e-mail: ryang@cs.uky.edu

H.M. Söderholm
The Swedish School of Library and Information Science, Göteborg University and the University
College of Borås, 50190 Borås, Sweden
e-mail: Hanna.Maurin@hb.se

S. Coquillart et al. (eds.), *Virtual Realities*, DOI 10.1007/978-3-211-99178-7_8,
© Springer-Verlag/Wien 2011

consultation; we describe the relevant computer vision/graphics, display, and networking research; we present a proof-of-concept prototype system; and we present some early experimental results supporting the general hypothesis that 3D remote medical consultation could offer benefits over conventional 2D televideo.

8.1 Introduction

We report here on a multi-year project to develop and evaluate technology for view-dependent 3D telepresence technology to support medical consultation across geographic distances. We refer to this technology as *three-dimensional medical consultation* (3DMC). Our long-term vision is to enhance and expand medical diagnoses and treatment in life-critical trauma situations. Our goal is to connect an advising health care provider, such as an emergency room physician, with a distant medical advisee and patient, such as a paramedic treating a trauma victim, using view-dependent 3D telepresence technology to provide a high-fidelity visual and aural sense of presence such that they can more effectively communicate and share information when diagnosing and treating the patient (see Fig. 8.1). Primarily, but not exclusively, we envision the technology enabling better patient healthcare through extemporaneous medical consultation across geographic distances in dynamic situations where patient diagnosis and treatment is time-critical and complex, but physical co-presence of medical experts and patients is not possible.

The basic technical idea for 3DMC is to use a relatively small number of cameras to "extract" (estimate) a time-varying 3D computer model of the remote environment and events. When coupled with head (or handheld viewer) position and orientation tracking, this should offer a consultant a continuum of dynamic views of the remote scene, with both direct and indirect depth cues through binocular stereo and head-motion parallax. Example scenarios are illustrated in Fig. 8.1. We believe that some day in the future such 3D technology could be a standard part of mobile emergency patient care systems (e.g., [6]) that today use 2D video technology.

We hypothesize that the shared sense of presence offered by view-dependent 3D telepresence technology will be superior to current 2D video technology, improving communication and trust between geographically-separated medical personnel, enabling new opportunities to share medical expertise throughout, between, and beyond medical facilities. To investigate this hypothesis our research addressed two fundamental questions: can we develop the technology for 3D telepresence in medicine, and will the technology be useful to the medical community? Thus our research consisted of three inter-related components: 3D technology research, prototype development, and evaluation.

Our 3D technology research explored the key technological barriers to 3D telepresence today, including real-time acquisition and novel view generation, tracking and displays for producing accurate 3D depth cues and motion parallax, and network congestion and variability. Our prototype development synthesized the results from our technology research efforts to create a system that aims to provide permanent,

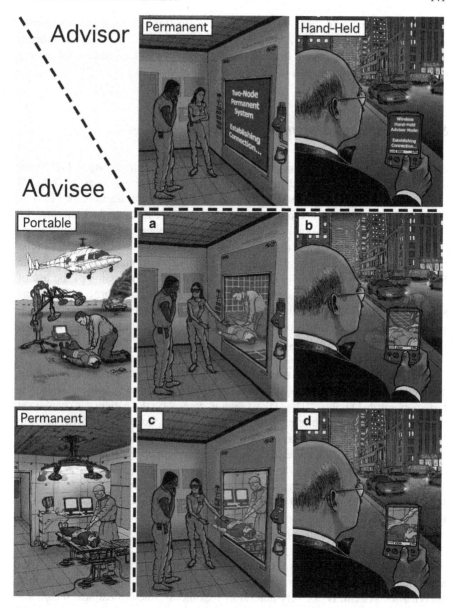

Fig. 8.1 Future vision of 3D telepresence for medical consultation. The *left column* illustrates examples of person-portable and permanent 3D telepresence technologies used by an *advisee*. The *top row* illustrates examples of permanent and hand-held technologies used by an *advisor*. Images (**a**)–(**d**) illustrate the shared sense of presence for corresponding advisor-advisee scenarios

portable, and hand-held access to 3DMC. Our evaluation effort assessed the potential effectiveness of 3DMC. Although some early results from each component have been reported elsewhere in conference papers, this is the first time all project components are presented in a holistic manner.

8.1.1 Medical Consultation via Video Technology

Medical consultation using two-dimensional (2D) video-conferencing and televideo technology has been explored in a variety of medical settings, such home-based health care [9, 20], prison-based healthcare [8, 10] and rural health care [23, 43]. Two limitations with respect to the technology arise repeatedly in the literature: the difficulty associated with obtaining the desired camera views and depth perception.

For example, camera view difficulties were mentioned in multiple places in the final report for the US National Library of Medicine's National Laboratory for the Study of Rural Telemedicine [23]. One example is in the discussion of the use of the 2D televideo system to observe children with swallowing disorders. The report states "Limitations of telemedicine services for management of feeding and growth issues include the need to rely on the interpretations of others during physical exams. At times the camera angles were not ideal to allow for clear pictures of the mouth during feeding" [23, p. 110].

The problem was also identified in [8] where they describe work using a computer-based telemedicine system for semi- and non-urgent complaints at a short-term correctional facility. "The lack of remote control on the patient care camera at the remote site by the examining emergency medical physicians requires the nurse to spend considerable time operating the camera and responding to technical instructions. This problem has been resolved in a recent system upgrade, but it was another important reason for nonuse" [8, p. 92].

Patients have also found this same limitation in 2D video technology. Georgetown University Medical Center [26] reports that in contrast to a face-to-face visit, the use of 2D video technology limits the physician's view of the patient, and as a result patients felt that the physician could not always "see" how the patient was "really doing."

One could try and address the visibility problem using multiple cameras. But switching between numerous disjoint views, as a security guard might with a surveillance system, is not very natural or feasible in time-critical health care situations. With a very large number of cameras and user head tracking, one could imagine automatic switching based on view position and orientation. But the quantity and configuration of cameras necessary to achieve smooth and appropriate switching over an operating room, as well as the 2D video storage and bandwidth needs, would be impractical. While pan-tilt-zoom cameras can help address this problem, they require additional technical skills, impose an additional cognitive load, and require additional time to adjust (which is difficult in a trauma situation).

In addition to the challenges in obtaining the desired 2D view of a remote patient, Tachakra states that "impaired depth perception is a significant problem in telemedicine." and notes that "the most important cue of depth is due to binocular disparity" [36, p. 77]. Similarly, a university "Clinical Studio" which used video conferencing to perform neurological examinations reported: "[Videoconferencing] technology is not difficult and can be [handled] by [Emergency Room] staff. However the images are in two-dimensions hence certain aspects of the exam could be enhanced by more than one camera angle" [36, p. 187].

In situations where depth perception would aid in the consultation, users must resort to secondary visual cues or verbal clarification from a remote collaborator, which both impose additional cognitive loads compared to the very natural views afforded if the consulting physician were able to "be there" with the patient and with the collaborating medical personnel. Tachakra describes several "coping strategies" that can be used to overcome the inherent limitation of 2D imagery. Chief among the coping strategies is the practice of "rotating the camera in the transverse plane about 30° at a time." Tachakra surmises that this controlled camera rotation "enables the consultant to build a three-dimensional mental image of the object by briefly storing a range of two-dimensional views" [36, p. 83]. This is not surprising given that object occlusion and motion parallax are two of the most powerful depth cues.

However it is often not realistic to require camera rotation as prescribed by Tachakra in emergency, time-critical health care situations in the field. For example, the time needed to rotate a camera and view the rotating imagery reduces the amount of time available to perform life-saving procedures. It reduces the number of on-site personnel who can provide assistance to a trauma victim as it requires the full-time effort of a trained on-site person. And, in some situations it may be physically very difficult to rotate a camera, e.g., when a victim of a car accident is lying on a hillside along the side of a road. To address these limitations, we developed 3D telepresence technology that provides depth perception and dynamic views.

8.1.2   Sense of Presence and Task Performance via 3D Technology

Previous research shows that 3D technology generally enables an increased sense of presence. For example, Hendrix and Barfield [16] report on three studies, in which they vary display parameters and attempt to assess a user's sense of presence. The results from the first and second study indicate that the reported level of presence is significantly higher when head tracking and stereoscopic cues are provided. The third study indicates that the level of presence increases with the visual field of view.

There is also evidence to suggest that view-dependent or immersive 3D displays increase users' task performance. For example, in a study of how various system parameters affect the illusion of presence in a virtual environment, Snow [32] reports a moderately positive relationship between perceived presence and task performance. Pausch and colleagues [29] found that users performing a generic pattern search task decrease task performance time by roughly half when they change from a stationary 2D display to a head-mounted (and tracked) 3D display with identical properties. Schroeder and colleagues [31] present the results of a study where distant collaborators attempted to solve a Rubik's cube type puzzle together. The authors compare face-to-face task performance with networked performance using both an immersive 3D display and a conventional 2D desktop display. They report that task performance using the networked immersive 3D display and in the face-to-face scenario were very similar, whereas desktop performance was "much poorer." Most recently, Mizell and colleagues [24] describe a careful 46-person user study aimed at determining whether or not immersive 3D virtual reality technology demonstrates a measurable advantage over more conventional 2D display methods when visualizing and interpreting complex 3D geometry. The authors report that the head-tracked 3D system shows a statistically significant advantage over a joystick-controlled 2D display.

Visual exploration of a 3D environment by means of a hand-held device, as illustrated in the right column of Fig. 8.1, has been previously proposed [14] and continues to be actively investigated [18, 19]. Applications include both viewing synthetic data and viewing computer-enhanced imagery of a user's real world surroundings. The latter is a very active research topic due to the growing interest in mobile (indoor or outdoor) Augmented Reality [30]. Today's mobile devices do not offer stereoscopic viewing (at least not a comfortable kind: the color anaglyph technique can of course be implemented on any platform), and so these types of displays can provide only (tracked) 2D perspective views into the remote environment. Yet even the earliest controlled study we are aware of [14] demonstrated good depth perception performance, comparable to typical desktop perspective displays such as the ones used in contemporary video games; a recent study [18] indicates that one can achieve a high degree of immersion and presence with "Hand-held Virtual Reality."

Thus previous research suggests that a 3DMC system may potentially improve information sharing and task performance in emergency medical situations, leading to improved patient health care. Yet there are significant technical challenges that must be overcome in order to create a 3DMC system.

8.1.3 3DMC Technical Challenges

To create a 3DMC system, we must reconstruct a dynamic remote 3D scene in real time. The most common approach to 3D scene reconstruction is to use cameras and effectively "triangulate" points in the scene. This involves automatically picking some feature in one camera's 2D image, finding the same feature in a second camera, and then mathematically extending lines from the cameras into the scene. The place where the lines intersect corresponds to the 3D location of the feature in the room. If one can do this reliably for a sufficient number of points in the scene, many times per second, then with some assumptions about the scene, and a lot of compute power, one can turn the dynamic collection of disjoint 3D points into a coherent dynamic 3D computer model that one can use like a flight simulator.

However there are at least three areas of fundamental difficulty associated with trying to reconstruct dynamic 3D models of real scenes: feature visibility, feature quality, and reconstruction algorithms. Features might not exist or might be confusing/ambiguous, they are hard to detect, isolate, resolve, and correlate, and automating the overall reconstruction process in light of these difficulties is a very hard problem. The state of the art is limited to static environments for large spaces, or dynamic events in relatively small controlled spaces.

8.2   Research

Three fundamental areas of technology research are required to create a 3DMC system: (1) computer vision methods for reconstruction of a 3D model/view of a dynamic scene; (2) remote consultation display paradigms; and (3) network resource management to support transmission of the 3D view to the remote consultant.

These areas and their relationships are reflected in Fig. 8.2 as follows: (a) and (b) on the left are associated with the reconstruction of a dynamic 3D model of the patient/procedure, (c) and (d) on the right are associated with the displays the remote consultant would use, and the networking research is associated with the geographical distance separation indicated in the middle.

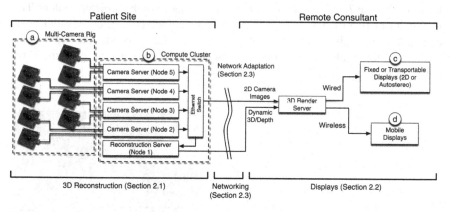

Fig. 8.2 System diagram showing the patient site components on the *left* and the remote consultant components on the *right*: (**a**) rigid multi-camera rig with eight Firewire cameras; (**b**) compute cluster with four camera nodes and one 3D reconstruction node; (**c**) a fixed or transportable viewing station with 2D or 3D (head tracked or autostereo) displays; (**d**) a mobile display such as a tracked PDA

8.2.1 3D Reconstruction

The 3D reconstruction process involves two major steps: the reconstruction of 3D *points* from 2D images and the reconstruction of 3D *surfaces* from the 3D points. To reconstruct 3D points from 2D images we developed a novel approach called *View-dependent Pixel Coloring* [41]. VDPC is a hybrid image-based and geometric approach that estimates the *most likely color* for every pixel of an image that would be seen from some *desired viewpoint*, while simultaneously estimating a 3D model of the scene. By taking into account object occlusions, surface geometry and materials, and lighting effects, VDPC can produce results where other methods fail: in the presence of textureless regions and specular highlights – conditions that are common in medical scenes.

As described in [42] we use the graphics hardware to perform the 3D reconstruction very quickly as the images arrive from the Camera Servers described in Sect. 8.3. The basic idea is to use the graphics hardware to rapidly render the camera images onto a series of virtual (computer graphics) planes swept through the scene, searching in parallel for the best color matches (least variance) at a dense set of points on the planes. As shown in Fig. 8.3, for a desired new view C_n (the red dot in Fig. 8.3), we discretize the 3D space into planes parallel to the image plane of C_n. Then we step through the planes. For each plane D_i, we project the input images on these planes, and render the textured plane on the image plane of C_n to get a image (I_i) of D_i. While it is easy to conceptually think of these as two separate operations, we can combine them into a single homography (planar-to-planar) transformation for which the graphics hardware is optimized to perform. For each pixel location (u, v) in I_i, we compute the mean and variance of the projected colors. The final color of (u, v) is the color with minimum variance in $\{I_i\}$, or the color most consistent among all camera views. The index i implicitly encodes the depth plane location, so the result contains both the most consistent color and the corresponding depth value at each pixel location.

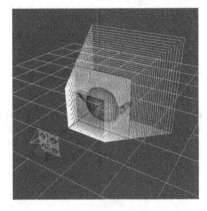

Fig. 8.3 A configuration where there are five input cameras, the small sphere in the lower left represents the new view point. Spaces are discretized into a number of parallel planes

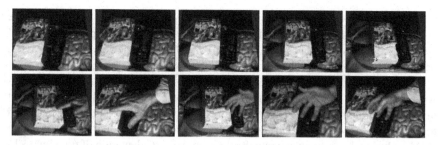

Fig. 8.4 A sequence of novel view images reconstructed using the system shown in Fig. 8.6. We set a box of Girl Scout cookies on top of the training torso to provide more obvious scene geometry

To achieve real-time performance we must make a few simplifying assumptions. First we assume that there are no occlusion problems, which allows us to compute photo-consistency values in a single pass. Second we assume that the scene is Lambertian, so that we can use color variance as the photo-consistency test. Third we use a smoothness constraint that aggregates weighted photo-consistency values from neighboring voxels, a practice commonly used in stereo. Under these assumptions, VDPC can be implemented entirely on commodity graphics hardware, taking advantage of the hardware's inherent parallelism.

When rendering stereoscopic views, we typically use VDPC to render one reference frame and then warp this frame to the second view based on the calculated depth map. In the places of occlusions we use neighboring pixels with large depth values (e.g., pixels further away from the center of projection) to fill in the gaps. Given the small baseline between the stereoscopic views, the artifacts caused by this in painting process are usually negligible. The final image quality depends on the displacement between the desired view and the input camera views. The larger baseline, the more artifacts are likely to become visible.

Figure 8.4 shows some results from our current prototype (Fig. 8.6). Those views were reconstructed on line, in real time. Note that the views were reconstructed and rendered from completely novel view points – none the same as any of the cameras, at different times during the live sequence.

8.2.2   Remote Consultation 3D Displays

When a medical advisor is on duty in a hospital, it is reasonable to expect that they might have access to facilities for stereoscopic, head-tracked viewing of dynamic 3D reconstructions of the remote patient and advisee. See, for example, Fig. 8.1a,c. Our current prototype addresses this scenario with a high-resolution monitor and a system for tracking the viewer's head position and orientation. The user wears a head band with three infrared LEDs that are tracked in real time by a small sensor unit. From this we compute the location of the user's dominant eye and render the reconstructed imagery from that point of view. Thus the user can observe the reconstructed view with natural/intuitive monoscopic head-motion parallax. We are also working on time-division multiplexing (shuttered) stereoscopic displays, and new autostereo displays that support multiple simultaneous viewers, with no glasses, and *independent* views.

We also want to provide the best possible 3D experience when the medical advisor is away from the hospital (Fig. 8.1, right). For a remote display we looked at *personal digital assistants* (PDAs). Most medical personnel are already accustomed to carrying a pager and mobile telephone, and some a personal digital assistant (PDA). Our goal was to investigate the development or adaptation of tracking technology and user interface paradigms that would allow a remote medical advisor to use a PDA as a "magic lens" [12, 13, 25, 28], providing a view of the remote patient, with natural interactive viewpoint control to help address occlusions and to provide some sense of depth.

We investigated a two-handed patient "prop" paradigm as shown in Fig. 8.5. Hinckley et al. introduced the idea, using a doll's head or rubber ball and various tools as 'props' for neurosurgeons visualizing patient data [17]. Hinckley found that users could easily position their hands relative to one another quickly – a task we all do frequently. For 3D medical consultation the advisor would have a physical prop that serves as a surrogate for the patient and a PDA that is tracked *relative to the prop*. For example the PDA cover could serve as the prop. The advisor would then hold the prop (PDA cover) in one hand and the PDA in the other, moving them around with respect to each other as needed to obtain the desired view. This paradigm provides the advisor with an instant visual target to aim their "magic lens" at, and also affords new ways of looking at the data. For example, an advisor can rotate the prop to quickly get a different view, rather than spending time and energy walking around to the other side. As a bonus, tracking a PDA relative to

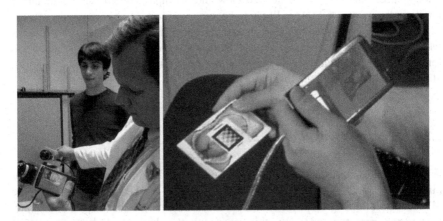

Fig. 8.5 *Left*: Our first tracked PDA prototype used a HiBall-3000™ tracking system [1], with sensors mounted on the PDA (Toshiba e800, *left hand*) and the surrogate (*right hand*). *Right*: Our current prototype uses a PointGrey DragonFly camera [3] mounted on the PDA (*left hand*). The prop (*right hand*) has a printed image of our training torso on it, along with a grayscale pattern. We use the ARToolkit [2] to track the surrogate with respect to the PDA (camera)

another object is a much more tractable problem than tracking a PDA relative to the world, opening up a number of potential tracking solutions that were otherwise not feasible [40].

We have developed three main software components: a Tracking Server; a PDA Server (that also acts as a client to the Tracking Server); and a PDA Client. The Tracking server gets images from the PDA camera, and uses ARToolkit [2] to track the surrogate (PDA cover) with respect to the PDA. The PDA Server, which currently runs on the viewing station server (Sect. 8.3), continually gets a complete representation of the reconstructed data from the compute/rendering cluster (b) via a dedicated Ethernet connection as described in Sect. 8.3. It also obtains the estimated position and orientation of the PDA from the Tracking Server using the Virtual-Reality Peripheral Network (VRPN) protocol [4]. It then renders a view of the most recent reconstruction from the estimated PDA position and orientation, and compresses the view to send to the PDA. The PDA Client (running on the PDA) receives compressed images and displays them, as well as relaying user input back to the PDA Server, such as thumbwheel-controlled field-of-view settings. Each of these components may be run on the same or separate machines.

8.2.3 Networking

In our target 3DMC scenarios the network path represents a significant bottleneck. We must carefully manage this resource in order to ensure that at all times we transmit the data that are most useful to the overall application and the goals of the user. In particular, 3DMC has the potential to generate many media streams with complex interstream semantic relationships, and the utility of the information from one data source may depend on the quality and utility of information from some other data source. For example, given two video cameras that share a significant overlap of field of view, it may be preferable to allocate available bandwidth to capture and transmit a high-quality image for only one of the two streams while allowing the quality of the other stream to degrade. Alternatively, it may be better to allocate bandwidth equally in order to achieve similar quality for both streams – useful for VDPC or stereo correlation and high-quality 3D reconstruction. Thus the challenge we face is twofold. First, how can we compactly and intuitively specify an adaptation policy to support specific user-level goals? Second, how can we efficiently evaluate that policy?

We need a framework for addressing the problems of adaptation that is more flexible than previous approaches, which often rely on statically defined priorities (e.g., prioritize audio over video) or simple rule-based decisions (e.g., when available bandwidth is X, do Y). In the framework we are developing, all possible trade-offs available to the application are mapped as nodes in an N-dimensional "utility space." Each dimension represents a particular axis for adaptation. Edges between nodes represent both encoding dependencies as well as encoding costs. The nodes and edges form a graph embedded within the utility space. The current information needs of the system are modeled as a "point of interest" within this space. The location of this point of interest changes to reflect the how the user is interacting with the system and the dynamics of the application. The utility of any given tradeoff is inversely proportional to the distance between the node that represents the tradeoff and the point of interest. Adaptation is now simply the process by which we select the most useful tradeoff available as defined by the ratio of utility to cost. Real-time evaluation is feasible since the adaptation is now a simple mechanical process of maintaining the set of possible tradeoffs in the graph and their distance to the point of interest. Additional technical details can be found in [15].

While the use of a utility space provides us with a mechanical means of driving adaptation and allows parsimonious specification of adaptation policy, the construction of a utility space for a specific application is more art than science. An application developer must incorporate appropriate domain knowledge in order to make choices about which adaptation dimensions are going to be modeled, how these dimensions are scaled relative to each other, the specific distance function that will be used to establish utility, and how the actions of the user are reflected by the point of interest. For 3DMC, we have identified five dimensions for adaptation: one each for time, video resolution, and relative change of visual content; and two that capture the notion of region of interest (i.e., field of view). Preliminary experiments show the system is able to make complex, non-trivial adaptation decisions in an emulated eight-camera setup such as in Fig. 8.6 [21]. Much of the remaining challenge is to develop and evaluate specific utility functions that correspond to the actual perceived quality of real users.

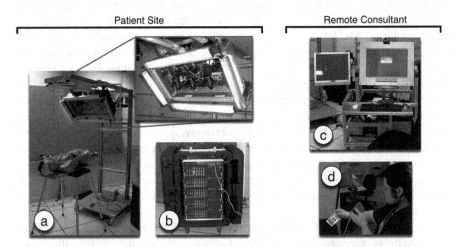

Fig. 8.6 Our proof-of-concept 3DMC prototype, with patient site components on the *left* and remote consultant components on the *right*: (**a**) portable camera unit with eight Firewire cameras and high-frequency area lights; (**b**) compute cluster; (**c**) a transportable consultant viewing station with 2D and 3D (head tracked or autostereo) displays; (**d**) a tracked PDA mobile display

8.3 Our 3DMC Prototype System

As shown in Fig. 8.6, our prototype consists of multiple components that would be associated with the patient site and the remote consultant: a portable camera unit (a), a portable compute/rendering cluster (b), and two consultant display device paradigms (c) and (d).

The portable camera unit (PCU) shown in (a) of Fig. 8.6 is a rolling unit holding a camera-lighting array with eight 640×480 resolution digital (IEEE 1394a) color cameras from Point Grey Research [3]. The cameras are currently mounted in two horizontal rows of four on a portable stand that can be positioned next to a patient. The cameras are positioned so their visual fields overlap the region of interest on the patient. Mounted around the cameras are multiple Stocker–Yale high-frequency fluorescent fixtures for flicker-free illumination. The entire array is mounted on a rolling cart with adjustable length and angle, and significant weight (underneath the base) to prevent tipping. The PCU includes an AC isolation transformer (mounted on the base) to meet the current leakage requirements of UNC Hospital's medical engineering staff.

The compute/rendering cluster (b) in Fig. 8.6 consists of five dual-processor servers in a transportable rack case. Four of the servers are connected to the PCU camera array via Firewire cables. These servers function as *Camera Servers*, compressing the PCU camera images and forwarding them via a dedicated gigabit Ethernet to the 5th server. Each camera server can optionally record the video streams to disk. The 5th server then decompresses the video streams, loading the color images into texture memory of the graphics card for view-dependent 3D reconstruction as described in Sect. 8.2.1. The unit also includes an AC isolation transformer. Note that because the PCU and the compute/rendering cluster in our prototype are connected via Firewire cables, they must generally be moved together. In the hospital we have placed the PCU inside a patient room, and the cluster just outside the door. In a real production system (in the future) the PCU (a) and compute/rendering servers (b) could be combined into a single unit.

The consultant viewing station (c) in Fig. 8.6 consists of a rolling cart with a dedicated server (lower shelf) that is connected to the compute/rendering cluster (b) by a single gigabit Ethernet cable. This Ethernet cable is the realization of the networking boundary shown in the middle of Fig. 8.2. It is the only link between the compute/rendering cluster (b) and the consultant viewing station (c). The connection could be across the hospital or across the world. The station has a high-speed and high-resolution 2D monitor (top right of cart), an Origin Instruments opto-electronic tracker (top of the 2D monitor) to track the viewer's head position and orientation, and an *autostereoscopic* display mounted on an articulated arm (left).[1] The unit also includes an AC isolation transformer.

---

[1] Autostereoscopic displays provide one more viewers with a fixed number of stereo views (for example eight) of a 3D scene, without the use of special user-worn glasses. See http://www.newsight.com.

The prototype of the tracked PDA mobile display (d) in Fig. 8.6 uses a DragonFly camera [3] mounted on a Toshiba e800 PDA. The camera is attached to the rendering PC (above) via a Firewire cable, which uses ArToolKit [2] to compute the relative position and orientation of the PDA. (This is discussed further in Sect. 8.2.2.) The current prototype is not truly portable because of the wired (Firewire) link to a computer, so we plan on implementing the tracking on a PDA with a built in camera in the future. Wagner and Schmalstieg have ported and optimized ArToolKit for PDAs [38, 39], and although their results indicated that the primary bottleneck is image capture rate, new PDAs are coming out with cameras better suited to video rate capture. This would allow a wireless interface.

Our 3DMC proof-of-concept system currently exhibits numerous shortcomings and limitations. Its acquisition system of eight cameras provides insufficient density for high quality reconstruction and insufficient range of views to enable reconstruction over a large viewing volume. The reconstruction algorithm (Sect. 8.2.1) makes simplifying assumptions in favor of speed, so the resulting 3D reconstructions often exhibit small gaps or other artifacts. The image quality of the reconstructions is often noticeably poorer than the quality of any of the eight input images.

The displays also exhibit several limitations. The commercial autostereo display, as virtually all such displays, presents fusible stereo imagery only within a range of distances from the display surface. Often a viewer instinctively moves closer to the display surface in an effort to more closely observe the medical scene, but is disappointed in losing the stereo imagery rather than gaining more detail. The PDA display exhibits even more severe limitations; it currently supports neither stereo nor head-tracking, although parallax is afforded through two-handed motions.

8.4 Evaluation

Because an extremely large amount of resources are needed to develop and deploy 3DMC we investigated its potential effectiveness already at this stage in its research and development cycle. If 3DMC has no possibility of having a positive impact on emergency medical care then there is no need to continue developing it. To evaluate its potential effectiveness we conducted a controlled experiment that compared the outcomes of a paramedic diagnosing and treating a trauma victim under one of the following three conditions: working alone, working in consultation with a physician using today's state-of-the-art video-conferencing, and working in consultation with a physician via a 3D proxy.

For the 3D proxy condition, the consulting physician was physically present in the same room as the mannequin and paramedic. The physician was allowed to freely move around in the room. However, the physician could not touch anything in the room and could only point to things using a laser pointer. This simulates the current vision and technical goals for 3DMC. Details regarding this approach and its validity can be found in [35].

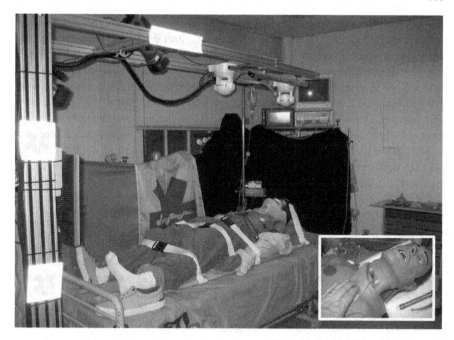

Fig. 8.7 *Human patient simulator* (HPS) staged as an accident victim for the experimental evaluation. Note the 2D video cameras and display mounted on the overhanging structure. Inset shows the HPS airway details

The experiment was a posttest, between-subjects design in which an emergency medical situation was realistically simulated. The medical situation involved the diagnosis and treatment of a trauma victim suffering from a blocked airway, when a victim's airway collapses. Each paramedic eventually had to perform a procedure beyond his/her level of everyday expertise – an emergency cricothyrotomy, i.e., make a surgical incision to open up the victim's windpipe, in order to save the victim's life. The victim was actually a METI human patient simulator, a sophisticated computerized mannequin that responds realistically to medicine and other treatments (Fig. 8.7). In all, 60 paramedics participated in the experiment; 20 per each condition.

Our evaluation measures included task performance and paramedics' perceptions of self-efficacy. A task performance protocol was developed in collaboration with emergency care physicians. It took into account task and subtask order, quality of task execution, harmful interventions performed, and task completion time. Each experiment session was recorded using four different video cameras (Fig. 8.7) that captured the monitor showing the victim's vital signs and multiple views of the paramedic, mannequin and physician (when present). These video-recordings were subsequently analyzed to grade task performance.

The theory of self-efficacy refers to a person's judgment of their capability to perform a certain task [5]. It fundamentally proposes that people are products as well as producers of their own environment and social systems. It suggests that people have self-beliefs that let them exercise control over their thoughts, beliefs and feelings which, in turn, effects how they behave. Self-efficacy affects a person's behavior such that people with high self-efficacy try harder when facing a difficult task and are less sensitive to failures and performance obstacles than people with low self-efficacy. Low levels of self-efficacy lead to more stress, slower recovery after failures, and higher likeliness to give up when facing problems. The primary, most influential source of self-efficacy is previous task performance experiences.

Self-efficacy is considered a major determinant of future task performance, i.e., task performance creates beliefs in ability which influence future task performance. There have been many studies investigating the validity of self-efficacy as a predictive measure. For example, Downey [11] compares and validates computer self-efficacy instruments with respect to predictive power on future performance, attitude and usage.

Because experiences, especially successful ones, are the strongest source of influence on self-efficacy [5] a paramedic's perceptions of self-efficacy after diagnosing and managing a difficult airway in a simulated medical scenario can help predict the paramedic's future performance in diagnosing and managing a difficult airway. That is, the theory of self-efficacy suggests that paramedics with higher levels of self-efficacy after diagnosing and managing a difficult airway will actually perform the same tasks better in the future.

After participating in a session each paramedic completed a self-efficacy post questionnaire. They also participated in a post interview, discussing their perceptions of the session.

Details of the data analysis can be found in [34]. The results illustrate that paramedics working in consultation with a physician via the 3D proxy tended to provide better medical care to trauma victims than paramedics working in consultation via today's 2D videoconferencing or paramedics working alone. Fewer subtask errors and harmful interventions were performed in the 3D proxy condition. Three paramedics working alone did not perform a cricothyrotomy, although a cricothyrotomy was required to save the victim. A total of eleven harmful interventions were performed when paramedics worked alone, and six were performed when paramedics consulted with a physician via 2D videoconferencing. In comparison only two harmful interventions were performed when the consultation occurred via the 3D proxy. However no statistically significant differences with respect to task performance times across conditions emerged from the data analysis.

Paramedics consulting with a physician via the 3D proxy reported the highest levels of self-efficacy. In comparison paramedics collaborating via 2D videoconferencing reported the lowest levels of self-efficacy. Furthermore the less work experience paramedics in the alone and 2D conditions had, the lower they rated their ability to treat similar patients in the future, whereas work experience had no impact at all on feelings of self-efficacy for paramedics in the 3D proxy condition. All of these results were statistically significant at the 0.05 level. These results suggest that the 3DMC may have a positive impact on future task performance, irrespective of a paramedic's years of professional experience.

However paramedics also mentioned several that 3DMC has the potential to make paramedics' work visible and subsequently evaluated in new ways that may have a negative impact on their careers. A paramedic explained:

> It kind of makes somebody nervous being monitored by a physician, someone of such higher training. And you're afraid to make a mistake because this person could be the person that ends up saying [whether] you get to do more, and where you work or not.

Ways to avoid such negative consequences that were mentioned by paramedics included opportunities for paramedics and physicians to get to know one another personally and professionally, open and non-judgmental communication practices, and increased understanding regarding joint responsibilities and priorities between paramedics in the field and physicians and nurses in the hospital.

Additional discussion regarding potential benefits and challenges of 3DMC from the perspective of physicians, nurses, medical center IT professionals, and large and small medical center administrators can be found in [33].

8.5   Cost Analysis

We generally adhere to the philosophy that to make something *cost*-effective one must first make it *effective*, and we are not yet prepared to make a strong argument that the systems we envision will be effective much less cost effective. Real-time on-line 3D telepresence is aimed at long-term needs for more efficient (timely and effective) medical consultation, improved health care, and (eventually) reduced costs. However the work is very early (beyond the current state of the art) which makes it difficult to assess the likely costs.

Several studies have attempted to quantify the cost effectiveness of conventional 2D televideo systems used for remote medical consultations, and we believe the end costs for 3D systems would be comparable. For example, [9, 10, 20, 37] and [43] concluded that the 2D systems they evaluated were (or would be) cost effective. In particular, Agha et al. concluded in [43] that "Telemedicine is a cost-effective alternative for the delivery of outpatient pulmonary care for rural populations with limited access to subspecialty services." They claim that the cost effectiveness is related to three major factors: (a) cost sharing; (b) effectiveness of telemedicine in terms of patient utility and successful clinical consultations; and (c) indirect cost savings accrued by decreasing cost of patients' lost productivity. We would expect the systems we propose to also benefit from these factors.

And while it would be imprudent at this point to make specific cost projections for 3D systems, it is possible that a "transportable" 3D telepresence node such as we describe could, in the future, be developed for roughly 2–5 times the fixed (one time) costs of a conventional 2D telemedical consultation system. This increased cost would be due almost exclusively to an increase in the number of cameras and computers, which (incidentally) are continually decreasing in price. One might add cost for networking infrastructure also, however it is possible (perhaps reasonable to assume) that future networking infrastructure between healthcare facilities will improve independently from this proposed work. For example, [27] points out how the Telecommunications Act of 1996 has and continues to improve access and reduce costs for urban and (explicitly in the act) rural health care providers. In any case, the networking techniques we developed (Sect. 8.2.3) are aimed at operation over a variety of capabilities, and as such could (if proven effective) perhaps support some functionality with the existing infrastructure.

8.6 Discussion

In the 2001 PITAC report to the President of the United States, Transforming Health Care Through Information Technology, recommendation five states that the US Department of Health and Human Services should establish an "aggressive research program in computer science" that addresses 'long-term needs, rather than the application of existing information technology to biomedical problems' [27, p. 13]. 3DMC is an aggressive research project in computer science addressing long-term needs for more effective medical consultation, improved health care, and (eventually) reduced medical care costs as described above. The work is in an early stage but we have made progress developing computer vision methods for reconstruction of a 3D model/view of a dynamic scene, remote consultation displays, and network resource management algorithms to support transmission of 3D views. The results were realized in a prototype system.

The Office for the Advancement of Telehealth [27] points out how the Telecommunications Act of 1996 has and continues to improve access and reduce costs for urban and rural health care providers. Our project builds on this tradition, discovering new ways technology can be used to provide emergency healthcare outside hospital settings to trauma victims. Trauma is a significant health problem, frequently referred to as the "hidden epidemic of modern society" because it is responsible for more productive years lost than heart disease, cancer and stroke combined [7,22]. 3DMC can potentially bring needed healthcare expertise to trauma victims before they are transported to hospitals. The sooner victims receive appropriate expert medical care, the shorter their recovery time and lower their medical care costs. Thus 3DMC could have a significant impact on patient healthcare in the future.

Acknowledgements At UNC-Chapel Hill we thank Jim Mahaney and John Thomas for their technical support; and former Graduate Research Assistant Max Smolens for his early contributions to the effort. We thank the paramedics who participated in the evaluation. This effort is primarily supported by National Library of Medicine contract N01-LM-3-3514: "3D Telepresence for Medical Consultation: Extending Medical Expertise Throughout, Between and Beyond Hospitals," and in part by NSF grant EIA-0303590: "Ubiquitous Pixels: Transforming Collaboration & Teaching with Pervasive Wall Displays."

References

1. 3rdTech, Inc. (2005). http://www.3rdtech.com/
2. ARToolkit (2005). http://www.hitl.washington.edu/artoolkit/
3. Point Grey Research (2005). http://www.ptgrey.com/
4. Virtual Reality Peripheral Network (2006). http://www.cs.unc.edu/Research/vrpn/
5. Bandura, A.: Self-efficacy: the exercise of control. W.H. Freeman, New York (1997)
6. Chu, Y., Huang, X., Ganz, A.: Wista: A wireless transmission system for disaster patient care. In: Proceedings of BROADNETS: 2nd IEEE/CreateNet International Conference on Broadband Networks, pp. 118–122. Omnipress, Boston (2005)
7. Coates, T., Goode, A.: Towards improving prehospital trauma care. Lancet **357**(9274), 2070 (2001)
8. David G. Ellis, M., James Mayrose, P., Dietrich V. Jehle, M., Ronald M. Moscati, M., Guillermo J. Pierluisi, M.: A telemedicine model for emergency care in a short-term correctional facility. Telemedicine Journal and e-Health **7**(2), 87–92 (2001)
9. Dimmick, S.L., Mustaleski, C., Burgiss, S.G., Welsh, T.S.: A case study of benefits and potential savings in rural home telemedicine. Home Healthcare Nurse **18**(2), 125–135 (2000)
10. Doty, E., L. H. Zincone, J., Balch, D.C.: Medicine Meets Virtual Reality: Healthcare in the Information Age, chap. Telemedicine in the North Carolina Prison System, pp. 239–241. IOS Press, Eds. J. Weghorst, Hans B. Sieburg, and Karen S. Morgan (1996)
11. Downey, J.: Measuring general computer self-efficacy: The surprising comparison of three instruments in predicting performance, attitudes, and usage. Hawaii International Conference on System Sciences **8**, 210a (2006). DOI http://doi.ieeecomputersociety.org/10.1109/HICSS.2006.268
12. Fitzmaurice, G.W.: Situated information spaces ad spatially aware palmtop computers. Communications of the ACM **36**(7) (1993)
13. Fitzmaurice, G.W., Buxton, W.: The chameleon: Spatially aware palmtop computers. In: ACM CHI94. Boston, MA USA (1994)
14. Fitzmaurice, G.W., Zhai, S., Chignell, M.H.: Virtual reality for palmtop computers. ACM Transactions on Information Systems **11**, 197–218 (1993)
15. Gotz, D., Mayer-Patel, K.: A general framework for multidimensional adaptation. In: MULTIMEDIA '04: Proc. of the 12th annual ACM international conference on Multimedia, pp. 612–619. ACM, New York (2004). DOI http://doi.acm.org/10.1145/1027527.1027671
16. Hendrix, C., Barfield, W.: Presence within virtual environments as a function of visual display parameters. Presence: Teleoperators and virtual environments **5**(3), 274–289 (1996)
17. Hinckley, K., Pausch, R., Goble, J.C., Kassell, N.F.: Passive real-world interface props for neurosurgical visualization. In: CHI '94: Proceedings of the SIGCHI conference on Human factors in computing systems, pp. 452–458. ACM, New York (1994). DOI http://doi.acm.org/10.1145/191666.191821
18. Hwang, J., Jung, J., Kim, G.J.: Hand-held virtual reality: A feasibility study. In: Proceedings of the ACM symposium on Virtual reality software and technology, pp. 356–363. ACM (2006)
19. Hwang, J., Jung, J., Yim, S., Cheon, J., Lee, S., Choi, S., Kim, G.J.: Requirements, implementation and applications of hand-held virtual reality. IJVR **5**(2), 59–66 (2006)
20. Kaiser Permanente: Outcomes of the kaiser permanente tele-home health research project. Archives of Family Medicine **9** (2000)
21. Krishnan, S., Mayer-Patel, K.: A utility-driven framework for loss and encoding aware video adaptation. In: MULTIMEDIA '07: Proceedings of the 15th international conference on Multimedia, pp. 1026–1035. ACM, New York, NY, USA (2007). DOI http://doi.acm.org/10.1145/1291233.1291459
22. Meyer, A.: Death and disability from injury: A global challenge. J Trauma **44**(1), 1–12 (1998)
23. Michael G. Kienzle, M.: Rural-academic integration: Iowas national laboratory for the study of rural telemedicine. Tech. rep., National Laboratory for the Study of Rural Telemedicine (2000)
24. Mizell, D.W., Jones, S.P., Slater, M., Spanlang, B., Swapp, D.: Immersive virtual reality vs. "flat-screen" visualization: A measurable advantage. (Submitted for publication). (2003)

25. Mohring, M., Lessig, C., Bimber, O.: Video see-through AR on consumer cell-phones. In: Proc. of the Third IEEE and ACM International Symposium on Mixed and Augmented Reality (ISMAR'04), pp. 252–253. IEEE Computer Society, Washington, DC, USA (2004). DOI http: //dx.doi.org/10.1109/ISMAR.2004.63
26. Mun, S.K.: Project phoenix: Scrutinizing a telemedicine testbed. final project report, national library of medicine, contract #n01-lm-6-3544. Tech. rep., Georgetown University Medical Center (2000)
27. Office for the Advancement of Telehealth: Telemedicine report to congress. Tech. rep., U.S. Department of Health and Human Services, Health Resources and Services Administration (2001)
28. Pasman, W., van der Schaaf, A., Lagendijk R.L., Jansen F.W.: Accurate overlaying for mobile augmented reality. Computers and Graphics 23, 875–881 (1999)
29. Pausch, R., Shackelford, M.A., Proffitt, D.: A user study comparing head-mounted and stationary displays. In: Proc. of IEEE Symposium on Research Frontiers in Virtual Reality, pp. 41–45. IEEE (1993)
30. Reitmayr, G., Drummond, T.W.: Going out: Robust modelbased tracking for outdoor augmented reality. In: Proceedings of 5th IEEE and ACM International Symposium on Mixed and Augmented Reality (ISMAR, pp. 109–118 (2006)
31. Schroeder, R., Steed, A., Axelsson, A.S., Heldal, I., Abelin, A., Wideström, J., Nilsson, A., Slater, M.: Collaborating in networked immersive spaces: As good as being there together? Computers & Graphics, Special Issue on Mixed Realities – Beyond Conventions 25(5), 781–788 (2001). http://www.elsevier.com/gej-ng/10/13/20/57/34/32/article.pdf
32. Snow, M.P.: Charting presence in virtual environments and its effects on performance. Ph.D. thesis, Virginia Polytechnic Institute and State University (1996)
33. Söderholm, H.M., Sonnenwald, D.H.: Visioning future emergency healthcare collaboration: Perspectives from large and small medical centers. Journal of the American Society for Information Science and Technology 61(9), 1808–1823 (2010).
34. Söderholm, H.M., Sonnenwald, D.H., Manning, J.E., Cairns, B., Welch, G., Fuchs, H.: Exploring the potential of video technologies for collaboration in emergency medical care. part ii: Task performance. Journal of the American Society for Information Science and Technology 59(14), 2335–2349 (2008). DOI 10.1002/asi.20939. http://www3.interscience.wiley.com/journal/121378034/abstract
35. Sonnenwald, D.H., Söderholm, H.M., Manning, J.E., Cairns, B., Welch, G., Fuchs, H.: Exploring the potential of video technologies for collaboration in emergency medical care. part i: Information sharing. Journal of the American Society for Information Science and Technology 59(14), 2320–2334 (2008). DOI 10.1002/asi.20934. http://www3.interscience.wiley.com/journal/121378032/abstract?CRETRY=1&SRETRY=0
36. Tachakra, S.: Depth perception in telemedical consultations. Telemed J E Health 7(2), 77–85. (2001)
37. Telemedicine Directorate: Advanced concept technology demonstrations letter of finding. Tech. rep., Walter Reed Army Medical Center (2000). http://www.salud.gob.mx/unidades/sic/cits/doctosFuente/2001REPO.pdf
38. Wagner, D., Schmalstieg, D.: First steps towards handheld augmented reality. In: ISWC '03: Proceedings of the 7th IEEE International Symposium on Wearable Computers International Symposium on Wearable Computers. IEEE Computer Society, Washington, DC, USA (2003)
39. Wagner, D., Schmalstieg, D.: Handheld augmented reality displays. In: G. Welch (ed.) Proceedings of 2nd Emerging Display Technologies Workshop (EDT 2006), pp. 35–36 (2006)
40. Welch, G., Noland, M., Bishop, G.: Complementary tracking and two-handed interaction for remote 3d medical consultation with a pda. In: G. Zachmann (ed.) Proceedings of Trends and Issues in Tracking for Virtual Environments, Workshop at the IEEE Virtual Reality 2007 Conference. Shaker, Charlotte, NC USA (2007)
41. Yang, R.: View-dependent pixel coloring—a physically-based approach for 2d view synthesis. Ph.d. thesis, University of North Carolina at Chapel Hill (2003)

42. Yang, R., Pollefeys, M., Yang, H., Welch, G.: A unified approach to real-time, multi-resolution, multi-baseline 2d view synthesis and 3d depth estimation using commodity graphics hardware. International Journal of Image and Graphics (IJIG) **4**(4), 1–25 (2004)
43. Zia Agha MD, M., Ralph M. Schapira, M., Azmaira H. Maker, P.: Cost effectiveness of telemedicine for the delivery of outpatient pulmonary care to a rural population. Telemedicine Journal and e-Health **8**(3), 281–291 (2002)

Chapter 9
SEE MORE: Improving the Usage of Large Display Environments

Achim Ebert, Hans Hagen, Torsten Bierz, Matthias Deller, Peter-Scott Olech, Daniel Steffen, and Sebastian Thelen

Abstract Truly seamless tiled displays and stereoscopic large high-resolution displays are among the top research challenges in the area of large displays. In this paper we approach both topics by adding an additional projector to a tiled display scenario as well as to a stereoscopic environment. In both cases, we have developed new focus+context screen approaches: a multiple foci plus context metaphor in the tiled display setup and a 2D + 3D focus+context metaphor in the stereoscopic scenario.

9.1 Introduction

Of the machine components that are part of human-computer interaction for visualization, the display has one of the largest effects. The display determines the physical size of the viewport, the range of effective field-of-view and resolution that is possible, and the types of feasible interaction modalities. All other interactions must be placed in the context of the display. If you have ever seen a movie on a large screen TV, then you have been surely impressed with the captivating display that makes the viewing innately attractive. This is not limited to entertainment alone. People get the same sensations, impressions, and further their understanding of displayed information in more serious applications. So we need to understand how we can use them most effectively and where the advantages and disadvantages

A. Ebert (✉), H. Hagen, P.-S. Olech, S. Thelen, and T. Bierz
University of Kaiserslautern, D-67663 Kaiserslautern, Germany
e-mail: ebert@cs.uni-kl.de, hagen@cs.uni-kl.de, olech@cs.uni-kl.de, s_thelen@cs.uni-kl.de, bierz@cs.uni-kl.de

M. Deller and D. Steffen
German Research Center for Artificial Intelligence (DFKI),
University of Kaiserslautern, D-67663 Kaiserslautern, Germany
e-mail: matthias.deller@dfki.de, daniel.steffen@dfki.de

S. Coquillart et al. (eds.), *Virtual Realities*, DOI 10.1007/978-3-211-99178-7_9,
© Springer-Verlag/Wien 2011

of this medium are. As large screens have become cheaper and more commonplace in our environments, the research need has become more urgent.

Large displays are either a single display device or an assembly of display devices. In their survey, Ni et al. [NSS+06] distinguish six display hardware configurations. In the context of this paper, the following two are the most important ones:

- Multi-monitor desktop, tiled LCD panels, projector arrays: Tiled displays are 2D arrays build of common LCD displays or projectors. Compared to projectors, LCDs usually are less expensive, easier to align, and take less space. On the other hand, projector arrays do not have bezels between each tile.
- Stereoscopic displays, CAVEs and derivatives: By computing an image for each eye, these displays provide three-dimensional visualizations to the viewer. In order to see the 3D effect, the user typically has to wear special glasses. Compared to 2D high-resolution displays, they usually have a much lower resolution.

In addition, Ni et al. present their top ten research challenges in the area of large high-resolution displays. The first two topics on their list are *truly seamless tiled displays* and *stereoscopic large high-resolution displays*. In this paper we present two new focus+context screen metaphors [BGS01a] which address both problems.

Our first metaphor focusses on LCD-based multi-monitor systems and makes a contribution to address the bezel problem, i.e., to cover the missing bezel information. For many applications, data is continuous and correct spatial relationships are needed to interpret information in the right way. Here, monitor bezels can be very distracting and interfere with the objective of providing precise visualizations of the data. Our approach is to enhance the bezel area by projecting the missing image information directly onto the bezels. Thereby we create a nearly seamless image, which is composed of the high-resolution information displayed on the monitors and somewhat lower resolution information projected onto the bezels to fill the gaps.

The second metaphor addresses large stereoscopic displays. The technical limitations of such projective systems usually result in a loss of detail and sharpness of the visualized information. These limitations especially disadvantageous, in cases where two-dimensional context information (like user manuals, measurements, menus, etc.), need to be displayed. To accommodate these problems, we present a novel approach called $5DF+C$, which introduces a focus+context screen for large virtual environments. The concept is implemented by enhancing a common 3D projective system with a third (high resolution) projector. Here, the additional projector is used for displaying an additional high resolution 2D focus area.

In the following we provide an overview of related work, explain addressed problems in detail and introduce our new concepts and their benefits for tiled resp. stereoscopic display environments. We also present results from user studies we conducted in order to evaluate the effectiveness of our approaches.

9.2   State of the Art

In our modern information society, large display systems are widely-used. Accordingly, a lot of research has been done in this area. Some of these approaches deal with effective visualization metaphors (e.g., focus+context techniques), while others are focussing on more hardware-related issues.

With the building of tiled display systems one tries to solve the problem of screen real estate combined with a moderate to high resolution, where regular single device resolutions reach their limits. Within the research area of tiled displays there have been several interesting approaches, for both projector-based and monitor-based tiled display systems. By using multiple projectors one bypasses the bezel problem associated with LCD-based systems, but however has to cope with several other issues. The calibration of the projectors is a major challenge in setting up a really seamless system (see, e.g., [SSM01, CCF+00], and [Sto01]).

For monitor-based tiled displays there have been several approaches trying to minimize or bypass the bezel problem. In Mackinley et al. [MH04] the bezel problem of the wideband display was approached by presenting novel interface techniques and seam aware applications. In the paper of Ball et al. [BVC+05] parts of the monitor frame were physically removed to minimize gaps between neighboring displays. Most other publications do not explicitly deal with the bezel problem and accept all consequences of monitor frames passing the display.

The bezel problem implies other challenges when setting up monitor-based tiled systems. For navigation tasks it is necessary that the pointer can cross monitor bezels when moving from one display to another without irritating the user. Baudisch et al. [BEHG04] compensate offset and warping effects by applying appropriate transformations to the movement of the cursor. The approach even works for multi-monitor systems having non-uniform screen resolutions.

Another interesting application with a certain relevance to our approach is the focus+context screen [BGS01b]. In the focus+context screen a large low-resolution area coming from a projector, is used to display context information. A small high-resolution screen integrated into the context area displays detailed information of the current focus. The combination of different display technologies is what makes the focus+context screen resemble the approach we are going to present.

A lot of research work is dealing with the problem of information overload. An overcoming way is presented in Shneiderman's guideline for design of information visualization [Shn96]: "overview first, zoom and filter, then details on demand". Seen from a more practical point of view, we can distinguish the approaches in zoomable interfaces, overview+detail, focus+context, and focus+context screens. Much research has been done in all of these areas. Therefore, the following considerations on the related work can only show a small excerpt.

Zoomable interfaces [PF93] display information objects sequentially by organizing them in space and scale. Panning techniques are used to change the visible area of the information space. In parallel, zooming allows the change of scale. The most common approach is geometric zoom. Here, the size of an object can be regulated on a linear scale. If the semantic of the objects is known, semantic zooming approaches can handle complex relations between scale and appearance. Other zoomable interfaces are constant density zooming [WLS98] and non-linear panning and zooming [FZ98]. Usually, zoomable interfaces are controlled by keyboard and mouse.

Overview and detail (o+d) techniques show an overview of the entire information space, together with a detailed view of part of the contents [HF01,PCS95]. They use a specialized multi-window arrangement to deal with the problem of information overload. A global view of the information space is given in an overview window. An additional detail window is allowing the user a close-up view. Users navigate using the overview window rather than using the detail window, which makes o+d interfaces improve the efficiency of the user's navigation [BW90]. A drawback of o+d interfaces is the demand of more screen space than interfaces without overviews. Also, the time used for visual search can increase because of the spatially indirect relation between overview and detail window [CMS99].

In contrast to o+d, *focus plus context* (f+c) approaches join the current focus of attention and its context, so the switching between windows is not required anymore. While the most important data at the focal point is shown at full size and detail, the context areas around the focal point are compressed to free valuable screen space for the focus. Examples for f+c techniques are Fisheye Views [Fur86, Fur99], Perspective Wall [MRC91], and Document Lens [RM99]. The main drawback of f+c approaches is the introduction of visual distortion. The degree of distortion increases with the distance from the focus point. Like other f+c approaches, *Focus+context screens* (f+c screens) can simultaneously display focus and context information. However, they provide both areas in a single, non-distorted view. F+c screens are low resolution displays with an embedded high resolution display, e.g. Baudisch et al. [BGS01a]. The main advantage in comparison to common f+c approaches is the preservation of the scaling of the content across the whole display. The geometry of the content is thereby preserved.

9.3   SEE MORE on Tiled Displays

The bezel problem of LCD-based tiled displays is caused by monitor frames that pass the screen and disturb the impression of a seamless display. Monitors with minimal bezel areas can reduce this effect but still the lattice they create is one of the major disadvantages of the LCD-based approach. There are usually two ways of dealing with this problem, each having its own advantage and disadvantages:

1. The *offset approach* simply ignores the bezels and their effect on the continuousness of a scene. A mouse cursor crossing the border of one monitor jumps into the neighboring one and objects in that region appear to be stretched by an offset that is equal to the bezel size of monitors plus the distance between them. This can create strange effects and seems to be intolerable at a first glance. However the offset approach has the advantage that no image information gets lost at the monitor borders.

2. The *overlay* approach tries to compensate the bezel problem by pretending the lattice to be an overlay of the image. In contrast to the offset approach mouse cursors and other objects will vanish under the bezels. The result is an overall continuous image with one having the impression of looking through a window with vertical and horizontal bars. While this seems to be preferable to the discontinuities that are caused by the offset approach, one has to keep in mind that potentially important information can be "hidden" by the bezels.

A choice between them depends on the particular application. In any case the perception of a scene will be affected by the technique being used. We would like to refer to this circumstance as *loss of semantics*.

Another, more subtle effect can lead to additional misinterpretation when using the overlay approach. In neurosciences it is known that two collinear oblique lines separated by two vertical parallels can cause failures of perception. The collinear lines appear to be offset, even if in fact they are aligned. This effect was first discovered in 1860 by the physicist Poggendorff and is therefore named *Poggendorff Illusion*. Although the reasons for the effect are not yet well understood, it has an impact on the visualization with LCD-based tiled display, for Poggendorff situations arise at the area of contact of two monitors.

In contrast to the aforementioned techniques, our approach combines the availability of all pixel information (offset) with the continuousness of the whole scene (overlay) and presents a technique that neither distorts objects across the boundary of monitors nor covers important information without giving a hint of what is happening beneath the bezels. The following section describes the idea of our approach.

9.3.1   The Tiled Focus+Context Approach

The screens of our tiled display (see Fig. 9.1) have bezels of approximately one inch size, so that we have to cope with offsets of about two inches between neighboring monitors (gaps caused by the monitor rack can increase the offset). We make a virtue out of this necessity and use the monitor frames as display areas for additional projectors. The monitors display the scene treating the bezels as overlays while at the same time missing information is provided by the projectors. The projectors only render those parts of a scene that would be hidden by the lattice and mask the LCD areas with black squads. We have bond the black frames of our displays with diffuse reflecting white cardboard and create a lattice-like reflective screen as illustrated in Fig. 9.1. The image parts displayed on the lattice provide missing information in a projector dependent resolution (e.g., $1{,}920 \times 1{,}080$), which is significantly lower than the single monitors (e.g., $2{,}560 \times 1{,}600$), so that the whole scene can be divided into regions of very high and rather low resolution. When using more than one projector each of them can be restricted to a predefined subset of monitors. Thereby the lattice resolution is increased.

Fig. 9.1 A 3 × 3 *TF+C* setup (*white bezels*)

Although high-resolution and low-resolution devices have been used together previously, e.g. in the focus+context screen [BGS01b], it has never been done with the intention of solving the bezel problem.

Regarding the calibration of our Tiled Focus+Context (*TF+C*) system, various methods for aligning projectors in terms of geometry, luminance and color can be found in literature. In principle every known technique for the calibration of multi-projector systems can be applied. However, since we focus on the *TF+C* approach in general and not on a fully sophisticated implementation we restrict ourselves to the *geometric* alignment of projectors to a certain cut-out of the display wall, knowing that additional techniques can be applied to make the transition between projectors and LCDs as seamless as possible.

The render framework for driving the system is implemented in C++ and OpenGL, and uses MPI (Message Passing Interface) for managing synchronization and communication between executing threads. Window and event handling is done via SDL (Simple Direct Media Layer). All software is open source and thus supports portability to different platforms. The framework is a master-slave system [NSS+06], i.e. all nodes execute an instance of the application while a dedicated node – the master – is responsible for processing user input and making it known to the slaves.

In order to show the flexibility of our approach, we have installed it on two prototypic systems of different size and resolution. The smaller one consists of 5 commodity PCs driving a 3 × 3 tiled LCD wall (Fig. 9.1) which are connected via Ethernet. The 30 in displays achieve a resolution of 2,560 × 1,600 pixels and have bezels of approximately one inch size. The LCD matrix achieves a combined resolution of 7,680 × 4,800 pixels. Monitor frames are enhanced by a projector with a resolution of 1,920 × 1,080.

The second and larger display is a 200 megapixel tiled display with a resolution of 25,600 × 8,000 pixels. 50 Apple Cinema Displays are arranged in a 10 × 5 grid and are driven by 25 Power Mac G5 computer nodes. A designated additional node is responsible for managing high-level display functions.

These two different display configurations show the high scalability of our approach. Multiple projectors can be used to fill the entire display bezel area of a very large display. The number of projectors necessary to cover the entire area mainly depends on the aspect ratio of the display as well as on the budget and on the desired resolution. However, a comparably small number of additional projectors is needed to cover a large number of monitors.

9.3.2 Examples

Provided with the enhanced tiled display wall, we wanted to investigate its benefits in different scenarios.

When working on construction plans it is necessary to display components without distortions. Figure 9.2 illustrates the results obtained when visualizing an engine block with different bezel strategies. With the offset approach, the drive shaft in Fig. 9.2a appears discontinuous and broken to the middle. While this is most obvious effect, further distortion artifacts among the components can easily be made out. Apparently the offset approach is not an adequate choice for visualizing proportion sensitive data.

In Fig. 9.2b some artifacts are eliminated with the overlay approach. Distortion effects are not existent but still black bars traverse the scene and disturb perception. The $TF+C$ approach in Fig. 9.2c outperforms the other two methods. Although bezels can still be made out by color and resolution, information provided on the lattice and the absence of severe optical artifacts make our projection-based approach superior to the other two.

Figure 9.3 demonstrates how the overlay approach causes another serious problem that goes beyond the pure loss of information about the *geometry* of an object. While it is sometimes possible to deduce missing parts from the information remaining (based on experience and assumptions about the geometry), the hiding of *higher order* information is more severe. In the picture, the front area of a car coincides with a bezel bar of the display wall. Radiator and headlights are invisible. At the same time some other important information is missing – namely the emblem identifying the car. As a consequence, someone unfamiliar with cars will find it hard to determine the manufacturer, especially because the shapes of most today's car resemble

Fig. 9.2 A CAD example demonstrating the three approaches: (**a**) Offset approach, (**b**) Overlay approach, (**c**) New $TF+C$ approach

Fig. 9.3 *TF+C* providing *important* image information, such as, in this case, a company logo

each other. With the *TF+C* system, this drawback is eliminated. The information provided on the lattice clearly identifies the car as a Volkswagen.

Both examples show that without correction the image is either ambiguous or impossible to interpret. In most cases failure to correct for missing pixels leads to undesired results, loss of image information, or discontinuities. *TF+C* is compatible with a large number of application areas, ranging from medical imaging to engineering, from design to visual analytics, and from advertising to signage.

9.3.3 Interacting with the TF+C Display

At first glance, using projectors to project onto the bezels of LCD-based tiled walls seems to impose constraints to the possibilities of interacting with the displays. For obvious reasons back projection is not an option for *TF+C*. With this, the problem arises that users enter the projection area and cast shadows on the silver screen lattice. Note, that only the bezels are affected by the shadow while the images displayed on the LCD panels remain the same.

Our projector alignment allows inclined positions of up to 10° between projectors and displays. Placing the projector collateral to the screen allows users to move in front of the displays at reasonable distances without shadowing the lattice. This supports a habit we observed when users interact in front of large displays. Users wanting to have an overview of the scene step back in order to gain a larger field of view and be aware of context information. A more detailed view requires them to step forward so that they can focus on the object of interest. Physical movement in front of large displays is a natural focus+context technique we would like to refer to as *human zooming*. Our *TF+C* approach supports human zooming as follows: Low resolution information on the lattice is essential to perceive a seamless image from a "context distance" away from the monitors. When stepping forward, the extremely high resolution of LCDs becomes more important and allows to investigate details of a scene. Information on the lattice is not necessarily needed anymore, as its resolution is much lower than that of the LCDs. Another option to minimize the effect of shadows is to overlay the projector image with a second projection from an opposite direction. Because the lattice is illuminated twice, users can touch the silver screen and still perceive information on it. Jaynes et al. [JWS$^+$01] described a refined implementation of this idea using cameras to detect and remove shadows.

9.3.4 Evaluating the TF+C Approach

The examples given in Sect. 9.3.2 show that the *TF+C* method is able to prevent loss of semantics and make presentation of information on multi-monitor systems appear more complete. Now we need to find out if our approach has an impact on how users are able to perform certain tasks using the enhanced display. We conducted a user study in order to quantify the effect of *TF+C* and compare it with the overlay and offset approach. We investigated users' performance in *navigation tasks* and *perception experiments*. Our main hypothesis was that additional information provided by *TF+C* displays and the lack of image distortions positively affect user performance. We expected them in general to perform faster and more precise.

The experiment was designed to investigate how users perform under the three different conditions. Because we did not want to focus on a particular visualization technique, we kept tasks visually as simple as possible.

For a navigation experiment we chose a variant of the commonly known game *HotWire*. HotWire is a game of skill in which users have to move a mouse cursor along a predefined track without leaving an area of tolerance around it. We considered the game suited for our experiment because it forces users to navigate across monitor frames and explicitly deal with the advantages and disadvantages of the different approaches. In this experiment the independent variable is the method being used expressed at three different levels (offset, overlay, *TF+C*). The dependent variable is the time spent to complete the task. While running a game we measure the time and record the locations where the tolerance area was left.

More subjective aspects were addressed through perception experiments. We asked users to rate the difficulty of assigning collinear lines in a *Poggendorff* test. We set up a scene consisting of multiple oblique white lines running across all monitors. At the bezels users were asked to identify corresponding lines which proved to be rather hard considering the Poggendorff illusion. They could verify their decision by adding color to the scene and thereby identify corresponding lines by identic color. Naturally the effect does not arise with the offset approach since no information gets lost and distortions are directly due to the technique. *TF+C* prevents the effect because all lines appear continuous.

We asked 20 volunteers to participate in our study, four of them being female. Most participants stated to have considerable knowledge with computers and to use multi-monitor systems never or only rarely. Participants had to pass each test three times – one time for each condition, which corresponds to one of the three approaches. In order to prevent learning effects and symptoms of fatigue, we

Table 9.1 Averages and standard deviations of performance time for HotWire

Approach	Mean time (s)	Standard deviation of time (s)
Offset	142.5	56.95
Overlay	263.15	142.40
TF+C	109.05	33.25

permanently changed the order of approaches. Further we constantly altered the sequence of tracks presented in HotWire.

Table 9.1 summarizes the average amount of time for HotWire, including the standard deviations. A one-way ANOVA (Analysis of Variance) study was conducted with the data from the navigation task. We found the effect of approaches on *how fast* users complete the task was significant, $F_t(2, 57) = 16.01$, $p_t < 0.001$. Tukey's HSD (honestly significantly different) post-hoc test revealed significant pairwise differences among the means of the offset and overlay methods and the overlay and $TF+C$ methods, respectively. No significant difference could be attested for offset and $TF+C$. The analysis of *error rates* coincides with these discoveries, i.e. $F_e(2, 57) = 19.52$, $p_e < 0.001$.

$TF+C$ clearly outperforms the overlay technique. The recordings of error positions show that with the overlay approach, 89% of errors occurred at the bezels of the tiled display. However, we found no significant difference between offset and $TF+C$. We conclude that the availability of the complete image information is the most important aspect for completing a given task in a reasonable time.

The Poggendorff illusion had a clear effect in our perception experiment. Participants stated to have moderate to high difficulties in assigning collinear lines at the vertical borders of screens. This shows the effect cannot be ignored when designing applications for LCD-based tiled display walls. Offsets made the task generally harder. Naturally the task was greatly simplified with the additional information on the lattice. Perception with $TF+C$ was rated highest with an average of 5.65 (1 = poor, 6 = excellent). The difference between overlay (3.25) and offset (2.55) was not significant. The efficiency rating shows that a majority of participants, about 90%, considers $TF+C$ to increase performance.

A more detailed description of the evaluation can be found in [ETO+10].

9.4 SEE MORE on Stereoscopic Screens

Humans organize data sets according to certain individual criteria. They have the ability to visually collect and evaluate the overall contents of illustrations and images very fast. Even if humans are most efficiently in performing those tasks, computers can even enhance and assist the capabilities of the user. An example is the providing of a quick notion of elements relevant for or related to his current task by using its search capabilities in sorted and unsorted data resources, and its ability to quickly access and sort large amounts of data. All elements in the data set and the queries are represented as vectors in a high-dimensional metric vector space that is, e.g., spanned by the set of unique terms occurring in our information space. The relevance of one element to another is then related to the angle between the two element vectors, where smaller angles indicate a higher similarity of the elements, and consequently in a higher relevance.

Based on the premise of a personal document-based information space [WH01], we have developed and implemented our idea of an immersive virtual environment for interacting with such an information space. The result is a three-dimensional virtual environment realizing an enhanced writing desk. Each document is represented with a thumbnail view of its first page as well as all additional markings and personal annotations. Documents with similar content are visually linked and emphasized according to their degree of similarity. The user can enter several queries resulting in change of relevance of the single documents. Additionally, the user can manually revaluate the importance of the selected document for his current task, thus also changing the relevance of the connected similar documents. During our research, we have implemented several metaphors for visualizing the relevance of documents. We found that – especially when showing larger data sets (e.g., 200–300 elements) – stereoscopic visualization of relevance outperforms other preattentive features like color, size, and orientation by far. Therefore, we have chosen a three-dimensional, stereoscopic projection screen (PowerWall) to represent the context area in our system, which will be referred as "5DF+C" [EDD⁺08].

The advantage of presenting the relevance as a 3D metaphor conflicts with visualizing detail views for manifold reasons. First, resolution of the common stereoscopic screens is very poor, especially when put into relation to the display's physical dimensions. Second, different images for the left and the right eye have to be computed and projected. Even if calibrated very well, the matching of both projectors' images is not at 100%, which result in the blurring of details. Therefore, we propose 5DF+C as a new way of adding detail to a stereoscopic visualization environment. This is done by adding a third, consumer-grade projector to the PowerWall setup, which integrates a two-dimensional focus area into the three-dimensional context projection. The setup is drafted roughly in Fig. 9.4.

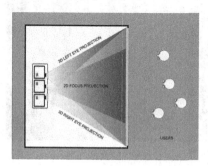

Fig. 9.4 Prototype setup

The stereoscopic image is rendered by two projectors with a $1{,}400 \times 1{,}050$ resolution onto a 2.9×2.3 m semi-translucent screen through circular polarizing filters of opposite handedness. The additional 2D projector provides a focus region of 0.9×1.3 m at a 3.5 times higher resolution.

Central system requirements are to integrate the 2D focus region into the 3D context region without any gaps, while avoiding multiple projections. In the system configuration described above, all projectors project onto the same screen. In order to avoid multiple interfering images, both stereoscopic projectors need to create a black object depending on the size of the focus region at the respective area. The synchronicity of the communication between the involved computers is achieved by using a dedicated sub-network of our LAN that does not have to handle any other traffic.

In order to integrate the 2D focus projection properly into the 3D virtual environment, the exact position of the focus region has to be known. This is necessary to enable a smooth transition between the view of a document in the 3D environment and the 2D focus region. These documents have to cover the same pixels to ensure the desired smooth transition. However, since the focus projector can be located freely somewhere behind the projection wall, both the position of the focus region and its dimensions within the virtual environment are not known a priori. Therefore, when setting up the projection hardware, the position and size of the focus region have to be made known to the software controlling the whole system (see Fig. 9.5). This is done in a manual calibration process. Therefore, the position of the 2D focus region must be mapped to the corresponding 3D position. For determining the x_{3D} and y_{3D} coordinates, the 3D coordinates that correspond to the upper left and lower right corners of the 3D focus region have to be determined. Once this information is available, the corresponding x and y 3D-coordinates for any pair (x_{2D}, y_{2D}) of 2D-coordinates can be easily computed. Based on this calibration information, the desired smooth transition between 3D and 2D view can be achieved by moving the selected focus object into the projection plane, enlarging it to the desired size and then changing to the high resolution 2D view.

Fig. 9.5 The 2D+3D focus+context environment

9.4.1 3D Context Information Space

Visual search is one of the most common activities in everyday life. Especially considering the multitude of visual distractions, humans are amazingly efficient at finding the objects they are looking for. Guided Search [Wol94] separates the whole process in two stages, preattentive and attentive. As the name suggests, preattentive vision is the process that operates before conscious attention is directed to an object. It describes the information available to the eye at a single glimpse. Visual features that enable the finding of target objects within this process are named preattentive cues. Some of the features that have been found to be preattentive include orientation, size, color, intensity, flicker, motion, and 3D depth cues including stereoscopic depth. Guidance mechanisms use the information acquired from preattentive vision to direct attention to objects or areas serially. During this attentive stage, the visual system examines objects it has been guided to during the preattentive stage to integrate different visual features of the object. The aspiration of using preattentive visual features for attention guidance in the context area is to assist the orienteering process by enhancing this mechanism with knowledge computed from the contents of the documents. After initiating a keyword search, the user is not presented with a descending list of document titles. Rather, he still has an overview of his complete document collection with the documents important for his current search being highlighted in a way to reflect their relevance to his search terms. If this is done using preattentive features in an advantageous way, the user can get a notion of which documents are relevant at a single glance.

In our research, we have explored and tested promising visual features for guiding the user's attention to document representations in an information-rich virtual environment [DEB+07]. We found that stereoscopic depth has been the most promising preattentive cue, emphasizing relevant documents effectively. Another advantage is the fact that the notion of important documents located closer to the user is a very intuitive way to visualize relevance.

9.4.2 Context Space Transformation

In our system, we use the 3D context visualization to interact with documents and with clusters of related documents on a more abstract level. When the user selects a document to request more details, the high resolution 2D focus area is blended in. In order to achieve the transition from the 3D context view to the 2D focus view, there are two general tasks to be done. First, the context space has to be distorted such that room for opening the document in the focus region becomes available. Since the 2D projector has got a fixed position, the maximal focus area is determined by the size and location of the 2D projector's image. Second, the selected document has to be moved into the focus region where it is scaled to fill it completely (see Fig. 9.6a). When this process is completed, the 2D high resolution view finally becomes visible.

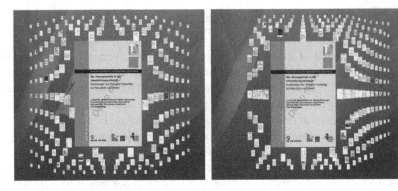

Fig. 9.6 (a) Distortion of the context area along the axis between center of the focus area and center of the document. (b) Distortion of the context area combined with tablecloth metaphor

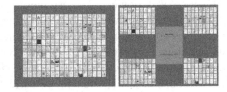

Fig. 9.7 (a) Selecting a document in the context (b) Highlighting the selected document and opening a copy in the focus area

In a first metaphor, the context space only is distorted in a way that space for the focus area opens up. The selected document is highlighted at its (distorted) position and a copy of this document is opened in the focus area. This approach is depicted in Fig. 9.7. However, when the documents in our context area are variously colored, highlighting the selected document may not have the desired effect since the highlighting color only is one among many others and it does not emphasize the highlighted document any more. In order to overcome this effect and to give an unambiguous hint which document is shown in the focus, we have realized the link between the document in the context and its copy in the focus area using the "Rubber Band" metaphor [BCR+03].

Our second metaphor moves the context space such that, before the distortion, the selected document is located in the center of the focus region. This approach is based on the tablecloth metaphor [RCB+05]. Now the whole context area is scaled and (in this example) moved upwards and to the right such that afterwards the selected document is located at the center of the focus region. The scaling (which of course again takes place in the focus plane) can easily be computed by the ratio between the x- and y-coordinates of the difference of the 3D context area in and the center of the 2D area. For the other three quadrants, the movements are performed symmetrically. A second distortion then moves the context documents away so that there again is space for displaying the complete focus region in high resolution (Fig. 9.8b). With

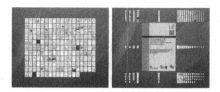

Fig. 9.8 (**a**) Selecting a document in the context. (**b**) Showing the focused document within its original context

this approach we preserve the original order of the documents and have realized a real f+c metaphor.

In order to generate the necessary space to display the focus region, we distort the context area in the projection plane. Additionally, the documents need to be scaled in order to be able to still show all the documents in the context area. In the example in Fig. 9.6a, we have only applied the distortion of the context area. Of course it is also possible to combine this distortion with the tablecloth metaphor, preserving the original context of the document viewed in the focus area (Fig. 9.6b).

When the above mentioned distortion of the context area is applied, the original arrangement of the documents in rows and columns is destroyed. In order to preserve the original alignment of the documents, we have also implemented another version of the distortion of the context area. This one is shown in Fig. 9.7b. Here, the context area is divided into octants. Within the single octants, the context area is either distorted only in one or in both directions, using the same principles as described above.

The distortions described so far are only valid for documents lying in the projection plane. However, our documents are ordered in a 3D document space. Therefore, we have extended the described distortions to documents lying before or behind this plane. To achieve this, the distortions are scaled according to central projection using the intercept theorem.

9.4.3   Focus Plus Context

Having identified size and arrangement of the focus-region, we place the desired document into the predetermined area of interest. For the purpose of providing a zero-gap integration, we initially show the stereoscopic visualization of the selection. Next, we use a so-called progressive multi-dimensional-transition technique (PMDT). This approach allows a smooth and continuous transition from the three-dimensional to the two-dimensional focus area.

After this, the stereoscopic representation of the document is faded out. At the same time the 2D focus is superimposed on the 3D focus-region. Initially, we use low resolution and cache-buffered document textures. By doing so, we can guarantee an optimal system performance and do not affect the user's potential for interacting and percepting. While the user's eyes linger on the document, the two-dimensional high resolution texture is then stepwise superimposed on the low resolution texture. Moreover, the user is able to browse the pages of the chosen document within the presented two-dimensional scope. We also use a two-dimensional progressive transformation technique while leaving through the document pages.

Finally, the specified focus region provides the possibility of a context-in-context visualization metaphor. Apart from the three-dimensional context environment, our interface offers the additional opportunity to visualize document specific information within the 2D focus-area. Thus, the user is provided with an intuitive and fast navigation through the selected document.

9.4.4 Experimental Evaluation

Our evaluation was conducted in the same virtual environment as described above. In [DEB+07] we have already shown that users can find the most relevant data better and faster in a stereoscopic representation. This is especially true for the context area, because a large number of objects is usually presented there. For focus-related tasks, we estimated that subjects would perform better in 2D instead of 3D. Additionally, we hypothesized that they would be able to work even more accurately if a high resolution 2D focus area is used.

We recruited 17 subjects, 41% of which were female. Only 18% had some experiences with virtual environments before our evaluation. The subjects were presented with 3D representations of several document collections containing about 150–300 documents. In the first step, they had to enter a number of search queries in order to find the documents that are best related to their search terms. Then the participants were asked to select the most important document, causing the selected document to appear in the focus area. Three different configurations of the focus area were shown to them:

- 3D mode: Like in any other common stereoscopic environment, the focus object is shown in 3D. To assure the best readability and as little stress for the human eye as possible, its stereo rendering parameters are computed so that it appears exactly on the projection plane.
- 2D low-res mode: Now our additional 2D projector is projecting the focus object. Compared to the 3D mode, the resolution of the projected object remains unchanged. Thus, we only apply a decrease in dimensionality.
- 2D high-res mode: The focus area is also projected by the 2D projector. But this time, the resolution of the focus is four times higher, taking advantage of the maximum native resolution of the projector.

For each variation the subjects were asked to read a small part of the document aloud, as accurately and quickly as possible. The whole evaluation process was recorded by video cameras, which made the analysis of reading times and error rates easier and more reliable.

Several reading tests were performed by each participant of our evaluation. In a first pass, they had to read the same text portion in all three different focus modes. The text was relatively short (number of words: 30) and written in the subjects' native language (German). Because the text stayed the same in each configuration, the measurements can be compared straightforward. However, we feared that the repetitive reading of the same paragraph would maybe influence the reading time and error rate (caused by memorizing the text). Therefore, in a second pass, different text passages were presented to them in each focus mode. The texts were carefully selected so that they were comparable in length and in degree of difficulty. We found no significant differences between the two passes.

In 3D focus mode, our subjects encountered serious problems in reading the example text. Only four subjects (23%) were able to fulfill the task completely. Three participants (18%) aborted the tests after reading a few words, the remaining ten subjects (59%) refused to read the texts. In the post-study questionnaire, they named the low resolution in combination with the blurring of the stereoscopic projection as the main reason. The average reading time was about 60 s (0.5 words/s) with a standard variance $\sigma = 11.15$.

In 2D low-res mode, all subjects were able to complete the reading tests. In addition, the reading was nearly three times faster compared to the 3D focus. The average reading time was about 22 s (1.4 words/s) with $\sigma = 6.02$. When only taking into account the subjects able to fulfill the 3D reading task, the improvement was even higher (average time = 17 s; 1.8 words/s; $\sigma = 3.59$).

Like in 2D low-res mode, all subjects completed the tests when using the high-res focus. Again, the overall reading performance was improved (by factor 3.7 compared to 3D, by factor 1.4 compared to the 2D low-res). The average reading time was 16 s (1.9 words/s) with $\sigma = 2.37$. As in 2D low-res mode, the subjects who were able to fulfill the 3D reading task performed better than the others (average time = 14 s; 2.1 words/s; $\sigma = 2.63$).

The subjects who finished the 3D reading task made four reading errors in average ($\sigma = 1.26$). When switching to the 2D low-res focus area, the error rate dropped to 0.33 ($\sigma = 0.65$). Like in reading time, the 2D high-res mode clearly outperformed both other focus modes: no participant made any mistakes (error rate = 0.0; $\sigma = 0.0$).

The results of our experimental evaluation support show that a 3D focus area not only results in a bad readability, but also in an extremely low efficiency. Both 2D modes significantly improve this situation. However, we have to note that the difference between 3D and 2D is by far higher than the difference between 2D low-res and 2D hi-res. In the latter, the most noticeable fact is that the performance differences among the subjects are conspicuously lower than with a low-res focus area (the standard variance drops from 6.02 to 2.37 in reading time and from 0.65 to 0.0 in error rate).

9.5 Conclusions and Future Work

In this paper, we have presented two approaches that contribute to two of the most important research challenges in the area of large displays: *truly seamless tiled displays* and *stereoscopic large high-resolution displays*. Both metaphors make use of an additional projector and result in two new focus+context screen approaches.

In multi-monitor systems, display frames distort scenes or cover important parts of them. This leads to potential misinterpretation of image information. We showed that it is possible to bypass the drawbacks of conventional tiled display techniques with minimal effort. Our hybrid approach combining different display technologies is able to produce an almost seamless tiled display avoiding discontinuities while at the same time maintaining a majority of pixel information.

In large stereoscopic environments, the technical limitations of such projective systems usually result in a loss of detail and sharpness of the visualized information. We introduced a focus+context screen approach that enhances a common 3D projective system with a third (high resolution) projector. We showed that our 2D+3D focus+context screen improves the users' performance with respect to both reading time and error rate significantly. In the future, we are planning to investigate how new interaction techniques specifically tailored to both setups can further improve the users' cognitive performance in complex scenarios. This aims at developing interaction metaphors that seamlessly support the user both in a 3D and in a 2D environment. We expect such new integrated interaction techniques to augment additionally the gain in performance and efficiency that we have already achieved with our presented approaches.

Acknowledgements We thank Nahum Gerson for his long time support, fruitful discussions, and constructive comments. We also thank all our study participants. This research has been funded by the Federal Ministry of Education and Research (BMBF) and DFG's International Research Training Group 1131.

References

[BCR+03] P. Baudisch, E. Cutrell, D. Robbins, M. Czerwinski, P. Tandler, B. Bederson, and A. Zierlinger. Drag-and-pop and drag-and-pick: Techniques for accessing remote screen content on touch- and pen-operated systems. In *Proceedings of Interact'03 (2003)*, pages 57–64, 2003.

[BEHG04] P. Baudisch, E. Cutrell, K. Hinckley, and R. Gruen. Mouse ether: accelerating the acquisition of targets across multi-monitor displays. In *CHI '04: CHI '04 extended abstracts on Human factors in computing systems*, pages 1379–1382, New York, NY, USA, 2004. ACM.

[BGS01a] P. Baudisch, N. Good, and P. Stewart. Focus plus context screens: combining display technology with visualization techniques. In *UIST '01: Proceedings of the 14th annual ACM symposium on User interface software and technology*, pages 31–40, New York, 2001. ACM.

[BGS01b] P. Baudisch, N. Good, and P. Stewart. Focus plus context screens: combining display technology with visualization techniques. In *UIST*, pages 31–40, 2001.

[BVC+05] R. Ball, M. Varghese, B. Carstensen, E. D. Cox, C. Fierer, M. Peterson, and C. North. Evaluating the benefits of tiled displays for navigating maps. In *IASTED International Conference on Human-Computer Interaction*, 2005.

[BW90] D. Beard and J. Walker. Navigational techniques to improve the display of large two-dimensional spaces. *Behaviour and Information Technology* 9(6):451–466, 1990.

[CCF+00] Y. Chen, D. W. Clark, A. Finkelstein, T. C. Housel, and K. Li. Automatic alignment of high-resolution multi-projector display using an un-calibrated camera. In *VIS '00: Proceedings of the conference on Visualization '00*, pages 125–130, Los Alamitos, CA, USA, 2000. IEEE Computer Society.

[CMS99] S. K. Card, J. D. Mackinlay, and B. Shneiderman, editors. *Readings in information visualization: using vision to think*. Morgan Kaufmann, San Francisco, CA, USA, 1999.

[DEB+07] M. Deller, A. Ebert, M. Bender, S. Agne, and H. Barthel. Preattentive visualization of information relevance. In *HCM '07: Proceedings of the international workshop on Human-centered multimedia*, pages 47–56, New York, 2007. ACM.

[EDD+08] A. Ebert, P. Dannenmann, M. Deller, D. Steffen, and N. Gershon. A large 2d+3d focus+context screen. In *CHI '08 extended abstracts on Human factors in computing systems*, pages 2691–2696, Florence 2008. ACM.

[ETO+10] A. Ebert, S. Thelen, P.-S. Olech, J. Meyer, and H. Hagen. Tiled++: An enhanced tiled Hi-Res display wall. *IEEE Trans. Vis. Comput. Graph.*, 16(1):120–132, 2010.

[Fur86] G. W. Furnas. Generalized fisheye views. In *CHI '86: Proceedings of the SIGCHI conference on Human factors in computing systems*, pages 16–23, New York, 1986. ACM.

[Fur99] G. W. Furnas. The fisheye view: a new look at structured files, pages 312–330, 1999.

[FZ98] G. W. Furnas and X. Zhang. Muse: a multiscale editor. In *UIST '98: Proceedings of the 11th annual ACM symposium on User interface software and technology*, pages 107–116, New York, 1998. ACM.

[HF01] K. Hornbæk and E. Frøkjær. Reading of electronic documents: the usability of linear, fisheye, and overview+detail interfaces. In *CHI '01: Proceedings of the SIGCHI conference on Human factors in computing systems*, pages 293–300, New York, 2001. ACM.

[JWS+01] C. Jaynes, S. Webb, R. M. Steele, M. Brown, and W. B. Seales. Dynamic shadow removal from front projection displays. In *VIS '01: Proceedings of the conference on Visualization '01*, pages 175–182, Washington, 2001. IEEE Computer Society.

[MH04] J. D. Mackinlay and J. Heer. Wideband displays: mitigating multiple monitor seams. In *CHI '04: CHI '04 extended abstracts on Human factors in computing systems*, pages 1521–1524, New York, 2004. ACM.

[MRC91] J. D. Mackinlay, G. G. Robertson, and S. K. Card. The perspective wall: detail and context smoothly integrated. In *CHI '91: Proceedings of the SIGCHI conference on Human factors in computing systems*, pages 173–176, New York, 1991. ACM.

[NSS+06] T. Ni, G. S. Schmidt, O. G. Staadt, R. Ball, and R. May. A survey of large high-resolution display technologies, techniques, and applications. In *VR '06: Proceedings of the IEEE conference on Virtual Reality*, page 31, Washington, DC, USA, 2006. IEEE Computer Society.

[PCS95] C. Plaisant, D. Carr, and B. Shneiderman. Image-browser taxonomy and guidelines for designers. *IEEE Softw.*, 12(2):21–32, 1995.

[PF93] K. Perlin and D. Fox. Pad: An alternative approach to the computer interface. In *Proceedings of the 20th Annual ACM Conference on Computer Graphics (SIGGRAPH '93)*, pages 57–64, New York, 1993. ACM.

[RM99] G. G. Robertson and J. D. Mackinlay. The document lens, pages 562–569, 1999.

[RCB+05] G. Robertson, M. Czerwinski, P. Baudisch, B. Meyers, D. Robbins, G. Smith, and D. Tan. The large-display user experience. *IEEE Comput. Graph. Appl.*, 25(4):44–51, 2005.

[Shn96] B. Shneiderman. The eyes have it: A task by data type taxonomy for information visu-
         alizations. In *VL '96: Proceedings of the 1996 IEEE Symposium on Visual Languages*,
         page 336, Washington, 1996. IEEE Computer Society.

[SSM01] R. Sukthankar, R. G. Stockton, and M. D. Mullin. Smarter presentations: Exploit-
         ing homography in camera-projectorsystems. In *Computer Vision, 2001. ICCV 2001.
         Proceedings. Eighth IEEE International Conference on*, pages 247–253 vol.1, Wash-
         ington, 2001. IEEE Computer Society.

[Sto01] M. C. Stone. Color and brightness appearance issues in tiled displays. *IEEE Comput.
         Graph. Appl.*, 21(5):58–66, 2001.

[WH01]   S. Whittaker and J. Hirschberg. The character, value, and management of personal
         paper archives. *ACM Trans. Comput.-Hum. Interact.*, 8(2):150–170, 2001.

[WLS98] A. Woodruff, J. Landay, and M. Stonebraker. Constant information density in
         zoomable interfaces. In *AVI '98: Proceedings of the working conference on Advanced
         visual interfaces*, pages 57–65, New York, 1998. ACM.

[Wol94] J. M. Wolfe. Guided search 2.0: A revised model of visual search. *Psychon. Bull. Rev.*,
         1(2):202–238, 1994.

Chapter 10
Inner Sphere Trees and Their Application to Collision Detection

Rene Weller and Gabriel Zachmann

Abstract We present a novel geometric data structure for approximate collision detection at haptic rates between rigid objects. Our data structure, which we call *inner sphere trees*, supports different kinds of queries, namely, proximity queries and the penetration *volume*, which is related to the water displacement of the overlapping region and, thus, corresponds to a physically motivated force. Moreover, we present a time-critical version of the penetration volume computation that is able to achieve very tight upper and lower bounds within a fixed budget of query time. The main idea is to bound the object from the *inside* with a bounding volume hierarchy, which can be constructed based on dense sphere packings. In order to build our new hierarchy, we propose to use an AI clustering algorithm, which we extend and adapt here. The results show performance at haptic rates both for proximity and penetration volume queries for models consisting of hundreds of thousands of polygons.

10.1 Introduction

Collision detection between rigid objects plays an important role in many fields of robotics and computer graphics, e.g. for path-planning, haptics, physically-based simulations, and medical applications. Today, there exist a wide variety of freely available collision detection libraries and nearly all of them are able to work at interactive rates, even for very complex objects [36]. Most collision detection algorithms dealing with rigid objects use some kind of bounding volume hierarchy (BVH). The main idea behind a BVH is to subdivide the primitives of an object hierarchically until there are only single primitives left at the leaves. Several kinds of bounding volumes have been proposed in the past, the most popular are axis aligned bounding boxes (AABBs), oriented bounding boxes (OBBs) [12], oriented polytopes (k-Dops)

R. Weller (✉) and G. Zachmann
Department of Computer Science, Clausthal University, D-38678 Clausthal-Zellerfeld, Germany
e-mail: rwe@tu-clausthal.de, zach@tu-clausthal.de

S. Coquillart et al. (eds.), *Virtual Realities*, DOI 10.1007/978-3-211-99178-7_10,
© Springer-Verlag/Wien 2011

[23] and spheres. BVHs guarantee very fast responses at query time, as long as no further information than the set of colliding polygons is required for the collision response. However, most applications require much more information in order to solve or avoid the collisions.

One way to do this is to compute the exact time of contact for the objects. This method is called continuous collision detection. Another approach, called penalty methods, is to compute repelling forces based on the penetration depth. However, there is no universally accepted definition of the penetration depth between a pair of polygonal models [30, 37]. Mostly, the minimum translation vector to separate the objects is used, but this may lead to discontinuous forces. Another approach is to avoid penetrations or contacts before they really happen. In this case, the minimum distance between the objects can be used to compute repelling forces.

Haptic rendering requires update rates of at least 200 Hz, but preferably 1 kHz to guarantee a stable force feedback. Consequently, the collision detection time should never exceed 5 ms.

One example of an approach that offers fairly constant query times are voxel-based methods like the Voxmap Pointshell algorithm (VPS), where objects, in general, have to be voxelized (the "voxmap") and covered by a point cloud (the "point shell"). This can be very memory consuming and produce aliasing artifacts due to the discretization errors.

10.1.1 Main Contributions

This chapter contributes the following novel ideas to the area of collision detection:

- A novel geometric data structure, the *Inner Sphere Trees (IST)*, that provides hierarchical bounding volumes from the *inside* of an object (Fig. 10.1).
- A method to compute a dense sphere packing inside a polygonal object.
- We propose to utilize a clustering algorithm to construct a sphere hierarchy.

Fig. 10.1 Our *Inner Sphere Trees* are based on sphere packings of arbitrary polygonal objects (*left*). They are suitable for different kinds of geometric queries, namely proximity queries (*middle*) and our new method for computing the penetration depth, the *penetration volume* (*right*)

- A unified algorithm that can compute for a pair of objects, based on their ISTs, both an approximate minimal distance and the approximate penetration volume; the application does not need to know in advance which situation currently exists between the pair of objects.
- A method to compute forces from the penetration volume that are continuous, both in direction and value.

The IST and, consequently, the collision detection algorithm is independent of the geometry complexity; they only depend on the approximation error.

The main idea is that we do not build an (outer) hierarchy based on the polygons on the boundary of an object. Instead, we fill the interior of the model with a set of non-overlapping simple volumes that approximate the object's volume closely. In our implementation, we used spheres for the sake of simplicity, but the idea of using inner BVs for lower bounds instead of outer BVs for upper bounds can be extended analogously to all kinds of volumes. On top of these inner BVs, we build a hierarchy that allows for fast computation of the approximate proximity and *penetration volume*.

The penetration volume corresponds to the water displacement of the overlapping parts of the objects and, thus, leads to a physically motivated and continuous repulsion force. According to [9, Sect. 5.1], it is "the most complicated yet accurate method" to define the extent of intersection, which was also reported earlier by [29, Sect. 3.3]. However, to our knowledge, there are no algorithms to compute it efficiently as yet.

While it is true that the penetration volume could actually decrease when the objects move further after an intersection has occurred, several definitions of penetration distance suffer from the same problem. This case usually only occurs when the objects are highly non-convex or when they are already "half-way through" each other.

Our data structure can support all kinds of object representations, e.g. polygon meshes or NURBS surfaces. The only precondition is that they be watertight. In order to build the hierarchy on the inner spheres, we utilize a recently proposed clustering algorithm that allows us to work in an adaptive manner.

In addition, inner sphere trees not only allow for computing both separation distance and penetration volume, but they also lend themselves very well to time-critical variants, which run only for a pre-defined time budget.

The results shows that our new data structure can answer both kinds of queries at haptic rates with very little loss of accuracy.

10.2 Previous Work

Collision detection has been extensively investigated by researchers in the past decades. There exist a large variety of freely available libraries for collision detection queries. However, the number of libraries that also support the computation of proximity queries or the penetration depth is manageable. Additionally, most of them are not designed to work at haptic refresh rates, or they are restricted to simple point probes [17], or require special objects, such as convex objects as input.

In the following, we will give a short overview of classical and also state of the art approaches to manage these tasks.

10.2.1 BVH Based Data Structures

Johnson and Cohen [18] present a generalized framework for minimum distance computations that depends on geometric reasoning and includes time-critical properties. The PQP library [24] uses swept sphere volumes as BVs in combination with several speed-up techniques for fast proximity queries. We used it in this chapter to compute the ground truth for the proximity queries. Sphere trees have also been used for distance computation [16,27,32]. The algorithms presented there are interruptible and they are able to deliver approximative distances. Moreover, they all compute a lower bound on the distance, while our ISTs derive an upper bound. Thus, a combination of these approaches with our ISTs could deliver good error bounds in both directions.

Johnson and Willemsen [19] computes local minimum distances for a stable force feedback computation and uses spatialized normal cone pruning for the collision detection.

Another classical algorithm for proximity queries is the GJK [3,11], which computes the distance between a pair of convex objects, by utilizing the Minkowski sum of the two objects. There also exist extensions to the GJK algorithms that allow to measure the penetration depth [6].

Zhang et al. [37] presented an extended definition of the penetration depth that also takes the rotational component into account, called the generalized penetration depth. However, this approach is computationally very expensive and, thus, might currently not be fast enough for haptic interaction rates.

Redon and Lin [33] approximate a local penetration depth by first computing a local penetration direction and then use this information to estimate a local penetration depth on the GPU.

Other GPU approaches with very similar problems have been presented by [21, 22] or [15] that also support proximity queries in image resolution.

The DEEP library [20] finds a "locally optimal solution" by walking on the surface of the Minkowski sums and uses a heuristic to estimate the initial features. However, it is restricted to convex polytopes.

Another interesting approach to avoid penetrations is the use of continuous collision detection. Ortega et al. [31] use a god-object based approach, that computes the collisions and the forces asynchronous in two different processes in order to guarantee constant updating rates.

There is very little literature on penetration volume computation. Hasegawa and Sato [14] explicitly construct the intersection volume of convex polyhedra. However, this method is applicable only to very simple geometries.

Fig. 10.2 The different stages of our sphere packing algorithm. First, we voxelize the object (*left*) and compute distances from the voxels to the closest triangle (second image; transparency = distance). Then, we pick the voxel with the largest distance and put a sphere at its center. We proceed incrementally and, eventually, we obtain a dense sphere packing of the object (*right*)

Faure et al. [8] compute an approximation of the intersection volume from layered depth images on the GPU. While this approach is applicable to deformable geometries, it is restricted to image space precision.

10.2.2 Voxel Based Data Structures

The Voxmap Pointshell approach [26] divides the virtual environment into a dynamic object, that is allowed to move freely through the virtual space and static objects that are fixed in the world. The static environment is discretized into a set of voxels. The dynamic object is described by a set of points that represent its surface. During query time, for each of these points it is determined with a simple boolean test, whether it is located in a filled volume element or not.

Renz et al. [34] presented extensions to the classic VPS, including optimizations to force calculation in order to increase its stability. However, even these optimizations cannot completely avoid the limits of VPS, namely aliasing effects, the huge memory consumption and the strict disjunction between dynamic and static objects.

Closely related to VPS are distance field based methods. Barbič and James [2] use a pointshell of reduced deformable models in combination with distance fields in order to guarantee continuous contact forces (Fig. 10.2).

10.3 Creation of the Inner Sphere Tree

In this section we describe the construction of our data structure. The goal is to fill an arbitrary object densely with a set of disjoint (i.e. non-overlapping) spheres such that the volume of the object is covered well while the number of spheres is as small as possible. In a second step, we build a hierarchy over this set of spheres. We chose spheres for volumes, because they offer a trivial and very fast overlap test. Moreover, since they are rotationally invariant, it is easy, in contrast to AABBs or OBBs, to compute the exact intersection volume when objects undergo rotations.

10.3.1 The Sphere Packing

Filling objects densely with spheres is a highly non-trivial task. Bin packing, even when restricted to spheres, is still a very active field in geometric optimization and far away from being solved for general objects [4, 35]. In our implementation of the inner sphere trees, we use a simple heuristic that offers a good trade-off between accuracy and speed in practice.

Currently, we voxelize the object as an intermediate step (by a simple flood filling algorithm). But instead of simply storing whether or not a voxel is filled, we additionally store the distance d from the center of the voxel to the nearest point on the surface, as well as the triangle that realizes this distance.

After the voxelization, we generate the inner spheres greedily. We choose the voxel V^* with the largest distance d^* to the surface. We create an inner sphere with radius d^* and centered on the center of V^*. All voxels whose center is contained in this sphere will not be considered any further. Additionally, we have to update all voxels V_i whose distance $d(V_i, V^*) < 2d$; their d_i must now be set to the new free radius. This is, because they are now closer to the sphere around V^* than to a triangle on the hull (see Fig. 10.3). This process stops, when there is no voxel left.

After these steps, the object is filled densely with a set of non-overlapping spheres. The density can be controlled by the number of voxels.

10.3.2 Building the IST

Our sphere hierarchy is based on the notion of a *wrapped hierarchy* [1], where inner nodes are tight BVs for all their leaves, but they do not necessarily bound their direct children (see Fig. 10.4). Compared to the more commonly used layered hierarchies, the big advantage is that the inner BVs are tighter. We use a top-down approach to create our hierarchy, i.e., we start at the root node that covers all inner spheres and divide these into several subsets.

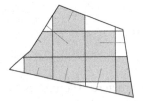 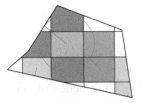 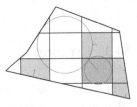

Fig. 10.3 The first steps of the creation of the inner spheres. First, the object is voxelized (*left*). Then, we compute the shortest distance to the surface (*lines emanating from voxel centers*) for interior voxel centers. Next, we place a maximal sphere at the voxel center with the largest radius (*large sphere*). Then, the *some voxels* are deleted, and the shortest distances of some voxels are updated, because they are closer now to an inner sphere. This procedure continues greedily as shown in the drawing to the *right*

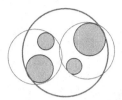

Fig. 10.4 In a wrapped hierarchy, the *large sphere* covers all its leaf nodes (*small solid spheres*), but not its direct children (*the two medium sized non-solid spheres*)

The partitioning of the inner spheres has significant influence on the performance during runtime. Previous algorithms for building ordinary sphere trees, like the medial axis approach [5, 16] work well if the spheres constitute a *covering* of the object and have similar size, but in our scenario we use disjoint inner spheres that exhibit a large variation in size. Other approaches based on the *k-center problem* work only for sets of points and do not support spheres.

So, we decided to use the *batch neural gas* clustering algorithm (BNG) known from artificial intelligence [7]. BNG is a very robust clustering algorithm, which can be formulated as stochastic gradient descent with a cost function closely connected to quantization error. Like *k-means*, the cost function minimizes the mean squared Euclidean distance of each data point to its nearest center. But unlike k-means, BNG exhibits very robust behavior with respect to the initial cluster center positions (the *prototypes*): they can be chosen arbitrarily without affecting the convergence. Moreover, BNG can be extended to allow the specification of the *importance* of each data point; below, we will describe how this can be used to increase the quality of the ISTs.

In the following, we will give a quick recap of the basic batch neural gas and then describe our extensions and application to building the inner sphere tree.

Given points $x_j \in \mathbb{R}^d$, $j = 0, \ldots, m$, and prototypes $w_i \in \mathbb{R}^d$, $i = 0, \ldots, n$, initialized randomly, we define the rank for every prototype w_i with respect to every data point x_j as

$$k_{ij} := \left| \{ w_k : d(x_j, w_k) < d(x_j, w_i) \} \right| \in \{0, \ldots, n\} \qquad (10.1)$$

In other words, we sort the prototypes with respect to every data point. After the computation of the ranks, we compute the new positions for the prototypes:

$$w_i := \frac{\sum_{j=0}^{m} h_\lambda(k_{ij}) x_j}{\sum_{j=0}^{m} h_\lambda(k_{ij})} \qquad (10.2)$$

These two steps are repeated until a stop criterion is met. In the original paper, a fixed number of iterations is proposed. We propose to use an adaptive version and stop the iteration if the movement of the prototypes is smaller than some ε. In our examples, we chose $\varepsilon \approx 10^{-5} \times \text{BoundingBoxSize}$, without any differences in the hierarchy compared to the non-adaptive, exhaustive approach. This improvement speeds up the creation of the hierarchy significantly (Fig. 10.5).

Fig. 10.5 This figure shows the results of our hierarchy building algorithm based in batch neural gas clustering with magnification control. All of those inner spheres that share the same color are assigned to the same bounding sphere. The *left image* shows the clustering result of the root sphere, the *right images* the partitioning of its four children

The convergence rate is controlled by a monotonically decreasing function $h_\lambda(k) > 0$ that decreases with the number of iterations t. We use the function proposed in the original paper: $h_\lambda(k) = e^{-\frac{k}{\lambda}}$ with initial value $\lambda_0 = \frac{n}{2}$, and reduction $\lambda(t) = \lambda_0 \left(\frac{0.01}{\lambda_0}\right)^{\frac{t}{t_{max}}}$, where t_{max} is the maximum number of iterations. These values have been taken according to [25].

Obviously, the number of prototypes defines the arity of the tree. If it is too big, the resulting trees are very inefficient. On the other hand, if it is too small, the trees become very deep and there exist a lot of levels with big spheres that do not approximate the object very well. Experiments with our data structure have shown that a branching factor of 4 produces the best results. Additionally, this has the benefit that we can use the full capacity of SIMD units in modern CPUs.

So far, the BNG only utilizes the location of the centers of the spheres. In our experience, this already produces much better results than other, simpler heuristics, such as greedily choosing the biggest spheres or the spheres with the largest number of neighbors. However, it does not yet take the extent of the spheres into account. As a consequence, the prototypes tend to avoid regions that are covered with a very large sphere, i.e., centers of big spheres are treated as outliers and they are thus placed on very deep levels in the hierarchy. However, it is better to place big spheres at higher levels of the hierarchy in order to get early lower bounds during distance traversal (see Sect. 10.4.1 for details).

Therefore, we use an extended version of the classical batch neural gas, that also takes the size of the spheres into account. Our extension is based on an idea of [13], where *magnification control* is introduced. The idea is to add weighting factors in order to "artificially" increase the density of the space in some areas.

With weighting factors $v(x_j)$, (10.2) becomes

$$w_i := \frac{\sum_{j=0}^{m} h_\lambda(k_{ij}) v(x_j) x_j}{\sum_{j=0}^{m} h_\lambda(k_{ij}) v(x_j)} \qquad (10.3)$$

In our scenario, we already know the density, because our spheres are disjoint. Thus, we can directly use the volumes of our spheres to let $v(x_j) = \frac{4}{3}\pi r^3$.

Summing up the hierarchy creation algorithm: we first compute a bounding sphere for all inner spheres (at the leaves), which becomes the root node of the hierarchy. To do that, we use the fast and stable smallest enclosing sphere algorithm proposed in [10]. Then, we divide the set of inner spheres into subsets in order to create the children. To do that, we use the extended version of batch neural gas with magnification control. We repeat this scheme recursively.

In the following, we will call the spheres in the hierarchy that are not leaves *hierarchy spheres*. Spheres at the leaves, which were created in Sect. 10.3.1, will be called *inner spheres*. Note that hierarchy spheres are not necessarily contained completely within the object.

10.4   BVH Traversal

During runtime, our new data structure supports different kinds of queries, namely proximity queries, which report the separation distance between a pair of objects, and penetration volume queries, which report the common volume covered by both objects. As a by-product, the proximity query can return a witness realizing the distance, and the penetration algorithm can return a partial list of intersecting polygons.

In the following, we describe algorithms for these two query types, but it should be obvious how they can be modified in order to provide an approximate yes-no answer. This would further increase the speed.

First, we will discuss the two query types separately, in order to point out their specific requirements and optimizations. Then, we explain how they can be combined into a single algorithm.

10.4.1   *Proximity Queries*

Our algorithm for proximity queries works like most other classical BVH traversal algorithms. We simply have to add the computation of lower bounds for the distance. If a pair of leaves, which are the inner spheres, is reached, we update the lower bound so far (see Algorithm 10.1). During traversal, there is no need to visit bounding volumes in the hierarchy that are farther away than the current minimum distance, because of the bounding property. This guarantees a high culling efficiency.

Algorithm 10.1: checkDistance(A, B, minDist)

---

input : A, B = spheres in the inner sphere tree
in/out: minDist = overall minimum distance seen so far
if A *and* B *are leaves* **then**
    // end of recursion
    minDist = min{distance(A, B), minDist}
else
    // recursion step
    forall *children* a[i] *of* A **do**
        forall *children* b[j] *of* B **do**
            if distance(a[i], b[j]) < minDist **then**
                checkDistance(a[i], b[j], minDist)

10.4.1.1 Improving Runtime

In most collision detection scenarios, there is a high spatial and temporal coherence, especially when rendering at haptic rates. Thus, in most cases, those spheres realizing the minimum distance in a frame are also the closest spheres in the next frames, or they are at least in the neighborhood. However, using the distance from the last frame yields a good initial bound for pruning during traversal. Thus, in our implementation we store pointers to the closest spheres as of the last frame and use their distance to initialize minDist in Algorithm 10.1.

Another speedup gives us the fact, that the traversal can be interrupted when the first pair of intersecting inner spheres is found if the objects overlap, that means the distance is smaller than zero and hence, the objects overlap.

Moreover, our traversal algorithm is very well suited for parallelization. During recursion, we compute the distances between 4 pairs of spheres in one single SIMD implementation, which is greatly facilitated by our hierarchy being a 4-ary tree.

10.4.1.2 Improving Accuracy

Obviously, Algorithm 10.1 returns only an approximate minimum distance, because it utilizes only the distances of the inner spheres for the proximity query. Thus, the accuracy depends on their density.

Fortunately, it is very easy to alleviate these inaccuracies by simply assigning the closest triangle (or a set of triangles) to each inner sphere. After determining the closest spheres with Algorithm 10.1, we add a subsequent test that calculates the exact distance between the triangles assigned to those spheres (see Fig. 10.6), which can only be smaller than the one derived using the inner spheres. This simple heuristic reduces the error significantly even with relatively sparsely filled objects, and it does not affect the runtime (see Fig. 10.13).

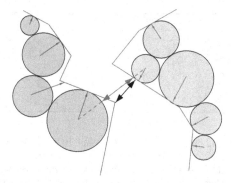

Fig. 10.6 Every inner sphere (*solid spheres*) is attached to its closest triangle (*solid polyline*). The distance between the closest spheres (*dashed line*) is an upper bound for the real distance between the closest triangles (*double arrow*)

Algorithm 10.2: computeVolume(A, B, totalOverlap)

---

input : A, B = spheres in the inner sphere tree
in/out: totalOverlap = overall volume of intersection
if A *and* B *are leaves* **then**
    // end of recursion
    totalOverlap + = overlapVolume(A, B)
else
    // recursion step
    forall *children* a[i] *of* A **do**
        forall *children* b[j] *of* B **do**
            if overlap(a[i], b[j]) > 0 **then**
                checkVolume(a[i], b[j], totalOverlap)

10.4.2 Penetration Volume Queries

In addition to proximity queries, our data structure also supports a new kind of penetration query, namely the *penetration volume*. This is the volume of the intersection of the two objects, which can be interpreted directly as the amount of the repulsion force, if it is considered as the amount of water being displaced.

Obviously, the algorithm to compute the penetration volume (see Algorithm 10.2) does not differ very much from the proximity query test: we simply have to replace the distance test by an overlap test and maintain an accumulated overlap volume during the traversal.

10.4.2.1 Filling the Gaps

The algorithm described in Sect. 10.3.1 results in densely filled objects. However, there still remain small voids between the spheres that cannot be completely compensated by increasing the number of voxels.

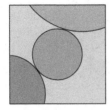

Fig. 10.7 After constructing the sphere packing (see Sect. 10.3.1), every voxel can be intersected by several non-overlapping spheres (*left*). These do not necessarily account for the whole voxel space (space not occupied by spheres in the *left picture*). In order to account for these voids, too, we simply increase the radius of the sphere that covers the center of the voxel (*right*)

As a remedy, we assign an additional, *secondary radius* to each inner sphere, such that the volume of the secondary sphere is equal to the volume of all voxels whose centers are contained within the radius of the primary sphere (see Fig. 10.7). This guarantees that the total volume of all secondary spheres equals the volume of the object, within the accuracy of the voxelization, because each voxel volume is accounted for exactly once.

Certainly, these secondary spheres may slightly overlap, but this simple heuristic leads to acceptable estimations of the penetration volume. (Note, however, that the secondary spheres are not necessarily larger than the primary spheres.)

10.4.2.2 Collision Response

In order to apply penalty forces in haptic environments or simulations, we also need the direction of the force in addition to its amount.

This can be easily derived from our inner sphere trees by considering all overlapping pairs of spheres (R_i, S_j). Let c_{R_i}, c_{S_j} be the sphere centers and $n_{ij} = c_{R_i} - c_{S_j}$. Then, we compute the overall direction of the penalty force as the weighted sum $\mathbf{n} = \sum_{i,j} \text{Vol}(R_i \cap S_j) \cdot \mathbf{n}_{ij}$ (see Fig. 10.8). Obviously, this direction is continuous, provided the path of the objects is continuous (see Fig. 10.9).

In case of deep penetrations, it can be necessary to flip some of the directions $\mathbf{n}_{ij}$. Computing normal cones for all spheres throughout the hierarchy can help to identify these pairs.

10.4.2.3 Improvements

Similar to the proximity query implementation, we can utilize SIMD parallelization to speed up both, the simple overlap check and the volume accumulation.

Furthermore, we can exploit the observation that a recursion can be terminated if a hierarchy sphere (i.e., an inner node of the sphere hierarchy) is completely contained inside an inner sphere (leaf). In this case, we can simply add the total volume of all of its leaves to the accumulated penetration volume. In order to do this quickly,

Fig. 10.8 The direction of
the penalty force can be
derived from the weighted
average of all vectors
between the centers of
colliding pairs of spheres,
weighted by their overlap

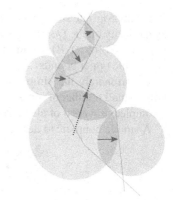

Fig. 10.9 Penetration
volume (*red*) and rotation of
the direction (*green*) during
the passing of a cow
alongside a pig by the size of
the whole bounding box (See
Fig. 10.11)

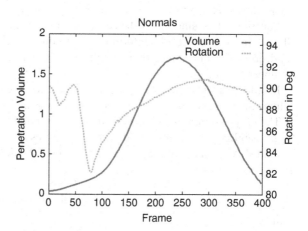

we store the total volume

$$\text{Vol}_l(S) = \sum_{S_j \in \text{Leaves}(S)} \text{Vol}(S_j), \tag{10.4}$$

where S_j are all inner spheres below S in the BVH.

This can be done in a preprocessing step during hierarchy creation.

10.4.2.4   Time-Critical Computation of Penetration Volume

In most cases, a penetration volume query has to visit many more nodes than
the average proximity query. Consequently, the runtimes are slower on average,
especially in cases with heavy overlaps.

In the following, we will describe a variation of our algorithm for penetration
volume queries that guarantees a predefined query time budget. This is essential for
time-critical applications such as haptic rendering.

An appropriate strategy to realize time-critical traversals is to guide the traversal by a priority queue Q. Given a pair of hierarchy spheres S and R, a simple heuristic is to use $\text{Vol}(S \cap R)$ for the priority in Q. In our experience, this would yield acceptable upper bounds.

Unfortunately, this simple heuristic also leads to very bad lower bounds, because only a small number of inner spheres will be visited (unless the time budget permits a complete traversal of all overlapping pairs).

A simple heuristic to derive an estimate of the lower bound could be to compute

$$\sum_{(R,S)\in Q} \sum_{\substack{R_i \in \text{ch}(R), \\ S_j \in \text{ch}(S)}} \text{Vol}(R_i \cap S_j), \tag{10.5}$$

where $\text{ch}(S)$ is the set of all direct children of node S.

Equation (10.5) amounts to the sum of the intersection of all direct child pairs of all pairs in the p-queue Q. Unfortunately, the direct children of a node are usually not disjoint and, thus, this estimate of the lower bound could actually be larger than the upper bound.

In order to avoid this problem, we introduce a new method to estimate the overlap volume more accurately: the *expected overlap volume*.

The only assumption we make is that for any point inside S, the distribution of the probability that it is also inside one of its leaves is uniform.

Let (R, S) be a pair of spheres in the p-queue. We define the *density* of a sphere as

$$p(S) = \frac{\text{Vol}_l(S)}{\text{Vol}(S)}. \tag{10.6}$$

with

$$\text{Vol}_l(S) = \sum_{S_j \in \text{Leaves}(S)} \text{Vol}(S_j), \tag{10.7}$$

where S_j are all inner spheres below S in the IST.

This is the probability that a point inside S is also inside one of its leaves (which are disjoint). Next, we define the *expected overlap volume* $\overline{\text{Vol}}(R, S)$ as the probability that a point is inside $R \cap S$ and also inside the intersection of one of the possible pairs of leaves, i.e.,

$$\begin{aligned}\overline{\text{Vol}}(R, S) &= p(S) \cdot p(R) \cdot \text{Vol}(R \cap S) \\ &= \frac{\text{Vol}_l(R) \cdot \text{Vol}_l(S) \cdot \text{Vol}(R \cap S)}{\text{Vol}(R) \cdot \text{Vol}(S)}\end{aligned} \tag{10.8}$$

(see Fig. 10.10).

In summary, for the whole queue we get an expected overlap volume by

$$\sum_{(R,S)\in Q} \overline{\text{Vol}}(R, S) \tag{10.9}$$

Clearly, this volume can be maintained during traversal quite easily.

Fig. 10.10 We estimate the
real penetration volume
during our time-critical
traversal by the "density" in
the hierarchy spheres (*large
spheres*) and the total volume
of the leaf spheres

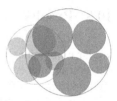

Algorithm 10.3: checkVolumeTimeCritical(A, B)

---

input : A, B = root spheres of the two ISTs
estOverlap = $\overline{\mathrm{Vol}}(A, B)$
Q = empty priority queue
Q.push(A, B)
while Q *not empty & time not exceeded* **do**
   (R, S) = Q.pop();
   if *R and S are not leaves* **then**
      estOverlap $- =$ $\overline{\mathrm{Vol}}(R, S)$
      forall $R_i \in$ *children of R*, $S_j \in$ *children of S* **do**
         estOverlap $+ =$ $\overline{\mathrm{Vol}}(R_i, S_j)$
         Q.push(R_i, S_j)

More importantly, this method provides a much better heuristic for sorting the
priority queue: if the gap between the expected overlap $\overline{\mathrm{Vol}}(R, S)$ and the overlap
$\mathrm{Vol}(R \cap S)$ is large, then it is most likely that the traversal of this pair will give the
most benefit towards improving the bound; consequently, we insert this pair closer
to the front of the queue.

Algorithm 10.3 shows the pseudo code of this approach. (Note that $p(S) = 1$
if S is a leaf, and therefore $\overline{\mathrm{Vol}}(R, S)$ returns the exact intersection volume at the
leaves.)

10.4.3 The Unified Algorithm

In the previous sections, we introduced the proximity and the penetration volume
computation separately. However, it is of course possible to combine both algorithms. This yields a unified algorithm that can compute both the distance and the
penetration volume.

To that end, we start with the distance traversal. If we find the first pair of intersecting inner spheres, then we simply switch to the penetration volume computation.

This is correct because all pairs of inner spheres we visited so far do not overlap
and thus do not extend the penetration volume. Thus, we do not have to visit them
again and can continue with the traversal of the rest of the hierarchies using the penetration volume algorithm. If we do not meet an intersecting pair of inner spheres,
the unified algorithm still reports the minimal separating distance.

10.5 Results

We have implemented our new data structure in C++ on a PC running Windows XP with an Intel Pentium IV 3 GHz dual core CPU and 2 GB of memory. We used a modified version of Dan Morris' *Voxelizer* [28] to compute the voxelization and the initial distances of the voxels.

We used several hand recorded object paths for benchmarking. In order to test the proximity queries, we moved the objects within a distance range of about 0–10% of the object's BV size. Here, we focused on very close configurations, because these are more stressing and also more interesting in real world scenarios. The paths for the penetration volume tests concentrate on light to medium penetrations of about 0–10% of the object's volume, because this resembles the usage in haptic applications best. But we also included some heavy penetrations of 50% of the object's volume so as to stress our algorithm.

We used several different objects to test the performance of our algorithms, like the armadillo or the torso (see Figs. 10.11–10.14). [1] The polygon count ranges from 50 to 700 k triangles per object. We voxelized each object in different resolutions in order to evaluate the trade-off between the number of spheres and the accuracy.

We used PQP to compute the exact distance and measure the quality of our distance approximation. The runtime of PQP is not directly comparable to approximative IST traversal. Just to give a sense of the speed-up when using our approximative method, we can say that it is between 10 and 120 times, depending on the density of the inner spheres.

To our knowledge, there are no publicly available implementations to compute the penetration volume efficiently. In order to evaluate the quality of our penetration volume approximation, we used a tetrahedralization in combination with a sphere hierarchy to compute the exact overlap volume. However, the runtime of this approach is not applicable to real-time applications due to bad BV fitting and the costly tetrahedron-tetrahedron overlap volume calculation (Fig. 10.12).

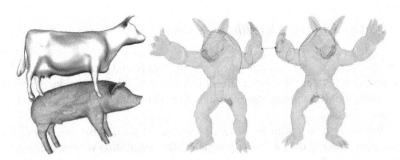

Fig. 10.11 Snapshots from our benchmarks: a pig and a cow (70 k polygons) and an armadillo (700 k). The *red* and *blue spheres* show the closest pair of spheres

---

[1] Please visit cg.in.tu-clausthal.de/research/ist/video to watch some videos of our benchmarks.

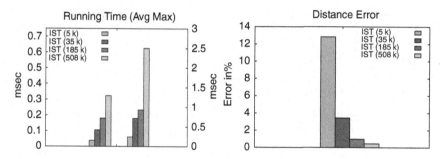

Fig. 10.12 Distance computations in the armadillo scene. *Left*: average and maximum time/frame. *Right*: relative error compared to accurate distance. (Numbers in parentheses denote the number of spheres)

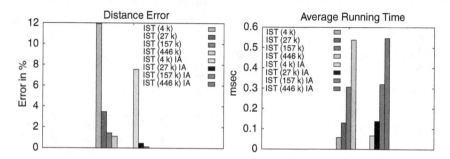

Fig. 10.13 *Left*: improvement of the accuracy (IA) in distance queries by the method described in (Sect. 10.4.1.2) in the pig scene with only one triangle stored for every sphere. *Right*: the improvement of accuracy does not significantly affect the runtime of our traversal algorithm

Fig. 10.14 More snapshots from our benchmarks: a torso (100 k) and a screwdriver (50 k). The *red* and *blue spheres* show the overlapping inner spheres

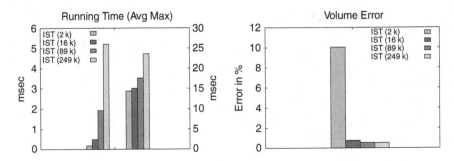

Fig. 10.15 Penetration volume computation in the screwdriver scene. *Left*: average and maximum time/frame. *Right*: relative error compared to accurate volume. (Numbers in parentheses denote the number of spheres)

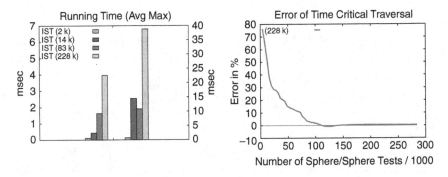

Fig. 10.16 Penetration volume computations in the torso scene. *Left*: average and maximum time/frame. *Right*: error relative to the exact penetration volume depending on the number of intersection tests

Our penetration volume algorithm is able to answer queries at haptic rates, even for very large objects with hundreds of thousands of polygons (see Fig. 10.15). In the case of deeper penetrations, our time-critical traversal guarantees acceptable estimations of the penetration volume even in worst-case scenarios and complex contacts (see Fig. 10.16).

10.6 Conclusions and Future Work

We have presented a novel hierarchical data structure, the *inner sphere trees*, that supports both proximity queries and penetration volume computations with one unified algorithm. Both kinds can be answered at rates of about 1 kHz (which makes the algorithm suitable for haptic rendering) even for very complex objects with several hundreds of thousands of polygons.

For proximity situations, typical average runtimes are in the order of 0.5 msec with 5,00,000 spheres per object and an error of about 0.5%. Obviously, the runtimes depend much more on the intersection volume in penetration situations; here, we are in the order of around 5 msec on average with 2,50,000 spheres and an error of about 0.7%. The balance between accuracy and speed can be defined by the user, and this is independent of the object complexity, because the number of leaves of our hierarchy is mostly independent of the number of polygons.

For time-critical applications, we describe a variant of our algorithm that stays within the time budget while returning an answer "as good as possible".

Our algorithm for both kinds of queries can be integrated into existing simulation software very easily, because there is only a single entry point, i.e., the application does not need to know in advance whether or not a given pair of objects will be penetrating each other.

Memory consumption of our inner sphere trees is similar to other bounding volume hierarchies, depending on the predefined accuracy (in our experiments, it was always in the order of a few MB). This is very modest compared to voxel-based approaches.

Another big advantage of our penetration volume algorithm is that it yields a continuous measure for penetration and force direction.

Last but not least, inner sphere trees are perfectly suited for SIMD acceleration techniques and allow algorithms to make heavy use of temporal and spatial coherence.

Our novel approach opens up several avenues for future work.

First of all, the intermediate step of voxelization in order to obtain a sphere packing should be replaced with a better algorithm. This is probably a challenging problem, because several goals should be met: accuracy, query efficiency, and small build times.

An interesting question is the analytical determination of exact error bounds. This could lead to an optimal number of inner spheres with well-defined errors, and it could further improve the heuristics for the time-critical traversal.

Finally, a challenging task would be to extend our approach also to deformable objects.

References

1. Agarwal, P., Guibas, L., Nguyen, A., Russel, D., Zhang, L.: Collision detection for deforming necklaces. Computational Geometry: Theory and Applications **28**(2–3), 137–163 (2004)
2. Barbič, J., James, D.L.: Six-dof haptic rendering of contact between geometrically complex reduced deformable models. IEEE Transactions on Haptics **1**(1), 39–52 (2008)
3. van den Bergen, G.: A fast and robust GJK implementation for collision detection of convex objects. Journal of Graphics Tools **4**(2), 7–25 (1999)
4. Birgin, E.G., Sobral, F.N.C.: Minimizing the object dimensions in circle and sphere packing problems. Computers & OR **35**(7), 2357–2375 (2008). URL http://dx.doi.org/10.1016/j.cor.2006.11.002

5. Bradshaw, G., O'Sullivan, C.: Adaptive medial-axis approximation for sphere-tree construction. In: ACM Transactions on Graphics, vol. 23(1), pp. 1–26. ACM press (2004). URL http://visinfo.zib.de/EVlib/Show?EVL-2004-1

6. Cameron, S.: Enhancing GJK: Computing minimum and penetration distances between convex polyhedra. In: Proceedings of International Conference on Robotics and Automation, pp. 3112–3117 (1997)

7. Cottrell, M., Hammer, B., Hasenfuss, A., Villmann, T.: Batch and median neural gas. Neural Networks **19**, 762–771 (2006)

8. Faure, F., Barbier, S., Allard, J., Falipou, F.: Image-based collision detection and response between arbitrary volumetric objects. In: ACM Siggraph/Eurographics Symposium on Computer Animation, SCA 2008, July 2008. Dublin, Irlande (2008)

9. Fisher, S.M., Lin, M.C.: Fast penetration depth estimation for elastic bodies using deformed distance fields (2001)

10. Gärtner, B.: Fast and robust smallest enclosing balls. In: J. Nesetril (ed.) ESA, Lecture Notes in Computer Science, vol. 1643, pp. 325–338. Springer, Berlin (1999) URL http://link.springer.de/link/service/series/0558/bibs/1643/16430325.htm

11. Gilbert, E.G., Johnson, D.W., Keerthi, S.S.: A fast procedure for computing the distance between complex objects in three-dimensional space. IEEE Journal of Robotics and Automation **4**, 193–203 (1988)

12. Gottschalk, S., Lin, M.C., Manocha, D.: OBBTree: A hierarchical structure for rapid interference detection. Computer Graphics **30** (Annual Conference Series), 171–180 (1996)

13. Hammer, B., Hasenfuss, A., Villmann, T.: Magnification control for batch neural gas. In: ESANN, pp. 7–12 (2006). URL http://www.dice.ucl.ac.be/Proceedings/esann/esannpdf/es2006-83.pdf

14. Hasegawa, S., Sato, M.: Real-time rigid body simulation for haptic interactions based on contact volume of polygonal objects. Computer Graphics Forum **23**(3), 529–538 (2004)

15. Hoff, K.E., Zaferakis, A., Lin, M., Manocha, D.: Fast 3d geometric proximity queries between rigid & deformable models using graphics hardware acceleration. Tech. Rep. TR02-004, Department of Computer Science, University of North Carolina – Chapel Hill (2002). URL ftp://ftp.cs.unc.edu/pub/publications/techreports/02-004.pdf. Friday, 8 March 2002 20:06:33 GMT

16. Hubbard, P.M.: Collision detection for interactive graphics applications. IEEE Transactions on Visualization and Computer Graphics **1**(3), 218–230 (1995)

17. Hudson, T.C., Lin, M.C., Cohen, J., Gottschalk, S., Manocha, D.: V-COLLIDE: Accelerated collision detection for VRML. In: R. Carey, P. Strauss (eds.) VRML 97: Second Symposium on the Virtual Reality Modeling Language. ACM, New York (1997)

18. Johnson, D.E., Cohen, E.: A framework for efficient minimum distance computations. In: Proceedings of the IEEE International Conference on Robotics and Automation (ICRA-98), pp. 3678–3684. IEEE Computer Society, Piscataway (1998)

19. Johnson, D.E., Willemsen, P.: Six degree-of-freedom haptic rendering of complex polygonal model. In: HAPTICS, pp. 229–235. IEEE Computer Society (2003). URL http://csdl.computer.org/comp/proceedings/haptics/2003/1890/00/18900229abs.htm

20. Kim, Y.J., Lin, M.C., Manocha, D.: Incremental penetration depth estimation between convex polytopes using dual-space expansion. IEEE Transactions on Visualization and Computer Graphics **10**(2), 152–163 (2004). URL http://visinfo.zib.de/EVlib/Show?EVL-2004-24

21. Kim, Y., Otaduy, M., Lin, M., Manocha, D.: Fast penetration depth computation for physically-based animation. In: S.N. Spencer (ed.) Proceedings of the 2002 ACM SIGGRAPH Symposium on Computer Animation (SCA-02), pp. 23–32. ACM, New York (2002)

22. Kim, Y., Otaduy, M., Lin, M., Manocha, D.: Fast penetration depth estimation using rasterization hardware and hierarchical refinement (short). In: COMPGEOM: Annual ACM Symposium on Computational Geometry (2003)

23. Klosowski, J.T., Held, M., Mitchell, J.S.B., Sowizral, H., Zikan, K.: Efficient collision detection using bounding volume hierarchies of k-dops. IEEE Transactions on Visualization and Computer Graphics **4**(1), 21–36 (1998). DOI http://dx.doi.org/10.1109/2945.675649

24. Larsen, E., Gottschalk, S., Lin, M., Manocha, D.: Fast proximity queries with swept sphere volumes. In: Technical Report TR99-018 (1999)
25. Martinetz, T.M., Berkovich, S.G., Schulten, K.J.: 'Neural-gas' network for vector quantization and its application to time-series prediction. IEEE Transactions on Neural Networks **4**(4), 558–569 (1993)
26. McNeely, W.A., Puterbaugh, K.D., Troy, J.J.: Six degrees-of-freedom haptic rendering using voxel sampling. In: A. Rockwood (ed.) Siggraph 1999, Annual Conference Series, pp. 401–408. ACM Siggraph, Addison Wesley Longman, Los Angeles (1999). URL http://visinfo.zib. de/EVlib/Show?EVL-1999-269
27. Mendoza, C., O'Sullivan, C.: Interruptible collision detection for deformable objects. Computers & Graphics **30**(3), 432–438 (2006). URL http://dx.doi.org/10.1016/j.cag.2006.02.018
28. Morris, D.: Algorithms and data structures for haptic rendering: Curve constraints, distance maps, and data logging. In: Technical Report 2006-06 (2006)
29. O'Brien, J.F., Hodgins, J.K.: Graphical modeling and animation of brittle fracture. In: SIGGRAPH '99: Proceedings of the 26th annual conference on Computer graphics and interactive techniques, pp. 137–146. ACM/Addison-Wesley, New York, NY, USA (1999). DOI http://doi.acm.org/10.1145/311535.311550
30. Ong, C., Gilbert, E.: Growth distances: New measures for object separation and penetration. T-RA **12**, 888–903 (1996)
31. Ortega, M., Redon, S., Coquillart, S.: A six degree-of-freedom god-object method for haptic display of rigid bodies with surface properties.
IEEE Transactions on Visualization and Computer Graphics **13**(3), 458–469 (2007). URL http://dx.doi.org/10.1109/TVCG.2007.1028
32. Quinlan, S.: Efficient distance computation between non-convex objects. In: Proceedings of International Conference on Robotics and Automation, pp. 3324–3329 (1994)
33. Redon, S., Lin, M.C.: A fast method for local penetration depth computation. Journal of Graphics Tools **11**(2), 37–50 (2006). URL http://jgt.akpeters.com/papers/RedonLin06/
34. Renz, M., Preusche, C., Pötke, M., peter Kriegel, H., Hirzinger, G.: Stable haptic interaction with virtual environments using an adapted voxmap-pointshell algorithm. In: Proc. Eurohaptics, pp. 149–154 (2001)
35. Schuermann, A.: On packing spheres into containers (about Kepler's finite sphere packing problem). In: Documenta Mathematica, vol. 11, pp. 393–406 (2006). URL http://arxiv.org/ abs/math/0506200
36. Trenkel, S., Weller, R., Zachmann, G.: A benchmarking suite for static collision detection algorithms. In: V. Skala (ed.) Inter'l Conf. in Central Europe on Computer Graphics, Visualization and Computer Vision (WSCG). Union Agency, Plzen, Czech Republic (2007). URL http://cg.in.tu-clausthal.de/research/colldet_benchmark
37. Zhang, L., Kim, Y.J., Varadhan, G., Manocha, D.: Generalized penetration depth computation. Computer-Aided Design **39**(8), 625–638 (2007). URL http://dx.doi.org/10.1016/j.cad.2007. 05.012

Chapter 11
The Value of Constraints for 3D User Interfaces

Wolfgang Stuerzlinger and Chadwick A. Wingrave

Abstract User interfaces to three-dimensional environments are becoming more and more popular. Today this trend is fuelled through the introduction of social communication via virtual worlds, console and computer games, as well as 3D televisions.

We present a synopsis of the relevant abilities and restrictions introduced by both input and output technologies, as well as an overview of related human capabilities and limitations, including perceptual and cognitive issues.

Partially based on this, we present a set of guidelines for 3D user interfaces. These guidelines are intended for developers of interactive 3D systems, such as computer and console games, 3D modeling packages, augmented reality systems, computer aided design systems, and virtual environments. The guidelines promote techniques, such as using appropriate constraints, that have been shown to work well in these types of environments.

11.1 Introduction

The interface is the bridge between the human and the effective use of their tools. In the beginning, the user interface for computers was text centric, constraining the human's expressiveness to command-line text. Later, two-dimensional graphical user interfaces (2D GUI's), using the WIMP (windows, icons, menus, pointer) metaphor became prevalent. GUI's offer precise tool control and have enabled many uses of computers in everyday life. Several post-WIMP interfaces operate outside these bounds, operating on human touch and voice modalities for multi-touch,

W. Stuerzlinger (✉)
York University, Toronto, Canada, www.cse.yorku.ca/~wolfgang,
e-mail: wolfgang@cse.yorku.ca

C.A. Wingrave
University of Central Florida, Orlando, FL, USA
e-mail: cwingrav@eecs.ucf.edu

S. Coquillart et al. (eds.), *Virtual Realities*, DOI 10.1007/978-3-211-99178-7_11,
© Springer-Verlag/Wien 2011

tangible, sketching and voice interaction [63]. In addition, Reality-Based Interfaces [31] incorporate the human's body and natural understanding of the world into the interface as exemplified by three-dimensional user interfaces (3D UIs) in Virtual and Augmented Reality (VR/AR). Unfortunately, these new interface modalities, while liberating and potentially far more expressive, establish fewer bounds for the interaction between the human and their tools. Consequently interface understandability and task performance suffer. The extra dimensionality in 3D raises issues not seen in command-line and 2D applications. In these cases, appropriate interface constraints can preserve precision while retaining the expressive interaction.

Today, examples of 3D user interfaces can be found in games, desktops, and computer-aided design (CAD) on a wide range of hardware configurations including traditional desktops, game consoles, and high-end virtual reality systems. These applications extend their interaction into 3D so as to gain some benefit of immersion, see e.g. [11]. Applications range from pure data visualization to highly interactive systems, with examples including static data visualization, architectural walkthroughs, and massively multiplayer online worlds for social and gaming purposes. Mobile devices also offer platforms more akin to 3D user interfaces as compared to their desktop predecessors.

However, creating effective user interfaces for 3D systems is a difficult problem [28,41,69]. The extra dimensionality of 3D gives the user much more freedom, raising issues not seen in 2D applications. Directly exposing all facets of the additional freedom of 3D to the user leads to extremely complex user interfaces, as evident in high-end CAD systems. Some recent systems have shown that it is possible to create user interfaces for 3D that are significantly less complex. For example, see Google Sketch-Up [24], SESAME [45], or the content editor in the Spore game [21]. Other examples use interaction techniques that are based on imagination to work around some of the issues [35].

In the following sections, we identify the challenges of creating interactive 3D applications. All of these challenges are based on the capabilities and limitations of humans and technical constraints. There are three main categories we will consider: input devices, display devices, and human issues. This is followed by a discussion of guidelines that can help constrain 3D interaction. This work amounts to a high-level overview of the state-of-the-art in 3D user interface technologies and human capabilities. For more details we refer the reader to technical survey articles, such as [14].

11.2 Capabilities and Limitations

Any user interface is part of a feedback loop, which involves a human reacting to system output and interacting with input devices to control the system. Hence, we discuss each of these three aspects here.

11.2.1 Input Devices

The variety of available 3DUI input devices is large. One factor is that applications have different requirements. Also the limitations and capabilities of each device class vary significantly. Hence, there is no single best input technology and no common hardware platform. Important to all input devices are their reported data in terms of degrees of freedom (DOF). Each degree is a dimension in which the device reports. A mouse is a 2DOF device, while a typical 3D UI input devices, often called a 3D tracker, provides 6DOF, for the 3 spatial dimensions and the rotations around each axis, i.e. heading, pitch, and roll. Additionally, devices can be described in terms of the independence of their dimensions, i.e. the number dimensions that can be controlled at once. For example, a mouse is a 2DOF device but the knobs on the child's toy Etch-a-Sketch are 1+1DOF. Moreover, and while several devices can track multiple points, the most common 6DOF devices track a single point of the physical device held by the user such as a pen, ball, or puck-shaped device.

The classic desktop input devices, the mouse and keyboard, are used in 3D UIs due to their ubiquitous availability and user familiarity. More commonly used, however, are position tracking systems that track multiple points in 6 degrees of freedom (6DOF). Between these extremes is a class of single point 6DOF devices, such as the Spaceball. Some of these 6DOF devices also provide haptic feedback. Input devices that operate on the surface are common as well, including sketch, touch and tangible input. Lastly, an emerging class of input devices, termed spatially convenient [70], is often used for gestures and basic input. A prominent example is the Nintendo Wii Remote (Wiimote).

Keyboards and mice vary in their utility in 3D UI's. Many CAD and modeling programs use them as the sole means of interaction with the third degree of freedom and rotations are made accessible via keyboard modifier keys, buttons, button combinations, or various on-screen manipulators such as 3D widgets [58]. Most 3D desktop games also use the mouse by constraining it to viewpoint control and the keyboard for travel and lateral motions, an interface made popular by id Software. Many console game controllers operate in a similar manner but replace the mouse with thumb-sticks. As many users of game "applications" play very frequently, they quickly evolve expertise. This has led to rapid interface enhancements in this domain, such as the differentiation between viewpoint and orientation control across devices.

However, many 3DUIs enable the user to physically move freely through space. Then the user will often find themselves away from surfaces that can support a mouse or keyboard. Hand-held chorded keyboards are an option but then the user's hands are tasked with holding the device and cannot perform natural actions such as grasping and releasing. One practical use of a mouse is to pair it with a 3D tracker and to use only the buttons or click-wheel of the mouse for discrete input. This is often called a flying mouse, "wand", or "bat" [64]. More and more frequently the Wiimote is used in such a role, see also below.

Between 2D devices and full 6DOF multi-point tracking are several other classes of devices. Among them are ball or puck shaped devices, such as the Spaceball, that sits on the desk. The user can apply isotonic forces in three dimensions, as well as twist in three dimensions for full 6DOF input. Through constraining the user's movements to a very small region there is little fatigue and natural control of more dimensions simultaneously compared to a mouse. However, the inherent sensitivity to small movements of this device often leads to a negative first-use experience [10]. 3D mice are also used to provide 6DOF input. These are often wireless and easily passed between users. Some devices, such as the InterSense Inertia Cube, only report orientation information, often sufficient for head orientation tracking or simple ray-casting pointing. The CubicMouse [23] allows for separate control of each dimension by having one manipulatable stick along each axis that can be pulled and twisted, translating these motions into 6DOF input.

Another class of input devices, called haptics devices, uses small robot arms and enable the user to move a pen or any other device attached to the end of the robot actuator. The range of motion is usually limited to a soccer-ball sized volume, unless one considers expensive high-end devices. Practically all of these devices also use the motors in the joints to "push back, which can provide the user with a haptic experience, i.e. the sensation of hitting the pen onto the surface of an object.

A more recent trend in input devices has been the use of commodity devices and sensors, as exemplified by the Wiimote. This class is termed Spatially Convenient devices [70]. Such devices are defined by three characteristics: often incomplete or limited spatial input, yet many useful functionalities and convenience in terms of commodity price, easy setup and high durability. The Wiimote is a game controller designed for the Nintendo Wii console and wirelessly provides acceleration and orientation change at a single point. It also uses an infrared camera to sense emitted IR light for a limited form of 3D tracking that works only when the device is pointed at the screen. The Wiimote has multiple buttons, a speaker, LEDs and a rumble device. It is now common for game controllers to contain similar functionality. High-end mobile phones contain similar functionality and hence can also be used as spatially convenient input devices. The iPhone 3GS includes additionally a multi-touch screen, a GPS, a magnetometer, and a significant amount of processing power. The impact of such devices onto 3D UI's is only starting to become apparent.

Gloves afford a natural approach to interaction. This makes them a common choice for 3D input devices. They vary in the form of data collected and ease of use. The discrete input of Pinchgloves can be easier to work with than other gloves, making it possible to create menu systems [12] or virtual keyboards [13]. The tactile feedback provided to the user makes it easy to understand when fingers touch and when they release. Some gloves return multiple dimensions of flex for each finger. However, this form of data is hard to handle and the sensors usually require periodic re-initialization to be accurate [34]. Moreover, long-term use can be problematic due to salt in the sweat affecting the sensors. Also, the lack of haptic feedback is an issue users report frequently. Mechanical tracking of finger bend angles can remove the re-initialization issue, but such gloves are cumbersome to put on and take off.

Free-space 6DOF tracking of a user's head, a hand, or a tool can be achieved with multiple approaches, each with associated tradeoffs [67, 70]. Free-space tracking generally suffers from decreased precision, increased jitter and noise, and also increased lag relative to desktop devices such as a mouse. In the best case, precision can be in the millimeter range, i.e. in a freshly and fully calibrated system under ideal conditions. Compare this to the precision needs of a mouse, where miniscule hand and finger motions need to be tracked to enable pixel-accurate pointing. Hence, mice offer resolutions up to 2,400 dpi and are generally one or two orders of magnitude more precise than trackers. Update rate is another important factor in these devices, with mice typically tracking at 125 Hz [1]. This is comparable to current 3D input devices. However, increased jitter, noise and latency in 3D trackers relative to common desktop devices have a significantly negative impact on human performance, see below. The technical alternative, algorithmic smoothing and filtering, trades off precision for latency, which again impacts performance.

An important use of free-space tracking is head tracking. Head tracking aligns computer-generated images with the user's current eye positions. The reduction of technical lag and other encumbrances, and the increase of precision and accuracy have lead to reasonable success of head tracking in VR applications. In Augmented Reality systems, the precision requirements are much higher, as the computer generated environment is superimposed onto the real world and humans readily identify inconsistencies in alignment. This is one of the challenges that AR faces [4].

Human gesturing is another form of input, which can use various forms of free-space tracking. Simple gestures include shakes or orienting, while more complicated gestures can incorporate multiple movements over time. Accelerometer and gyroscopic sensors are an alternative to recognize such gestures, and these sensors require no external frame of reference. This approach has been used for games and mobile devices, for example on the Wii or iPhone. Existing work using paired accelerometers and gyroscopes have achieved user-independent 95% recognition accuracy for a set of 25 gestures with a small training set [30]. This corresponds to a 5% failure rate, which is still high enough to significantly impact user performance, see e.g. [2].

A final class of input devices is the tangible, surface and sketch-based hardware. Seen as research fields on their own, the potential benefit of these devices for 3D interaction, and the benefit to them, in understanding 3D interaction, is high. For instance, the tangible nature of near-field haptics has improved 3D UIs such as holding a clipboard to perform pen and tablet operations [12] or a baby head prop to improve a neurosurgery application [29]. The naturalness of writing notes and sketching in a virtual environment can have a lot of potential but is limited to hardware configurations that do not block the user's view of the work.

11.2.2   Display Devices

Display devices are the most readily identifiable aspect of 3D UIs, and are considered by some to be the first indication of the 3D experience to come. More importantly, displays influence the interaction to such an extent that it would be appropriate to say they shape the type of possible interactions. A wide range of devices exist for 3D UIs, from head mounted displays (HMDs), large projected displays such as CAVEs or multi-walled systems, desktops, to volumetric displays [42]. The qualities of these displays will be discussed below, followed by display capabilities and limitations.

Two complimentary characteristics of displays include field of view (FOV) and field of regard (FOR). FOV is the viewing area from the user's viewpoint as measured in degrees. While this is typically measured diagonally so as to appear larger, vertical and horizontal FOV are actually important requirements for different applications, such as larger horizontal FOV for greater peripheral vision [18]. Field of regard is the amount of usable space around the user in degrees, which the display can provide. These are important for contrasting the capabilities between common displays such as CAVES which provide a large FOVs, equal to its FOR, and HMDs which provide relatively small FOVs (dependent upon the HMD) with complete FOR when a 6DOF head tracker is used.

Other qualities of displays are also important factors. They include display size, pixel density, brightness, costs, and 3D capabilities. Additionally, it matters how the displays are used and arranged. For instance, placing displays side-by-side in a tile-like fashion can create large high-resolution displays. Large displays, despite comparable viewing angles to smaller-up close displays, can be more engaging [52].

There are many output devices that can be used for 3D systems. The ubiquitous desktop monitors are the most commonly used form of display and continue to decrease in cost while increasing in size and resolution. Another cost-effective alternative is projected displays on a screen or wall, which easily creates very large displays. These too continue to drop in cost while increasing in resolution. One notable issue of projectors is that their resolution and update rates, important for stereo displays, are lower than desktop monitors. Additionally, they suffer from distortion due to off-axis key-stoning effects, colors, and marks on display surfaces and also the prominent need for large spaces for projection [51]. Additional issues, include heat, size and noise of these projectors. Inexpensive commercial 3D displays have appeared recently, brought to market for 3D gaming and entertainment purposes. They use either an internal projector or LCD display in conjunction with stereo glasses to achieve their effect.

Immersive projection systems such as CAVE's [17] or large immersive projection walls frequently use stereo projectors to immerse the user. However, all these systems are essentially single-user devices, as they afford only one perspectively correct image. While a few two-user systems have been demonstrated [39], they are exceedingly rare, as they require projection systems with more than 120Hz. Moreover, all these systems have large space requirements (6-sided CAVEs usually need a room that is three stories high), are very expensive to build and to maintain. The benefits of these systems are the wide field of view, completely surrounding for 6-walled CAVEs.

HMDs, whether stereo or not, can completely block-out the real world to allow the user to focus on the 3D world. Also HMDs require minimum instrumentation of the surrounding space to operate. However, the devices are often bulky on the user's head and the benefit of blocking out the real world is also a drawback: (1)

an immersed collaborator can't see surrounding collaborators and (2) it can restrict users from walking simply because they don't feel like they can. Moreover, most devices have a very small field-of-view, 30–40°, which is equal or less than what a typical computer monitor affords. A particularly insidious effect is that a smaller field-of-view also inhibits peripheral vision, e.g. [3], and/or spatial memory, e.g. [5], both of which greatly affect navigation. Head-mounted displays with a full field-of-view for each eye, approximately 110°, are now available, but are still expensive and heavy. On the positive side, head-mounted displays with head tracking can provide a field of regard only comparable with the most expensive six-walled surround-screen systems. Lastly, Augmented Realty see-through HMDs are a class of HMD where the user looks into the real world with the virtual world superimposed on top. These devices add virtual content to the real-world scene, but have issues regarding brightness, tracking latency, weight, and accuracy. Consequently, hand-held displays have been used more and more for Augmented Reality in recent work.

Lastly, there are true 3D display systems typically referred to as volumetric displays. A variety of technologies exist for this, and can generate "glowing points" inside a volume where these points are equally visible from every direction. The main issue with this concept is that users then see the front *and* back of objects simultaneously. However, this is something that the human visual system is not capable of interpreting for the general case. Hence, these displays are generally only usable for displaying wire frame or point-cloud data and/or require head tracking. For more issues with current 3D display technologies, such as low brightness, instable display, see [26]. One new class of system that has been demonstrated recently generates different images for different viewing directions by extending the concepts used in auto-stereoscopic displays, e.g. the Holografika 3D display systems and the USC Lightfield Display [32]. These technologies project many images into many (typically horizontal) directions simultaneously, which allows the viewer to move freely (typically side-to-side) without head tracking. However, they are not yet at a stage where they can be used in office or home settings.

11.2.2.1 Stereo

Stereo displays are often seen as a critical component of applications with 3D user interfaces. There are multiple technologies capable of generating a stereoscopic display; that is, the generation of a separate images for each eye. The most commonly used technology is stereo glasses, where different images are displayed and the glasses separate a left and right image for the user. Active stereo glasses, i.e. glasses synced to the display to shutter between displaying two separate images, typically necessitate twice the frame rate of normal displays. CRTs, DLP TVs, and recently LCD displays offer sufficiently high update rates for stereo display (120 Hz) and higher with affordable projectors lagging behind. This type of approach is often used in large surround-screen systems, created with tiled or projected displays. Passive stereo glasses typically used polarized light or filtered light approaches to achieve different views per eye. Polarized light approaches require display surfaces that retain polarization and often twice as many projectors, one for each eye.

A problem common to all glasses is that they negatively impact collaboration by making the eyes less visible. Yet, eye contact is very important to humans; well known to researchers of computer-mediated communication systems such as video conferencing. Another indication is that it is usually not socially acceptable to wear sunglasses indoors. Lastly, and with the exception of people already used to wearing glasses, most users prefer not to wear gear on their head.

Auto-stereoscopic displays generate different images that can be seen from different viewpoints by redirecting the light emitted by pixels on the screen in selected directions. In this way, different images can be created for the two eyes of a human. This is typically achieved via a lenticular screen in front of the actual display. Most technologies require that the user hold their head stable in a relatively small region to achieve a good stereo effect. Some create multiple "sweet spots" to allow for multiple users. As these sweet spots are usually relatively small, this leads to neck strain, prohibiting long durations of use. As such, some of the newest prototypes track the user's eyes and then "aim" images at the user in an active manner.

Image generation for 3D interactive systems normally involve the use of 3D graphics hardware. Great advances in performance and image quality have been achieved and image generation is usually not the bottleneck of 3D user interfaces, unless photorealism is a hard requirement. Hence, we do not discuss image generation for these displays.

11.2.2.2   Displaying 3D Text

Text never truly left the 2D desktop. It has been used in 3D interfaces, but mostly in labels or icons. One fundamental difference between 2D and 3D interfaces is the orientation of text and the variations in scale. Where 2D text is almost always parallel to the display surface, 3D text is often found at various orientations. This leads to sub-optimally rendered text as well as text smaller than the resolution of the display. Both effects make 3D text significantly less readable.

Words become less readable when they are perspectively distorted or rotated in any direction on the screen. Because of technical limitations in anti-aliasing methods, 3D text is normally rendered sub-optimally. These methods blur the content and hence decrease readability. For angles less than about 60° there is only a relatively small decrease in reading speed, which can be compensated by magnifying the text proportionally. For rotations larger than about 60° there is a sharp decrease in readability, even with optimal anti-aliasing methods [36]. This effect has even been verified in 3D displays [27].

Much more important however, is that perspective distortion causes large parts of the characters in a window to become extremely small – often smaller than a pixel. Imagine a page of text on a screen, rotated around the vertical axis by 45° so that the left side of the page is closer to the viewer. Then the beginning of each line is easily readable, but the text at the end of each line is practically guaranteed to be too small to be readable as the resolution of the screen is not sufficient. Hence it is not realistic to expect longer text to be readable in 3D unless it directly faces the user. Applications that display rotated text can hence really only use text for mnemonic or iconic reminders for the original content. In summary, and as information density is critical for many applications and unless significant increases in screen resolution occur, 3D text will continue to be problematic.

11.2.3 Human Issues

In this section we first mention "low-level" issues, i.e. motor skills and perceptual issues, and then discuss issues that are based on cognitive capabilities.

11.2.3.1 "Low-Level" Issues

Sensitivity to latency or lag is a property of the human "system" that affects both input and output devices simultaneously. Any non-trivial delay in the handling of movements, regardless if it is in the tracking system, the VR simulation, or on the display side, has negative effects on human performance [22] and presence [40]. This applies both to head as well as hand movements. The negative effects of lag and variations in lag for head movements are well documented in Virtual Reality research and are believed to be one of the main causes of cybersickness, see e.g. [37]. Beyond this, we highlight in this document the effect of lag on human manipulation performance, a topic that is well known in 2D user interface research [38], but has received only recently attention in 3D user interfaces [62]. For manipulation, measurements have shown that even delays as small as 16 milliseconds can affect performance adversely [22]. Systematic studies of the effects of latency and (spatial) jitter/noise show clearly that they have a negative effect on human performance [48, 62]. While humans are able to sense constant latency, they are able to adapt to it to some degree, but still rate it negatively. However, any substantial *variation* in latency usually has disastrous effects for manipulation [22, 66].

   As for 3D manipulation, humans are good at manipulating an object in 6DOF if they can grab it up close, make use of small and large movements, and are able to pair the manipulation with proprioceptive cues, i.e. feedback about the position of their limbs and the forces applied to them. Consider the task of plugging an illfitting electric plug into a wall-socket. The feedback provided by bumping into the socket is picked up by the fingers and responded to by fine-grained manipulations to guide the plug down the slopes of the socket. This also involves knowing how much force to apply, and that when too much resistance is encountered, the plug may be upside-down. Consider the difficulty orienting the plug properly without finger manipulations and/or without a second hand to assist. Consider how, without two hands, reorienting the plug would require awkward "clutching" movements (releasing, repositioning, and re-grabbing). Contrast this with typical 3D interfaces where users manipulate objects by a single tracked *point* or a long *ray* extending from their hands. Another related fact is that depth perception of humans is relatively less accurate compared to the accuracy across the visual field [68]. Moreover, if a contact surface is available, humans can leverage it to greatly simplify manipulation [53]. In summary, humans are not necessarily as proficient in full 6DOF manipulation tasks as many believe, see also below. They are just good at reacting to feedback and the use of the highly specialized sensing and actions of the body.

Fatigue and/or hand tremor is another problem that affects performance with 3D input devices. Devices held away from the user's body, such as 3D wands, 3D gloves and similar devices, cause fatigue. People are not designed to holding their hands in the air for extended periods of time, without some form of support. As an exercise, try extending your arm straight out to the side for a minute or two and you will quickly find how fatiguing this is. As well, we ask the reader to reflect on how many real-world professions exist that require this. One of the few examples is a conductor, but even they drop their hands to their sides as often as possible. Regarding hand tremor, it is hard to hold a hand at a constant location in space if there is nothing to position the hand against. Many professions address this by using various forms of support. One good 3D example is a sculptor, who uses the surface of the object itself to stabilize their hands and tools before modifying the object.

Humans also prefer strongly to interact with objects that they can see directly. If something is invisible, people will either rotate the object or move themselves to see their focus of attention before working on it. The way a plumber works is a good example here. In other words, we argue that manipulation of invisible objects is the exception, not the rule.

11.2.3.2   3D Cognition

As far as cognition is concerned, we point out that humans are not "naturally" proficient at full 3D navigation. Most human environments are not fully 3D, nor do they require full 6DOF navigation as people constrain themselves to 4DOF, i.e. walking in the plane and looking around. Tilting the head is unusual and changing the height of the viewpoint is usually accommodated with a complete change of posture. People in "full" 3D professions, such as astronauts, divers, and fighter pilots, usually need extensive training (hundreds to thousands of hours) to do their job. Astronauts also need training because they work in an environment without gravity, and they have to "un-learn" their reliance on gravity. One profession that uses limited 6DOF navigation is a plumber, who contorts his body to see under a sink or in a tight space – but many people prefer not to do this. Lastly, consider that although systems such as Google Earth afford 3D navigation, most people use this only within a very small region. Larger travel is usually handled by "jumping" to a new location, either via search or bookmarks. In other words, people prefer to "teleport" for larger distances rather than navigate.

Moreover, 3D spatial memory is not *that* much better than 2D spatial memory. The main reason for this is that the world is only a restricted 3D environment.

Consider that buildings have *numbered* floors, connected by elevators and stairs. Hence, most humans remember the floor number and the 2D location on that floor, but not the spatial location in 3D. Similarly, furniture has drawers or doors that are only accessible from the front, which forms again a 1D or 2D indexing system. And objects are organized inside the drawers to simplify access, too – very frequently in a 1D or 2D layout. Hence, most people are not trained to fully utilize 3D spatial memory, as the world around them doesn't require it. Another indication for this is that experiments comparing information retrieval times across 2D, $2^1/_2$D, and 3D interfaces showed that 3D interfaces were the slowest alternative, regardless if computers were involved or not [16]!

Last, but not least, we have to consider how "natural" user interface mechanisms need to be, see e.g. [55]. Consider for example that engineers need training to understand wireframe views or orthogonal projections. In other words, such displays are not appropriate for the average person. Or consider that 3D handles that move objects along the coordinate system axes or planes [15, 58] require that the user has an understanding of the concept of local and global coordinate systems – something that again needs training for most people. Finally, many computer-aided design systems offer manipulation methods that are a one-to-one mapping of the underlying mathematics or a very thin layer above it. Then the user needs to understand the mathematics to be able to use such a system effectively, which is often not practical. Consider, for example, how difficult it is to put a particular kind of crease into a NURBS surface in current CAD systems.

After having established the above list of challenges, it becomes easier to see why certain 3D user interfaces are more successful than others. In the following section we put forth guidelines that encapsulate the most important lessons learned.

11.3 Guidelines for Constraining 3D Interaction

Three-dimensional user interfaces have not fully matured despite years of research [7]. Part of the problem is that 3D hardware technologies are still too immature to set up and keep running on a daily basis without incurring significant overhead [57]. Another problem is that many user interface techniques are implemented as a thin layer on top of the mathematical foundations. A good example is the use of handles to constrain movement along one of the three major coordinate axes or on a plane, see e.g. [15, 58]. Consequently, only users who understand the underlying concepts, such as local coordinate frames in tilted surfaces, can effectively use such a system. Hence, naïve people cannot quickly interact with and change 3D content – all novices can do is "experience" a largely static world [14] in Virtual Reality systems. This is a primary barrier to broad acceptance.

In contrast, many 3D games and online virtual worlds offer easy access to 3D content. Most people adapt quickly to the way such systems afford interaction with 3D worlds. The content editor in the Spore game, also known as Spore Creator [21], is a good example as it enables even naïve users to perform a large range of 3D operations. To illustrate the difference, we encourage readers to compare this content creator with traditional CAD tools targeted at the same purpose. There is no fundamental reason why traditional CAD tools cannot adopt such an interface to simplify common operations. Moreover, most successful games and virtual worlds use essentially only 2D input for interaction, which involves the additional overhead of finding a good mapping of 2D interaction to the 3D scene depicted on the screen. Driven by market forces, a large number of games share the same fundamental user interface paradigms, which in turn encourages re-use of skills across games. A similar evolution is happening for online 3D worlds.

Here we present ten guidelines. They are based on the issues identified above, but are also based on knowledge present in the community of 3D games and online 3D worlds. Others are based on results of user studies with novice participants, i.e. persons without VR knowledge, or research in VR, perception, kinesiology, and 2D GUIs. These guidelines will help drive 3D UIs toward broader accessibility and will form a basis for the next generation of 3D UI techniques. The order of these guidelines corresponds largely to the sequence of issues identified above.

11.3.1 2D Input Devices are Advantageous

Input devices such as the Personal Interaction Panel, which use a pen on a 2D tablet to provide interaction in a VR system, have been shown effective for 3D worlds [60]. Also, constraining the input to 2D reduces hand fatigue and provides more accuracy. While it may be possible to do symbolic input with a Wiimote or other accelerometer-based systems, and has been done with 3D trackers [13], such approaches are not optimal and should be reserved for special cases such as short text input.

Moreover, a comparison of input device specifications between mouse- or pen-based systems and 3D technologies reveals that 2D technologies are one to two orders of magnitude more precise and have much less latency [61,62]. This research also shows initial evidence that these technological differences are one of the main reasons why 2D input devices outperform 3D input devices for tasks that require only 2D motion and even for 3D tasks [6]. Combinations between 3D tracking and an interactive tablet with a tracked pen are a sensible approach.

11.3.2 Perspective and Occlusion are the Most Appropriate Depth Cues

Motion parallax, either induced through self-motion or through moving objects, is the strongest depth cue [68]. However, most 3D user interfaces that afford interaction rely on a quasi-static viewpoint, as it is hard to manipulate objects with precision while in motion. Also, manipulating an object that is moving is similarly hard. Hence, most 3D user interfaces permit only interaction in a quasi-static view and scene or at least indirectly encourage a static view position.

In that situation, and for manipulation of objects beyond arm's length, perspective and occlusion are the strongest depth cues [68]. Assuming that there are no floating objects and sufficient texture is available, these two cues are usually sufficient to accurately and quickly judge an object's 3D position in an environment, unless optical illusions are involved. Although stereo display is valuable, it matters only for objects fairly close to the viewer [68]. Given that most 3D systems target large spaces, stereo display does not provide a clear value for 3D user interfaces. Last, but not least, stereo technologies are far from mature and are tiresome or problematic if used daily [20, 65].

11.3.3   Interact Only with Visible Objects

Users interact with what they see. As such, they prefer to navigate so as to see or better see objects before interacting with them [49, 64]. This is especially important when the 3D environment has no tactile feedback. There are several consequences of this guideline. First, it points to the importance of easy navigation. Second, because a 2D manifold can fully describe the set of all visible objects, 2D input is sufficient to select an object. This is also documented by the success of ray-casting and occlusion based techniques relative to point-based virtual hand techniques [8, 50]. This also means that 2D input devices are sufficient to select objects in a 3D world – assuming that adequate 3D navigation techniques exist. Practically all current 3D games use this to simplify the interaction with the content.

11.3.4   People See the Object, not the Cursor

Research into primate vision has demonstrated that monkeys attend visually to not only the tip of a tool in their hand but also the whole tool and the hand. This indicates that a cursor might not be the best choice for 3D UIs – a cursor is effectively a point, while an object covers an area in the visual field. The sliding technique introduced in the SESAME (Sketch, Extrude, Sculpt, and Manipulate Easily) system analyzes the visual-area overlap between the manipulated object and the static scene to determine a moving object's position. The associated user studies demonstrate that users can easily use and learn such techniques and that such methods provide clear performance benefits [44].

11.3.5 Floating Objects are the Exception

In the real world, few floating objects exist, and almost all objects are attached to
other objects. However, the default in most 3D systems is that every object floats.
In the real world, gravity ensures that objects float only for short periods of time,
unless they are attached to something else. Hence, and to leverage this experience
from the real world, the better default for a 3D system is for objects to always attach
to other objects in normal operation. There are clear performance benefits to this
[54], as also documented through the interaction possibilities in most games. User
interfaces can provide *secondary* user interface mechanisms to make objects stay in
midair for the exceptional cases where this is warranted.

11.3.6 Objects don't Interpenetrate

Solid objects – including the viewers themselves – can't interpenetrate each other.
Humans are used to this and deal with it every day. However, many VR systems
allow object interpenetration by default. Interpenetration leads to confusing visual
display, and many novice users cannot easily recover from such situations. For
example, consider the negative effect of users being "trapped" behind a wall in a
game or a small object disappearing inside a larger – most novices need help to
recover from such a situation. Real-time effective collision detection and avoidance for large environments is currently possible with the help of graphics hardware
[19, 25]. As an added benefit, collision detection and avoidance enables sliding contact, an efficient way to position objects in the real world [33]. These effects are
frequently used in games to simplify the user interface.

11.3.7 2D and $2^1/_2$ D Tasks are Simpler than 3D

Most real-world tasks aren't fully 3D; they are 2D or $2^1/_2$ D, as the real world is
often a subset of full 3D. For example, blueprints of buildings abstract the height
dimension so as to better focus on 2D spatial relationships. Multistory buildings
are layers of 2D floor plans. When needed, crosscuts show alternate dimensions or
perspective drawings show 3D. Real 3D structures in buildings exist, but they are
again the exception, not the rule. Consequently, most humans are used to dealing
with 2D or $2^1/_2$ D and don't have the skills necessary to deal with problems that are
fully 3D. There is experimental evidence that underlines this, e.g. [16].

Another example is the way stacks of objects, such as paper, clothes, cards, are
handled. People quickly learn that one can't just pull an object out of a stack. Instead

one has to lift the top of the stack away to reveal the desired object then work with that object and finally reassemble the stack. One example for a 3D UI that exploits this is the SESAME system, which analyzes the scene structure to afford quick and easy manipulation of such stacks [46]. Related to this are techniques for the easy manipulation of common object groups such as cabinets or chairs [43, 59]. Hence, offering 2D methods to achieve most tasks is an excellent way to increase usability for 3D user interfaces.

11.3.8 Constrained Navigation and Rapid Transportation is Good

In the real world, navigation rarely requires unconstrained manipulation of all 6 DOFs. And all professions that (can potentially) use true 6DOF navigation, such as fighter pilots, night and wreck divers, and astronauts, require large amounts of training. Furthermore, physics limits even a fighter plane to essentially 4DOFs of freedom in navigation. Helicopter pilots can access more degrees of freedom simultaneously, but require even *more* training. In general, most navigational tasks have 4 or less DOF's, a fact that can and should be used to simplify the user interface, as this makes navigation much more accessible.

As navigation for larger distances is cumbersome, many systems provide a means of instant transportation to different locations. This is usually associated with a search feature that allows users to specify a name for a location. One issue with teleportation is that users may become disoriented [9], and as such, cues to assist user's understanding of orientation should be provided. A reasonable mechanism is to provide an overview/radar view that highlights the users' current position in the larger environment or an animation transferring the user into a new position, as introduced in the World-In-Miniature technique [47].

11.3.9 Full 3D Rotations aren't Always Necessary

Many common objects, such as chairs, desks, and shelves, have a clear "up" orientation. Other objects, such as hanging lamps and whiteboards, also have clear orientations. These objects are all attached to other objects. This attachment provides appropriate constraints for rotation – a chair is on its side only in exceptional cases. Consequently, providing a simple user interface to rotate an object around the axis afforded by that object's main attachment is a good design alternative for easy-to-use systems [56]. Although a 3D UI should support full 3D rotations, this option should not be the primary mode as full 3D rotations are best delegated to secondary user interface mechanisms.

11.3.10 Reality Simulation isn't Always Appropriate

One option for 3D user interfaces is to simulate reality more or less completely. However, besides being technically challenging, this is not appropriate for many applications. Consider e.g. an object being bumped off a table and rolling under a cupboard, or even breaking upon impact. Retrieving or repairing that object is cumbersome and not necessary in a 3D user interface – unless the application focus is on the retrieval task. Additionally, the more realistic the environment, the more users expect of it. Then, if the interaction fails to live up to expectations, they become frustrated. Hence, we suggest that reality be simulated as far as necessary to afford good skill transfer from a user's previous experience and easy manipulation, but not necessarily further.

11.4 Conclusions and Directions for Future Work

The next generation of 3D UIs can greatly benefit from user interface techniques that are adapted to how humans perceive and interact with the real world. Moreover, novel 3D UIs should leverage the strengths of humans and existing technologies – for both input and output – as far as possible and avoid known weaknesses. This will maximize the chances for skill transfer, thus increasing the usability of all developed techniques. This will lead to better 3D applications, a broader range of applications that use 3D productively, and increased adoption of 3D UIs.

In the following list, we target the main 3D user interface application domains with specific advice. Note that this is general advice that applies to the field as a whole, not necessarily to individual systems. As a disclaimer, we state that some of the advice listed is not necessarily always backed up fully by scientific inquiry, and we do not expect all of the items to stand the test of time.

11.4.1 Games

Most 3D games already include simple-to-use 3D user interfaces that follow directly or indirectly many of the above-mentioned guidelines. One challenge that we would like to pose to this community is to push the interactivity of games further, in the sense that in many games most of the environment is quite static and cannot be interacted with, or has only limited interaction possibilities. Pushing this limit will enable new kinds of game paradigms, as evidenced e.g. by the Spore content creator. Another boundary that is already being explored is new kinds of interaction devices, as evidenced by the Wiimote.

11.4.2 Virtual Reality

Most traditional VR systems employ a user interface based on the wand-in-hand paradigm and with stereo displays. Depending on the application area it may be worthwhile to revisit these decisions, as there are alternatives that necessitate less training and offer much better usability. E.g. is stereo really necessary or helpful for the application area? Would an interactive tabled tracked in 3D offer a simpler user interface for the domain and also afford more efficient interaction at the same time? Another direction to explore is haptic interfaces. However, only systems that can track both hands and fingers simultaneously with high accuracy can expect to benefit from effective skill transfer from human experience in 3D manipulation of objects.

11.4.3 Augmented Reality

With the transition to hand-held devices the user interface needs for this field have changed radically. This is visible by the fact that most AR systems are "view-only", i.e. not fully interactive. However, interactive manipulation of the content in a "live" setting is exactly one of the areas where AR systems can distinguish themselves from other approaches!

11.4.4 3D Desktops

On the one hand there are many 2D desktop windowing systems that have recently added 3D effects to increase visual attractiveness. This kind of pseudo-3D system has no real need for a 3D user interface, except to deal with the "stacking" of windows that occurs naturally in these systems. In this context it is interesting to point out that this "stacking" of 2D windows makes the normal desktop window-ing system already a $2^1/_2$ D environment! On the other hand there are the "real" 3D desktop windowing systems that allow traditional 2D windows to be rotated and moved in 3D. Given that the readability of textual content suffers very significantly by this, we suggest that either live "icon" previews or similar thumbnails be consid-ered – they may well offer all the benefits for a smaller price in terms of usability. Interaction with content in windows that are perspectively distorted and/or rotated is not a good idea in general. Finally, one of the drawbacks of 3D desktops is that the user needs to spend more effort on navigation and on the landmarks that aid that navigation, which may well cancel any benefits gained through the transition to a 3D world [16]. The concept of virtual desktop managers/spaces is a competi-tive concept that seems to have higher end-user acceptance, yet still leaves room for quasi-3D effects during transitions.

11.4.5 Computer Aided Design

In general, this class of systems can benefit greatly from a general refresh of the underlying assumptions and defaults. Google SketchUp is a great example of such a refresh. We believe that the additional introduction of a contact assumption will very likely improve manipulation performance for the most common interactions in practically all CAD systems. The work on SESAME [45] points to the potential gains. Clearly, CAD systems will have to enable the user to create floating objects. However, this should not be the default and should only be possible through secondary user interface mechanisms. It is far more efficient to provide primary user interface techniques that directly support and maintain the more common case of objects in contact.

Acknowledgements Many thanks to the reviewers for the suggestions that helped greatly to refine the structure of this work.

References

1. Agilent ADNS-3080 Optical Mouse Sensor datasheet, Agilent Technologies, (2005), http://www.alldatasheet.com/datasheet-pdf/pdf/193358/HP/ADNS-3080.html. Cited 13 April 2010.
2. A.S. Arif, W. Stuerzlinger, *Predicting the Cost of Error Correction in Character-Based Text Entry Technologies*, In ACM CHI 2010, (April 2010).
3. R. Arsenault, C. Ware, *Frustum View Angle*, Observer View Angle and VE Navigation, Proceedings of SVR, (2002).
4. R. Azuma, *A Survey of Augmented Reality*. In Presence: Teleoperators and Virtual Environments 6, 4 (August 1997), pp. 355–385.
5. J. Bakdash, J. Augustyn, D. Proffitt, *Large displays enhance spatial knowledge of a virtual environment*. In Symposium on Applied Perception in Graphics and Visualization, (2006), pp. 59–62.
6. F. Bérard, J. Ip, M. Benovoy, D. El-Shimy, J. Blum, J. Cooperstock, *Did "Minority Report" Get It Wrong? Superiority of the Mouse over 3D Input Devices in a 3D Placement Task*. In Interact 2009, pp. 400–414.
7. D. Bowman, J. Chen, C. Wingrave, et al., *New Directions in 3D User Interfaces*, In International Journal of Virtual Reality, 5(2), (2006), pp. 3–14.
8. D. Bowman, D. Johnson, L. Hodges, *Testbed Evaluation of Virtual Environment Interaction Techniques*, In Virtual Reality Software and Technology, (1999), pp. 26–33.
9. D. Bowman, D. Koller, L. Hodges, *Travel in Immersive Virtual Environments: An Evaluation of Viewpoint Motion Control Techniques*, In VRAIS, (1997), pp. 45–52.
10. D. Bowman, E. Kruijff, J. LaViola, I. Poupyrev, *3D User Interfaces: Theory and Practice*. (Addison-Wesley, Reading, 2005).
11. D. Bowman, R. McMahan, *Virtual Reality: How Much Immersion is Enough?*, In IEEE Computer, 40(7), (2007), pp. 36–43.
12. D. Bowman, C. Wingrave, *Design and Evaluation of Menu Systems for Immersive Virtual Environments*. In Proceedings of IEEE Virtual Reality, 2001, pp. 149–156.
13. D. Bowman, C. Wingrave, J. Campbell, V. Ly, *Using Pinch Gloves^{TM} for both Natural and Abstract Interaction Techniques in Virtual Environments*. In Proceedings of HCI International, 2001, pp. 629–633.

14. F. Brooks, *What's Real About Virtual Reality?*, In IEEE Computer Graphics & Applications, 19(6), (Nov. 1999), pp. 16–27.
15. J. Chen, D. Bowman, J. Lucas, C. Wingrave, *Interfaces for Cloning in Immersive Virtual Environments*, In Eurographics Workshop on Virtual Environments, (2004), pp. 91–98.
16. A Cockburn, B McKenzie, *Evaluating Spatial Memory in Two and Three Dimensions.* In International Journal of Human-Computer Studies, 61(30), (2004), pp. 359–373.
17. C. Cruz-Neira, J. Sandm, T. A. DeFanti, *Surround-Screen Projection-Based Virtual Reality: The Design and Implementation of the CAVE*, In Computer Graphics, ACM SIGGRAPH, (August 1993), pp. 135–142.
18. M. Czerwinski, D. Tan, G. Robertson, *Women take a wider view.* In Proceedings of the SIGCHI Conference on Human Factors in Computing Systems: Changing Our World, Changing Ourselves, (2002), pp. 195–202.
19. K. Dave, K. Dinesh, *CInDeR: Collision and Interference Detection in Real-time using graphics hardware*, In Graphics Interface, (2003), pp. 73–80.
20. D. Diner, D. Fender, *Human Engineering in Stereoscopic Viewing Devices.* (Plenum Press, New York, 1993).
21. Electronic Arts, Spore, http://www.spore.com/, Cited 4 April 2010.
22. S. Ellis, M. Young, B. Adelstein, S. Ehrlich, *Discrimination of Changes of Latency During Voluntary Hand Movement of Virtual Objects*, In Human Factors and Ergonomics Society, (1999), pp. 1129–1136.
23. B. Fröhlich, J. Plate, *The cubic mouse: a new device for three-dimensional input*, In ACM CHI, (2000), pp. 526–531.
24. Google, Google SketchUp, http://sketchup.google.com/. Cited 4 April 2010.
25. N. Govindaraju, S. Redon, M. Lin, D. Manocha, *Cullide: Interactive Collision Detection between Complex Models in Large Environments Using Graphics Hardware*, In SIGGRAPH Workshop on Graphics Hardware, (2003), pp. 25–32.
26. T. Grossman, R. Balakrishnan, *An evaluation of depth perception on volumetric displays*, In AVI, (2006), pp. 193–200.
27. T. Grossman, D. Wigdor, R. Balakrishnan, *Exploring and reducing the effects of orientation on text readability in volumetric displays*, In ACM CHI, (2007), pp. 483-492.
28. K. Herndon, A. Van Dam, M. Gleicher, *Workshop on the Challenges of 3D Interaction*, In SIGCHI Bulletin, 26(4), (1994), pp. 1–9.
29. K. Hinckley, R. Paush, J. Goble, N. Kassell, *Passive Real-World Interface Props for Neurosurgical Visualization*, In CHI, (1994), pp. 452-458.
30. M. Hoffman, P. Varcholik, J. LaViola, *Breaking the Status Quo: Improving 3D Gesture Recognition with Spatially Convenient Input Devices*, In Proceedings of IEEE Virtual Reality, (March, 2010), pp. 59–66.
31. R.J.K. Jacob, A. Girouard, L.M. Hirshfield, M.S. Horn, O. Shaer, E.T. Solovey, J. Zigelbaum, *Reality-Based Interaction: A Framework for Post-WIMP Interfaces*, In CHI, (2008), pp. 201–210.
32. A. Jones, I. McDowall, H. Yamada, M. Bolas, P. Debevec, *Rendering for an interactive 360° light field display*, In ACM SIGGRAPH, (2007), article no. 40.
33. Y. Kitamura, F. Kishino, *Consolidated Manipulation of Virtual and Real Objects*, In VRST, (1997), pp. 133–138.
34. G. Kessler, L. Hodges, N. Walker, *Evaluation of a Whole-Hand Input Device*, In ACM Transactions on Computer- Human Interaction, 2(4) (Dec. 1995), pp. 263–283.
35. A. Kulik, *Building on Realism and Magic for Designing 3D Interaction Techniques*, In IEEE Computer Graphics & Applications, 29(6), (November/December 2009), pp. 22–33.
36. K. Larson, M. van Dantzich, M. Czerwinski, G. Robertson, *Text in 3D: some legibility results*, In ACM CHI Extended Abstracts, (2000), pp. 145–146.
37. J. LaViola, *A Discussion of Cybersickness in Virtual Environments*, In SIGCHI Bulletin 32(1), (Jan. 2000), pp. 47–56.
38. I. S. MacKenzie, C. Ware, *Lag as a determinant of human performance in interactive systems*, In ACM CHI, (1993), pp. 488–493.

39. J. Marbach, *Image Blending and View Clustering for Multi-Viewer Immersive Projection Environments*, In IEEE Virtual Reality, (2009), pp. 51–54.
40. M. S. Meehan, S. Razzaque, M. Whitton, F. Brooks, *Effects of Latency on Presence in Stressful Virtual Environments*, In IEEE Virtual Reality, (2003), pp. 141–148.
41. B. Myers, *Why are Human-Computer Interfaces Difficult to Design and Implement?*, In Technical Report CMU-CS-93-183, (1993).
42. T. Ni, G. Schmidt, O. Staadt, M. Livingston, R. Ball, R. May, *A survey of large high-resolution display technologies, techniques, and applications*, In IEEE Virtual Reality, (2006), pp. 223–236.
43. J.-Y. Oh, W. Stuerzlinger, *Intelligent Manipulation Techniques for Conceptual 3D Design*, In Human Computer Interaction: Interact, (2003), pp. 319–326.
44. J.-Y. Oh, W. Stuerzlinger, *Moving Objects with 2D Input Devices in CAD Systems and Desktop Virtual Environments*, In Graphics Interface, (2005), pp. 195-202.
45. J.-Y. Oh, W. Stuerzlinger, J. Danahy, *SESAME: Towards Better 3D Conceptual Design Systems*, In ACM Designing Interactive Systems, (2006), pp. 80–89.
46. J.-Y. Oh, W. Stuerzlinger, D. Dadgari, *Group Selection Techniques for Efficient 3D Modeling*, In IEEE Symposium on 3D User Interfaces, (2006), pp. 95–102.
47. R. Pausch, T. Burnette, D. Brockway, M. Weiblen, *Navigation and locomotion in virtual worlds via flight into hand-held miniatures*, In SIGGRAPH, (1995), pp. 399–400.
48. A. Pavlovych, W. Stuerzlinger, The Tradeoff between Spatial Jitter and Latency in Pointing Tasks, ACM Symposium on Engineering Interactive Computing Systems 2009, 187–196.
49. C. Phillips, J. Granieri, N. Badler, *Automatic viewing control for 3D direct manipulation*, In Symposium on Interactive 3D Graphics, (1992), pp. 71–74.
50. I. Poupyrev, S. Weghorst, M. Billinghurst, T. Ichikawa, *Egocentric Object Manipulation in Virtual Environments: Empirical Evaluation of Interaction Techniques*, In Siggraph/Eurographics Workshop Graphics Hardware, (1998), pp. 41–52.
51. R. Raskar, G. Welch, M. Cutts, A. Lake, L. Stesin, H. Fuchs, *The office of the future: A unified approach to image-based modeling and spatially immersive displays.* In SIGGRAPH, (1998), pp. 179–188.
52. B. Reeves, A. Lang, E. Y. Kim, D. Tatar, *The Effects of Screen Size and Viewer Contents on Attention and Arousal.* In Journal of Media Psychology, 1(1), (1999), pp. 49–67.
53. G. Robles-De-La-Torre, *The Importance of the Sense of Touch in Virtual and Real Environments*, In Special issue on Haptic User Interfaces for Multimedia Systems, IEEE Multimedia, 13(3), (2006), pp. 24–30.
54. T. Salzman, S. Stachniak, W. Stuerzlinger, *Unconstrained vs. Constrained 3D Scene Manipulation*, In Engineering for Human-Computer Interaction, (2001), pp. 207–219.
55. B. Shneiderman, *Why Not Make Interfaces Better than 3D Reality?*, In IEEE Computer Graphics and Applications, 23(6), (Nov./Dec. 2003), pp. 12–15.
56. G. Smith, T. Salzman, W. Stuerzlinger, *3D Scene Manipulation with 2D Devices and Constraints*, In Graphics Interface, (2001), pp. 135–142.
57. A. Steed, *Some Useful Abstractions for Re-Usable Virtual Environment Platforms*, In IEEE Virtual Reality Workshop for Software Engineering and Architectures for Realtime Interactive Systems, (2008).
58. P. Strauss, R. Carey, *An object-oriented 3D graphics toolkit*, In SIGGRAPH, (1992), pp. 341–349.
59. W. Stuerzlinger, G. Smith, *Efficient Manipulation of Object Groups in Virtual Environments*, In IEEE VR, (2002), pp. 251–258.
60. Z. Szalavári, M. Gervautz, *The Personal Interaction Panel—a Two-Handed Interface for Augmented Reality*, In Computer Graphics Forum, 16(3), (1997), pp. 335–346.
61. R. Teather, W. Stuerzlinger, *Assessing the Effects of Orientation and Device on (Constrained) 3D Movement Techniques*, In IEEE Symposium on 3D User Interfaces (2008), pp. 43–50.
62. R. Teather, A. Pavlovych, W. Stuerzlinger, S. MacKenzie, *Effects of tracking technology, latency, and spatial jitter on object movement*, In IEEE Symposium on 3D User Interfaces (2009), pp. 43–50.

63. A. van Dam, *Post-WIMP user interfaces*. Commun. ACM, 40(2), (Feb. 1997), pp. 63–67.
64. C. Ware, K. Lowther, *Selection Using a One-Eyed Cursor in a Fish Tank VR Environment*, In ACM Transactions on Computer-Human Interaction, 4(4), (1997), pp. 309–322.
65. Z. Wartell, L.F. Hodges, W. Ribarsky, *A Geometric Comparison of Algorithms for Fusion Control in Stereoscopic HTDs*, In IEEE Trans. Visualization & Computer Graphics, 8(2), (2002), pp.129–143.
66. B. Watson, *The Effects of Variation of System Responsiveness on User Performance in Virtual Environments*, Human Factors, 40, (1998), pp. 403–414.
67. G. Welch, E. Foxlin, *Motion Tracking: No Silver Bullet, but a Respectable Arsenal*, In IEEE Computer Graphics and Applications, 22(6), (2002), pp. 24–38.
68. C. Wickens, J. Hollands, *Engineering Psychology and Human Performance*, 3rd ed., (Prentice-Hall, NJ, 1999).
69. C. Wingrave, J. LaViola, *Reflection on the Design and Implementation of Virtual Environments*. In Special Issue of Presence: Teleoperators and Virtual Environments: Reflections on the Design and Implementation of Virtual Environment Systems, 19(2), (2010).
70. C. Wingrave, B. Williamson, P. Varcholik, J. Rose, A. Miller, E. Charbonneau, J. Bott, J. LaViola, *Wii Remote and Beyond: Using Spatially Convenient Devices for 3DUIs*. In IEEE Computer Graphics and Applications, 30(2), 2010, pp. 71–85.

Chapter 12
Evaluation of a Scalable In-Situ Visualization System Approach in a Parallelized Computational Fluid Dynamics Application

Sebastian Manten, Michael Vetter, and Stephan Olbrich

Abstract Current parallel supercomputers provide sufficient performance to simulate unsteady three-dimensional fluid dynamics in high resolution. However, the visualization of the huge amounts of result data cannot be handled by traditional methods, where post-processing modules are usually coupled to the raw data source, either by files or by data flow. To avoid significant bottlenecks of the storage and communication resources, efficient techniques for data extraction and preprocessing at the source have been realized in the parallel, network-distributed chain of our *Distributed Simulation and Virtual Reality Environment* (DSVR). Here the 3D data extraction is implemented as a parallel library (libDVRP) and can be done in-situ during the numerical simulations, which avoids the storage of raw data for visualization at all.

In this work we evaluate our current techniques of flow visualization via parallel generation of pathlines and volume visualization via parallel extraction of isosurfaces in a realistic scenario. The *Parallelized Large-eddy Simulation Model* (PALM) serves here as a typical example application of numerical simulation of unsteady flows. Our special attention we payed to the evaluation of the influence of the additional in-situ visualization on the parallel speed-up of PALM. Finally it can be shown that this influence is neglectable small for parallel runs with up to over 80 cores.

S. Olbrich (✉)
Regional Computer Center and Department of Computer Science, Scientific Visualization and Parallel Processing, University of Hamburg, 20146 Hamburg, Germany
e-mail: stephan.olbrich@rrz.uni-hamburg.de

M. Vetter
Department of Computer Science, Scientific Visualization and Parallel Processing, University of Hamburg, D-20146 Hamburg, Germany
e-mail: michael.vetter@uni-hamburg.de

S. Manten
Center of Information and Media Technology, Heinrich Heine University Duesseldorf, 40225 Duesseldorf, Germany
e-mail: manten@uni-duesseldorf.de

S. Coquillart et al. (eds.), *Virtual Realities*, DOI 10.1007/978-3-211-99178-7_12,
© Springer-Verlag/Wien 2011

12.1 Introduction

Coming along with the compute power of modern supercomputers numerical simulations can produce a huge amount of data. Approaches for scientific visualization
on the other hand often consist of two working steps. First, the raw data is computed
and stored to disk by the simulation environment. Afterwards in a post-processing
step the 3D geometries are extracted from the raw data and used for rendering. In
typical scenarios, the visualization mapping and the 3D rendering are done in a separate process after the simulation. This may lead to a capacity bottleneck on the
storage side.

The *Parallelized Large-eddy Simulation Model* (PALM)[1] is a typical application which does numerical simulation of unsteady flows in high resolution. It is
required that simulation and visualization has to be coupled, in order to explore the
time-dependent scalar and vector fields as navigatable 3D virtual reality movies. On
massively-parallel computers, PALM simulates computational fluid dynamics on a
rectilinear grid which contains up to 10^{10} data points, each containing several scalar
and vector values. For simulation of non-stationary phenomena about 10^4 time steps
are required. This results in raw data sets in the order of 1 PBytes for one scenario,
which cannot be stored on disk in adequate time during the simulation.

Even if the volume of raw data is one or two magnitudes smaller – like in simulations with a lower number of data points – there still remain problems in classical
post-processing scenarios. Now the raw data can be stored on supercomputers in
adequate time by a parallel I/O, but – like the simulation itself – the extraction of 3D
geometries from the raw data cannot be done in real-time on conventional graphics
workstations.

So the graphical post-processing has to be divided again into two separate sub-
steps, the extraction of 3D geometries and the rendering of the 3D geometries, and
only the rendering is done in real-time on graphic systems.

The distributed visualization environment DSVR [3, 9, 10] take these challenges
by the use of a parallel and network-distributed processing chain. The extraction
of 3D geometries is realized in a parallel software library libDVRP, which is called
directly by the application that is doing the simulation on the parallel supercomputer.
So instead of realizing the visualization as a separate post-processing step, it is done
in-situ during the simulation. This avoids the storage of raw data for visualization
and of course I/O bottlenecks, too.

In this work PALM is used as an example application to evaluate our approach
in a realistic scenario. As test scenario we have chosen a parallel simulation of
atmospheric convection cells. During this simulation isosurfaces and pathlines are
extracted from the generated volume and flow data by our parallel software library
libDVRP. The parallel isosurface extraction includes a integrated parallel polygon

---

[1] Developed by Institute of Meteorology and Climatology, Leibniz University of Hannover,
Germany.

simplification step to reduce additionally the volume of 3D data [11]. The parallel pathline extraction [19] is based on a parallelized Runge–Kutta integration.

For both techniques, the parallel pathline and the parallel isosurface extraction, we payed special attention to the evaluation of the influence of the additional in-situ visualization on the parallel speed-up of PALM and also to the overhead caused by the visualization. We have examined also the effect of a varying amounts of generated 3D data on the performance.

12.2   Related Work

Since numerical simulations of unsteady flows in high resolution take advantage of parallel high performance computing, it is very desirably to do so also for particle tracing, pathline extraction, and isosurface extraction.

A common method for the extraction of isosurfaces of scalar fields on rectilinear grids is the marching cubes algorithm [5]. This algorithm generates the isosurface as a triangle mesh and is easy to parallelize, because it extracts the isosurface grid cell by grid cell without using any information about neighbouring cells. So a parallel marching cubes algorithm is discussed in [7] for example. But for large grids the number of triangles in the extracted mesh is so large, that it cannot be rendered in real-time even if current high end graphics hardware is used.

So the data volume of the generated polygon mesh has to be reduced. For this reason a lot of polygon simplification techniques have been developed. An overview about these different techniques can be found in [6]. There are also some parallelized approaches for polygon simplification [4, 15, 17]. Most of them are developed for shared memory systems and cannot be applied on cluster architectures. They work only if the complete mesh in the full resolution is given as input. Furthermore all known simplification approaches realize the polygon simplification as a separate computing step after the polygon generation and are not able to take advantage of intermediate data and results in the mapping process.

Parallel simulation and parallel visualization of particle traces, which could render up to 60,000 particles, have been discussed in [1]. In [14] real-time flow visualization is done by analyzing regions of interest on a high-performance computer and do the flow visualization on a graphic frontend. In [21] a hierarchical representation is introduced into parallel visualization environments to increase scalability.

In these approaches the complete visualization is done as a separate post-processing task and all raw data have to be stored permanently, which may lead to a capacity bottleneck on the storage side. The same problem occurred during the volume visualization via isosurfaces, if it is done as a separate post-processing step.

Recently the standard visualization tools Paraview [12] and VisIt [20] are used for in-situ visualization in massively parallel high performance computing scenarios [8, 18]. But these tools do not support the generation and storing of navigatable 3D virtual reality movies by extracting 3D scenes during each time step of the simulations, neither in synchronous live nor in batch processing scenarios.

12.3 Concept and Design of DSVR

High-performance numerical simulation applications are typically run on massively parallel computers, which are realized as clusters of multi-core processor nodes, supported by message passing infrastructure and programming library (MPI).

Due to Amdahl's Law, the parallel speed-up is limited to the reciprocal value of the sequential fraction of the computation. For this reason, efficient utilization can only be achieved if also the data extraction and visual data analysis components of the complete process chain are parallelized adequately. To avoid sequential bottlenecks, tight integration and parallelization of visualization filtering and mapping are essential.

In order to create a highly interactive virtual reality environment, not only efficient 3D scene generation (simulation and data extraction) is an issue, but also the limitation of response and update time budgets, especially for exploration cycles and 3D navigation (rendering). Latency can be reduced by pipelining and data streaming instead of file transfer, by increasing the network throughput, and by increasing the rendering performance. Dependent on these infrastructure parameters, the number of 3D primitives or the data volume has to be limited, respectively. In the case of applying geometric simplification or compression algorithms, this has to be parallelized efficiently, too.

A scalable approach including flexible support for batch, tracking, and computational steering scenarios is realized by our networked process chain:

1. Data extraction and creation of 3D scenes, which represent features of the raw data, are efficiently implemented by parallel processing of the data parts – using a parallel software library libDVRP – corresponding to the domain decomposition of the parallelized simulation. This significantly reduces the data volume, while 3D interaction support is preserved. For larger numbers of parallel processes the parallel speed-up of libDVRP can be improved by splitting a single process from the MPI communicator. This process does the transmission to the streaming server asynchronously, while the other processes does the calculation of the next 3D scene [3].
2. The generated sequence of 3D files is stored on a separate 3D Streaming Server, which provides RTSP-based (Real-Time Streaming Protocol [16]) play-out capabilities for continuous 3D media streams, especially in high-performance IP networks.
3. The 3D scene sequence is presented as an animation in a virtual reality environment with an interactively configurable frame rate. This step has been implemented as a web-based 3D viewer plug-in, taking advantage of stereoscopic displays and interactive tracking devices.

So in the *Distributed Simulation and Virtual Reality Environment* (DSVR) all parts of the visualization pipeline are implemented as three networked instances (Fig. 12.1). These components are the 3D generator (data source, filter, mapper), the 3D streaming server, and the 3D viewer (rendering, presentation). The 3D generator

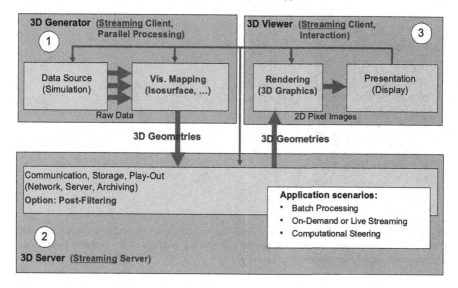

Fig. 12.1 Realization of the visualization pipeline in DSVR

and the 3D viewer are streaming clients which generate and consume sequences of 3D scenes, respectively, tightly connected to the 3D streaming server over TCP/IP. They can be operated in asynchronous (3D movies "on demand") or synchronous scenarios (real-time, "live" visualization). By implementing a back-channel, we also support computational steering scenarios or interactive control of filtering and mapping parameters.

In graphics based approaches for flow field visualization like streamlines or path-lines one of the most discussed problems is the initial placement of these lines, which is normally solved by calculating adequate seedpoints via different techniques of numerical flow field analysis. But an interactive, numerical flow field analysis is not possible without storing the raw data. Additionally, for unsteady high-resolution flow fields with huge amounts of raw data the flow analysis can not be done in real-time on current graphic workstations.

So 3D streaming server and viewer client were recently extended by a post-filtering approach [19], which still avoids the storing of raw data and also allows a high degree of interaction in real time and also in 3D video-on-demand scenarios. In the new approach property-enhanced traced particles or pathlines are used, and subsets of pathlines can be selected according to additionally given or calculated properties in the local environment and history of the pathlines in form of a "query over a stream" (Fig. 12.2).

In the following Sects. 12.3.1 and 12.3.2 two parallelized, geometrically scalable approaches are described, that we have implemented for flow and volume visualization. Results of an evaluation in a test case are given in Sect. 12.4.

Fig. 12.2 Pathline visualization in a flow field, the simulation of atmospheric convection cells. Complete pathlines scene based on a generalized seeding strategy (*left*). Property-based post-filtered scene, exploring convection cells (*right*)

12.3.1 Parallel Isosurface Extraction, Integrating Flexible Polygon Simplification

Our scalable method for the isosurface extraction combines the marching-cubes algorithm [5] with configurable polygon simplification, based on vertex clustering [13]. A flexible polygon simplification is important to adapt the number of primitives in the 3D scenes to the bandwidth of the IP network and rendering limits of the graphics environment. Like the parallel pathlines extraction our parallel isosurface algorithm is based on the decomposition of the rectilinear grid that is given by the calling application. By contrast with [15] our MPI-based approach supports also massively-parallel distributed memory cluster architectures.

Doing the remeshing of the cluster vertices in the clustering step in the classic way leads to some problems in the parallel algorithm. Caused by the domain decomposition not all vertices of neighbouring clusters are known at the domain borders. Two neighboured domains have normally only one common plane of grid points, but not a common plane of clusters. So an additional communication between the compute nodes is necessary to achieve coherent surfaces by boundary-overlapping (marked section in Fig. 12.3, left side).

To avoid these additional communications we recently developed a parallel iso-surface extraction method, which avoids exchanging data between neighboured nodes at the boundaries [11]. Due to a new kind of clustering scheme and remeshing, the vertex clustering can be done completely locally, cluster by cluster, without involving neighbours, and no boundary-overlapping is necessary.

Additional vertices are placed at the positions where the isosurface cuts the edges of the clusters and remeshed with the representative point of the cluster. So coherent surfaces are generated because the points of intersection on the edges are the same for neighboured clusters (Fig. 12.3, right side). With the same cluster size this

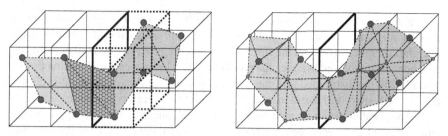

Fig. 12.3 Remeshing at the domain borders by boundary-overlapping (*dotted region*) in the old algorithm (*left*) and the local remeshing in the new algorithm (*right*). In the old algorithm the rastered triangles (*left picture*) would not be generated without boundary-overlapping

Fig. 12.4 Part of an isosurface of temperature extracted from an atmospheric convection cells simulation. The *left image* shows the scene in the original marching cubes resolution, the *right image* the same scene with an integrated vertex clustering using 4 × 4 × 4 clusters, which reduces the 3D data volume and polygon count to 10% of the original volume

algorithm generates a higher number of triangles because of the additional vertices placed at the edges of the clusters. Using the new algorithm for $\mathbf{d} \times \mathbf{d} \times \mathbf{d}$ clustering, we typically get a reduction to $2d^{-2}$-times of the original polygon count of the unmodified Marching Cubes method instead of a reduction to d^{-2}-times. But the quality of the generated isosurfaces is higher, too. Comparing isosurfaces with a similar level of reduction – configuring a bigger cluster size for the new algorithm shows that with both algorithms a similar quality of isosurfaces is achieved at the same level of reduction (Fig. 12.4).

12.3.2 Parallel Pathline Extraction

The extraction and visualization of pathlines is a common method for visualizing unsteady flow fields. Thereby a pathline shows the way of one particle released at a certain timestep at one point – called seedpoint – and observed for several timesteps. The pathline extraction, which we have implemented as part of the lib-DVRP, uses selectively the Euler or Runge–Kutta (2nd or 4th order) integration. Since the numerical simulation on parallel computers typically provides the high-resolution data fields as parts on separate compute nodes corresponding to domain decomposition, we also focus on a parallelization in that way.

Our approach is implemented on top of MPI [2], which is also used in most parallel simulation codes. The global rectilinear grid is distributed in partial grids over the compute cluster and the simulation's resulting data will be neither stored on disk nor communicated between the parallel cores. This means that the extraction of a pathline in the distributed grid can be done only on that core of the parallel cluster that holds the part of the grid in which the pathline is currently placed in.

So the parallelization is ruled by the domain decomposition of the applications, and during integration of the trajectory three cases for data locality in the compute cluster have to be considered:

1. The pathline will still stay in the partial grid volume, that is simulated by the actual process.
2. The pathline will leave the global area of the simulation.
3. The pathline will leave the area simulated by the actual process but still stay in the global grid.

In the third case the pathlines are transferred between processes. So a pathline is always hosted by the process which also holds the currently needed raw data. Using Runge–Kutta for integration, a transfer could also be necessary during a Runge–Kutta substep.

The pathline extraction is implemented as on-the-fly processing, directly accessing the transient raw data of the respective time step in main memory, according to the underlying domain decomposition.

As a result, we get an interleaved data stream, containing 3D geometry and additional property elements. Assuming a constant number of pathlines, $O(n^3)$ grid points and $O(n)$ supporting points per pathline, the data volume is reduced by a factor of $O(n^2)$. Assuming a constant number of supporting points per pathline, which can be easily achieved by neglection of intermediate points, the data volume will be constant.

12.4 Evaluation in the Context of PALM

For performance evaluation we have used a linux cluster consisting of 12 Bull NovaScale R422-E1 nodes. Each of the nodes contains 2 Intel Quad-Core Xeon Harpertown CPUs 2.8 GHz and 8 GB memory. The nodes are connected by Infiniband (QDR) based MPI-Interconnects and running currently under Intel MPI Library 3.1 for Linux using RDMA shared memory and socket data transfer modes. For all parallel runs we "round robin" the processes across the hosts.

In case of 10 or more parallel processes the "split mode" of libDVRP was used [3]. So one process – P0 in Fig. 12.5 – was split from the MPI communicator and the transmission to the streaming server was done asynchronously by this process, while already continue with the next simulation step. The streaming server and this process was running exclusively on the same compute node.

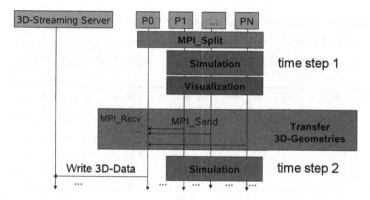

Fig. 12.5 Communication scheme of libDVRP using the "split mode"

As test scenario we choose a parallel simulation of atmospheric convection cells using PALM and extract isosurfaces of temperature and a set of traced pathlines using libDVRP. The parallelisation in PALM bases on a domain decomposition. For each time step in the simulation the parallel library libDVRP is called for isosurface or/and pathline extraction. The measurement of the runtimes was always done over 100 timesteps. All runs were done in batch mode. The threshold for the isosurfaces and the seed points of the pathlines were set by libDVRP calls at the beginning of the simulation.

The memory requirements of PALM for single and double process runs limit the possible grid size. The additional memory requirement of the visualization library libDVRP is neglectable. In no case more than 10% of the memory requirement of PALM was needed additionally.

We decide to use a grid consisting of $720 \times 720 \times 180$ data points for most of the calculations. For this grid size single process runs are not possible because of the limited amount of system memory on the nodes. So the runtimes for the single process runs are estimated from double process runtimes, assuming the same speed-up as in runs with a grid size of $500 \times 500 \times 180$.

First we have evaluated the influence of the additional in-situ visualization on the parallel speed-up of PALM. For speed-up measurement four different computing series were done.

In the first sequence we have started PALM without libDVRP calls to get the parallel speed-up without additional extraction of 3D scenes. In the second sequence a isosurface of temperature was extracted by libDVRP during the PALM run. The communication avoiding algorithm was used here with $4 \times 4 \times 4$ clustering in the integrated polygon simplification. An in-situ extraction of approximately 5,000 pathlines – each with 30 supporting points – using the Runge–Kutta 4th order integration was done in the third sequence and at last isosurface and pathlines were extracted together in a fourth sequence. Parameters are chosen here in a way that the extracted 3D scenes can be rendered without any problems in real-time on current graphics hardware.

Table 12.1 Runtimes per frame and parallel speed-up of PALM without and with additional in-situ extraction of isosurfaces and pathlines with libDVRP

No. of cores	Runtime (s)				Parallel speed-up			
	PALM	PALM + DVRP			PALM	PALM + DVRP		
		iso.	path.	iso.+path.		iso.	path.	iso.+path.
1	211.67	218.02	222.36	224.64	1.00	1.00	1.00	1.00
2	106.91	110.11	112.30	113.45	1.98	1.98	1.98	1.98
9	25.07				8.44			
10		25.59	25.66	25.84		8.52	8.67	8.69
25	11.43				18.52			
26		11.05	12.12	11.14		19.74	18.34	20.16
42	8.31				25.49			
43		8.54	8.47	8.58		25.54	26.24	26.17
64	5.86				36.13			
65		5.95	6.02	6.06		36.62	36.94	37.07
80	5.40				39.23			
81		5.57	5.61	5.67		39.11	39.63	39.61

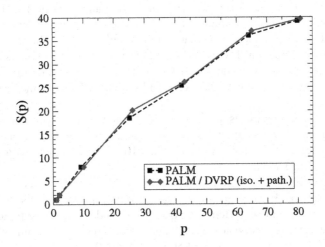

Fig. 12.6 Comparison of the parallel speed-up $S(p)$ of PALM without and with additional in-situ visualization using libDVRP (p: number of cores)

Table 12.1 shows the measured runtimes and speed-up for the four series. Speed-ups of series 1 and 4 are also compared in Fig. 12.6. On our computing cluster the parallel speed-up of PALM itself is limited by the given Quad-Core technology. The cache line of the Quad-Core CPUs is a bottleneck, especially if more than two cores of a CPU are used.

Additionally we have measured the fractions of the total runtime for the libDVRP calls in all these runs (Fig. 12.7, left).

It is a typical problem that the API of a library, like libDVRP, cannot be generally adapted to any proprietary data structure of calling applications. Furthermore

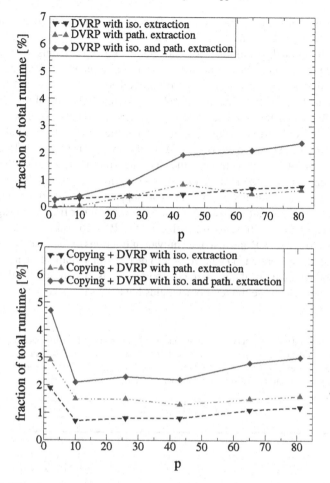

Fig. 12.7 Relative time consumption of libDVRP (*top*) and relative time consumption of libDVRP including partial copying of raw data into temporary fields according to libDVRP's data format (*bottom*) in relation to the simulations total time

libDVRP uses single precision as sufficient accurateness, while PALM needs double precision.

So the parts of original data, that are used by libDVRP, has to be type-converted and copied into temporary data fields for the libDVRP calls. To evaluate this overhead we also have measured the fractions of total runtime for the complete additional work including the partial copying of the raw data into the temporary data fields (Fig. 12.7, right).

Two main results can be summarized from the presented calculations. First, under the chosen conditions there is no significant effect on the parallel speed-up by the additional in-situ visualization. As second the part of the in-situ visualization at the total runtime is small and rises only slowly with the number of cores that are used for the parallel runs. This means that an efficient parallel in-situ visualization will remain efficiently even on more than 100 cores.

We also focus on the examination of the effect of raising amounts of generated 3D data on the performance. So a group of test runs was done with a varying extracted 3D data volumes. All these test runs are done on 80 (+1) cores, and libDVRP's fraction of the total runtime was measured for different 3D data volumes.

Table 12.2 shows the influence of a rising extracted 3D data volume in the case of an isosurface extraction. Table 12.3 shows the same for an extraction of pathlines. For the isosurface extraction the vertex clustering is varied between $2 \times 2 \times 2$, $3 \times 3 \times 3$ and $4 \times 4 \times 4$ clustering to modify the 3D data volume. In case of the pathline extraction the data volume is increased by seeding more pathlines. The number of points per frame is calculated according to 30 supporting points for each line.

Here the most relevant measurements are the volume per frame (averaged about 100 time steps) and the time used for the libDVRP. A comparison shows that the time needed for libDVRP and also the equivalent fractions of the total time increases linearly with the generated 3D data volume. The time for visualization includes time for the copying of the raw data into the temporary fields, which should take the same time in all cases, because the temporary fields have the same size.

Table 12.2 Dependency of libDVRP's time consumption per frame for isosurface extraction from the extracted 3D data volume per frame (3D volume). The volumes of raw data (raw volume) are listed also. The vertex clustering is varied between $2 \times 2 \times 2$, $3 \times 3 \times 3$ and $4 \times 4 \times 4$ clustering to modify the 3D data volume. All runs are done with 81 parallel tasks. All values are averages over 100 frames (timesteps)

Grid	Clusters	Raw volume [MB]	#Triangles	3D volume [MB]	Time [s] Total	vis.	DVRP	Time [%] vis.	DVRP
$500 \times 500 \times 128$	$4 \times 4 \times 4$	170.9	114800	5.3	2.74	0.036	0.027	1.3	1.0
$500 \times 500 \times 128$	$3 \times 3 \times 3$	170.9	224500	10.3	2.74	0.047	0.038	1.7	1.4
$500 \times 500 \times 128$	$2 \times 2 \times 2$	170.9	445600	20.4	2.79	0.074	0.061	2.7	2.2
$720 \times 720 \times 128$	$4 \times 4 \times 4$	253.1	233500	10.7	5.57	0.067	0.043	1.2	0.8
$720 \times 720 \times 128$	$3 \times 3 \times 3$	253.1	446300	20.4	5.61	0.094	0.070	1.7	1.3
$720 \times 720 \times 128$	$2 \times 2 \times 2$	253.1	911900	41.7	5.66	0.162	0.136	2.9	2.4

Table 12.3 Dependency of libDVRP's time consumption per frame for pathlines extraction from the extracted 3D data volume per frame. The volumes of raw data (raw volume) are listed also. All runs are done with 81 parallel tasks. All values are averages over 100 frames (timesteps)

Grid	#Pathlines	Raw volume [MB]	#Points	3D volume [MB]	Time [s] Total	vis.	DVRP	Time [%] vis.	DVRP
$500 \times 500 \times 128$	4850	683.6	145500	2.5	2.74	0.051	0.030	1.9	1.1
$500 \times 500 \times 128$	9640	683.6	289200	4.9	2.76	0.065	0.049	2.3	1.8
$500 \times 500 \times 128$	19540	683.6	586200	9.8	2.78	0.078	0.064	2.8	2.3
$720 \times 720 \times 128$	4850	1012.5	145500	2.5	5.61	0.091	0.036	1.6	0.6
$720 \times 720 \times 128$	9640	1012.5	289200	4.9	5.59	0.104	0.047	1.9	0.8
$720 \times 720 \times 128$	19540	1012.5	586200	9.8	5.60	0.115	0.057	2.0	1.0

Since one separate process does the transmission to the streaming server asynchronously, while the other processes do the calculation of the next 3D scene, the streaming has no effect on the runtime. So especially for isosurface extraction, for which the most time-consuming steps do not depend on the size of the vertex clusters, the linear increasing of libDVRP's fraction of the total runtime with the volume of the extracted 3D data must be widely caused by the collection of the extracted 3D data via MPI. This makes the use of optimized MPI communication techniques in this part of the framework essential for scenarios with a higher degree of parallelization in the future.

12.5   Conclusion and Future Work

Tests with PALM as a typical example application of numerical simulation of unsteady flows show that in realistic scenarios the fraction of the in-situ visualization at the total runtime is small and rises only slowly with the number of cores that are used for the parallel runs. So in-situ visualization with libDVRP works efficiently on more than 80 cores. There is also no significant effect on the parallel speed-up by the additional in-situ visualization.

For future work there exist same options for improvement in the DSVR framework. The collection of 3D data in libDVRP can be improved by the use of optimized MPI communication for example. Furthermore parallel streaming and data compression techniques can be introduced to enlarge the throughput of 3D data in the framework.

After these improvements a switch to massively parallel application examples running on parallel supercomputer systems with over 1,000 cores seems to be possible.

Acknowledgements The authors are grateful to PD Dr. Siegfried Raasch and his group for sharing the PALM software and for fruitful discussions.

Computational support and infrastructure was provided by the Center of Information and Media Technology (ZIM) at the Heinrich Heine University of Duesseldorf (Germany).

This work is partly supported by the DFG (German Research Foundation) under Grant No. OL 241/1-1 (Project EVITA).

References

1. Bruckschen, R., Kuester, F., Hamann, B., Joy, K. I.: Real-time out-of-core visualization of particle traces. In PVG '01: Proceedings of the IEEE 2001 Symposium on Parallel and Large-Data Visualization and Graphics, pp. 45–50. IEEE Press, Piscataway (2001)
2. Gropp, W., Lusk, E., Skjellum, A.: Using MPI: Portable Parallel Programming with the Message-Passing Interface. The MIT Press, Cambridge (2000)
3. Jensen, N., Olbrich, S., Pralle, H., Raasch, S.: An efficient system for collaboration in tele-immersive environments. In: Bartz, D. et al (eds.): Eurographics Workshop on Parallel

Graphics and Visualization 2002, pp. 123–131. Eurographics Association, Aire-la-Ville, Swiss (2002)

4. Langis, C., Roth, G., Dehne, F.: Mesh simplification in parallel. In: Proceedings of the 4th International Conference on Algorithms and Architectures for Parallel Processing (ICA3PP 2000), pp. 281–290. World Scientific Publishing, Singapore (2000)

5. Lorensen, W. E., Cline, H. E.: Marching Cubes: A High Resolution 3d Surface Construction Algorithm. Computer Graphics **21**(4), 163–69 (1987)

6. Luebke, D. P.: A Developer's Survey of Polygonal Simplification Algorithms. IEEE Computer Graphics and Applications **21**(3), 24–35 (2001)

7. Miguet, S., Nicod, J. M.: Complexity Analysis of a Parallel Implementation of the Marching-Cubes Algorithm. International Journal of Pattern Re-cognition and Artificial Intelligence **11**(7), 1141–1156 (1997)

8. Moreland, K., et al.: Large Scale Visualization on the Cray XT3 Using ParaView In: Cray User's Group 2008

9. Olbrich, S., Pralle, H.: Virtual Reality Movies – Real-Time Streaming of 3D Objects. Computer Networks: The International Journal of Computer and Telecommunications Networking **31**(21), 2215–2225 (1999)

10. Olbrich, S., Pralle, H., Raasch, S.: Using streaming and parallelization techniques for 3d visualization in a high-performance computing and networking environment. In: Lecture Notes in Computer Science, Vol. 2110, pp. 231–240. Springer, Berlin (2001)

11. Olbrich, S., Manten, S., Jensen, N.: Scalable isosurface extraction in a parallelized streaming framework for interactive simulation and visualization. In: Proceedings of the 10th International Conference on Humans and Computers (HC-2007), pp. 147–152. (2007)

12. Paraview project: http://www.paraview.org/

13. Rossignac, J., Borrel, P.: Multi-resolution 3d approximations for rendering complex scenes. In: Geometric Modeling in Computer Graphics, pp. 455–465. Springer, Berlin (1993)

14. Schirski, M., Bischof. C., Kuhlen, T.: Interactive exploration of large data in hybrid visualization environments. In: Proceedings of the IPT-EGVE 2007 Symposium, pp. 69–76. (2007)

15. Schmidt, O., Rasch, M.: Parallel mesh simplification. In: Proceedings of the International Conference on Parallel and Distributed Processing Techniques and Applications (PDPTA 2000), pp. 1361–1367. (2000)

16. Schulzrinne, H., Rao, A., Lanphier, R.: Real Time Streaming Protocol (RTSP). Internet RFC 2326 (1998)

17. Soetebier, I., Birthelmer, H., Sahm, J., et al.: Managing Large Progressive Meshes. Computers & Graphics-UK **28**(5), 691–701 (2004)

18. Thomas, K.: Porting of VisIt parallel visualization tool to the Cray XT3 system. In: Cray User's Group 2007

19. Vetter, M., Manten, S., Olbrich, S.: Exploring unsteady flows by parallel extraction of property-enhanced pathlines and interactive post-filtering. In: Proceedings of 14th Eurographics Symposium on Virtual Environments (EGVE 2007), (Posters) pp. 9–12. (2008)

20. VisIt project: https://wci.llnl.gov/codes/visit/

21. Yu, H., Wang, C., Ma, K.-L.: Parallel hierarchical visualization of large time-varying 3d vector fields. In: Proceedings of ACM/IEEE Supercomputing 2007 Conference, pp. 24–35. ACM, New York (2007)

Author Index

Aarts, E., 17
Abelin, A., 144
Acquisti, A., 33
Adelstein, B.D., 45, 211
Agarwal, P., 186
Agne, S., 173, 176
Allard, J., 8, 185
Allbeck, J., 65, 99, 110
Amor, H.B., 103, 108, 113
Anderson, J., 130
Anderson, L., 40
Antley, A., 66
Araya, C., 23
Arbib, M.A., 100
Arif, A.S., 207
Aronson, J., 45, 82
Arsella, S.M., 64
Arsenault, R., 209
Ascher, U., 131
Augustyn, J., 209
Avery, B., 72
Axelsson, A.S., 144
Azarbayejani, A., 125
Azmaira, H.M., 142, 155
Azuma, R.T., 13, 207

Bérard, F., 214
Babu, S., 66
Badler, N.I., 65, 99, 110, 215
Baillot, Y., 23, 30
Bakdash, J., 209
Bakker, P., 101
Balakrishnan, R., 209, 210
Balch, D.C., 142, 155
Ball, R., 162, 163, 166, 208
Bandura, A., 153, 154
Baraff, D., 126
Barakonyi, I., 16

Barba, C., 66
Barbič, J., 185
Barbier, S., 185
Barfield, W., 143
Barnes, T., 66
Barr, A., 126
Barsky, E., 17
Barthel, H., 173, 176
Baudisch, P., 162–164, 166, 174
Bauhs, J., 33
Bay, H., 31
Baylor, A.L., 71
Beard, D., 164
Beckhaus, S., 40, 41, 82, 84, 87–89
Bederson, B., 174
Belhumeur, P., 60
Ben-Joseph, E., 90, 93
Bencina, R., 89
Bender, M., 173, 176
Benovoy, M., 214
Berghoff, M., 89
Berkovich, S.G., 188
Bhat, K., 125, 131
Biderman, A., 90, 93
Billard, A., 100
Billinghurst, M., 23, 24, 26, 32, 33, 46, 89, 215
Bimber, C., 14, 16
Bimber, O., 148
Bindiganavale, R., 65, 99, 110
Birgin, E.G., 186
Birthelmer, H., 227
Bischof. C., 227
Bishop, G., 149
Bismpigiannis, T., 31
Bitouk, D., 60
Blom, K.J., 84, 87, 88
Blum, J., 214
Boj, C., 69
Bolas, M., 209

S. Coquillart et al. (eds.), *Virtual Realities*, DOI 10.1007/978-3-211-99178-7,
© Springer-Verlag/Wien 2011

Subject Index